ENDURING HOSTILITY

Enduring Hostility

THE MAKING
OF AMERICA'S
IRAN POLICY

DALIA DASSA KAYE

STANFORD UNIVERSITY PRESS
Stanford, California

Stanford University Press
Stanford, California

Library of Congress Cataloging-in-Publication Data
Names: Kaye, Dalia Dassa author
Title: Enduring hostility : the making of America's Iran policy / Dalia
    Dassa Kaye.
Description: Stanford, California : Stanford University Press, [2026] |
    Includes bibliographical references and index.
Identifiers: LCCN 2025008564 (print) | LCCN 2025008565 (ebook)
    | ISBN 9781503643901 cloth | ISBN 9781503644595 paperback |
    ISBN 9781503644601 ebook
Subjects: LCSH: United States—Foreign relations—Iran | Iran—Foreign
    relations—United States
Classification: LCC E183.8.I55 K39 2026 (print) | LCC E183.8.I55 (ebook)
    | DDC 327.73055—dc23/eng/20250408
LC record available at https://lccn.loc.gov/2025008564
LC ebook record available at https://lccn.loc.gov/2025008565

Cover design: Bob Aufuldish, Aufuldish & Warinner

The authorized representative in the EU for product safety and compliance
is: Mare Nostrum Group B.V. | Mauritskade 21D | 1091 GC Amsterdam
| The Netherlands | Email address: gpsr@mare-nostrum.co.uk | KVK
chamber of commerce number: 96249943

To David, Danielle, and Abe for all the joy and encouragement that only a family can bring

CONTENTS

PREFACE

One of my early forays into U.S. policy on Iran was a 2007 conference in Washington, D.C. that I helped organize as a mid-career political scientist at the RAND Corporation. I was fortunate to work with my colleague, the late Jim Dobbins, a prominent former U.S. diplomat with a renowned reputation for troubleshooting conflict and postconflict crises, from the Balkans to Somalia and many places in between. Iran policy wasn't new to me by any measure, but my previous academic work centered more on Arab-Israeli peacemaking. I had also written a book about track two diplomacy, informal dialogues among experts and former officials that aim to create channels of communication that can help prevent and resolve conflicts. I had taught and written about international affairs, Middle East politics, and peace processes as an assistant professor at George Washington University before returning to my home state of California to join RAND at its headquarters in Santa Monica.

The question of what moves adversaries from conflict toward peace is what motivated me to study international relations in the first place. In the late 1980s I studied for a year in Jerusalem during the first Palestinian uprising (the *intifada*), which I believed demonstrated that the conflict was unsustainable. The onset of the Oslo peace process in the early 1990s seemed to validate that belief and offer hope that the parties were finally moving toward resolving this seemingly intractable conflict. I even wrote my doctoral dissertation and published my first book on the subject of regional cooperation "beyond the handshake" between Israeli prime minister Yitzhak Rabin and Palestine Liberation Organization chairman Yasser Arafat on the White House lawn. Tragically, those heady days passed, and by the late 1990s and early 2000s, especially after the second *intifada*, the outlook for peace appeared far bleaker. Working on the subject had become enervating, even if it kept drawing me back in.

So when I arrived at RAND in 2005, it was somewhat of a relief to find there was more demand for research on Iran and related regional security issues than on the Arab-Israeli conflict. These were still the early years of the United States dealing with the aftermath of its disastrous invasion of Iraq in 2003, which led to rising Iranian influence across the region. Iran's growing nuclear ambitions also posed a significant threat, not just to the United States, but also to the global nonproliferation regime. Having lived in the Netherlands in the early 2000s to work on projects related to European policy in the Middle East, I was familiar with the difficult European diplomatic outreach to Iran on the nuclear challenge and other areas of concern.

Dobbins, no naïve optimist by any stretch, nonetheless believed that governments needed to engage adversaries to solve problems, a position that strongly resonated with me. And yet, as we were organizing that event in Washington nearly twenty years ago, I was struck by how difficult even rudimentary dialogue with Iranian counterparts could be. We had hoped, for example, to convene a panel via videoconference—at the time a novel feature—where senior U.S. diplomat Nicholas Burns, then the undersecretary of state for political affairs, and seasoned Iranian diplomat Mohammad Javad Zarif, then Iran's permanent representative to the United Nations, could speak to each other directly. Despite our entreaties, the political sensitivities about public direct engagement made it impossible to convene the conversation, even via video link. Instead, each addressed the conference separately. This incident only underscored for me how important developing channels of communication would be if the United States and Iran were ever to start chipping away at one of the most deeply rooted adversarial relationships in the world.

My participation in several dozen track two meetings involving Iranians and other regional participants over two decades has deepened my conviction in the importance of dialogue to better understand the perceptions and motivations driving American adversaries. I also came to understand just how challenging it would be to deal with Iran, given the deep well of animosity toward the country in Washington. Iran's conduct from the earliest days of its revolution—hostage taking, support for terrorism, repression at home—provided plenty of ammunition to fuel the hostility. But what I never understood was how not talking to Iranians would make them less dangerous. Even as I continued years of policy research on Iran's conduct in the region, its nuclear advances and its adversarial relationship with Israel and other states in the region, I wondered why the U.S. relationship with Iran was so resistant to change, given how much damage this hostility has caused—to us, to them, to the region, and indeed to the world.

When I left RAND in late 2020 to pursue other initiatives, I finally had the opportunity to step back and reflect on this question. I began what would become this book while a fellow at the Wilson Center in Washington, D.C., and continued to work on the project intermittently over the next several years, collecting and reading a wide array of existing material on the topic as well as conducting interviews with many of the leading American policymakers who helped shape U.S. policies on Iran over the years. The outbreak of the Gaza war after the Hamas attack on Israel on October 7, 2023, only accentuated the dangers of this fraught relationship.

U.S.–Iran hostility has now endured—and Americans and Iranians have had to endure it—for longer than the Cold War between the United States and the Soviet Union. After many years of trying to help inform U.S. policy options on Iran, I wanted to use the book as a way to better understand why the U.S.–Iran relationship was so deeply adversarial in the first place. Why hadn't transformational geostrategic shifts or leadership changes significantly altered the relationship after so many years? Even with the occasional modest bilateral engagement, and more significant dialogue in the Iran nuclear talks during the Obama administration, what accounted for the overarching and consistent antagonism of the relationship? Why, in short, was the hostility so enduring?

The conventional answer—"It's them, not us"—does not tell the full story. To be sure, an "It's Iran, stupid!" explanation is compelling given the Islamic Republic's long history of reprehensible activities, from its own external terrorism and support for terrorist groups to domestic repression, not to mention the hostage crisis of 1979 to 1981. No doubt that plays a major role in contemporary American policy, a story of Iranian bad behavior that is well documented and often told. Less well understood is the American side of the story—because the enduring hostility is not just about them, it is also about us. Without looking into the policymaking system within the United States, we cannot fully understand the depth and duration of the hostility. Given my decades-long engagement with the American foreign policy community, I felt this was an angle I could uncover and explain in ways that illuminate not only U.S. Middle East policy but also, more generally, how Washington works when a foreign policy subject has deep domestic resonance.

Ultimately, the result is a book about American foreign policy and the people who make it. I have always believed that we cannot fully understand foreign policy, or likely any area of public policy, without understanding the people who shape it. And the prevailing beliefs of the policymakers who have shaped America's Iran policy for decades have remained remarkably consistent. Perhaps the second Trump presidency, just starting as I write these words, will prove disruptive enough to foreign policy orthodoxies to chart a different path, for better or worse. But if nearly a half-century of U.S.–Iran hostility has taught us anything, the underlying dynamics that influence foreign policy in Washington will prove difficult to change. My hope is that this book offers both a cautionary tale and also the prospect that change is possible, even between the most intractable of enemies.

ACKNOWLEDGMENTS

Writing a book is a solitary endeavor but, as all authors know, it is not possible without a lot of help along the way. I am grateful for the time and space to start the research for this book as a visiting scholar at the Wilson Center, and to the "Covid cohort" of fellows encouraging one another's book projects despite the pandemic setbacks. The Wilson Center's library staff offered excellent research support and I am also thankful to Robert Litwak and Merissa Khurma for providing a welcoming environment during my visit. Jonah Kaufman-Cohen was a stellar research assistant during the early stages of the project. The Wilson Center's demise in the early months of the second Trump administration is a deep loss for the foreign policy community and wider public understanding of global issues.

The UCLA Burkle Center for International Relations has provided an intellectual home for me throughout the writing of this book and as I simultaneously pursued other research projects. Its director, Kal Raustiala, and deputy director, Alexandra Lieben, are steadfast friends and supporters of my work.

While I researched and wrote the book after leaving the RAND Corporation, my fifteen years of experience there was critical to my career development. I will always value the friendship and wisdom of the board members of RAND's Center for Middle East Public Policy (CMEPP) both during and after my time as director, and the many RAND colleagues whom I worked closely with over the years. I am particularly grateful to

Peter Richards for providing critical feedback on early iterations of the book proposal. Fred Wehrey has been a consistent collaborator, sharing his deep knowledge of the region and the publishing world, and Shira Efron, a supportive friend and research partner, helped connect me to many of the Israeli policymakers whom I interviewed for the book.

I have also greatly benefited from the insights and support of my Swedish friends and colleagues during a research visit as a Fulbright scholar at Lund University in 2023–2024, hosted by the Center for Middle Eastern Studies (CMES) and its director, Karin Aggestam. The vibrant research environment and supportive colleagues enabled me to make significant progress on this book and gain new insights into the changing landscape in both the Middle East and Europe.

Stanford University Press editor Dan LoPreto's support throughout the publication process has proved invaluable, offering both substantive and procedural feedback that helped move the project seamlessly from early drafts to the final manuscript. I am also grateful to SUP's editing, production, and marketing teams for seeing the manuscript through to publication. The input from anonymous reviewers was also extremely helpful in improving the book as I moved toward the final editing stages.

I am in debt to the many policymakers and experts I interviewed over the course of writing this book, some of whom are acknowledged by name but many of whom preferred to remain anonymous. Their insights provided a window into internal dynamics shaping U.S. policy that was absolutely critical to the analysis that resulted in these pages.

Last, but most important of all, my husband David Kaye encouraged me at every stage of the project, reading and editing far too many drafts and allowing me to talk through challenges at critical points. He has always been and continues to be my biggest booster in work and life.

INTRODUCTION

Iran as the Ultimate Rogue

The 1991 Gulf War ended with a promise of peace in the Middle East, an American commitment to shepherd Israelis and Arabs into a peace conference that would jump-start not just an Israeli-Palestinian agreement but also wider regional security and development. The United States, under the no-nonsense guidance of Secretary of State James Baker, organized the conference in Madrid in October of that year with an ambition to redefine the region for a world after the Cold War. The meeting, co-chaired by President George H. W. Bush and Soviet president Mikhail Gorbachev, brought together the principal adversaries as well as representatives from the United Nations, the European Community, and dozens of governments from inside and outside the region.

One government was conspicuously absent: the Islamic Republic of Iran. During a wide-ranging discussion with the late Martin Indyk, one of the most prominent former U.S. officials involved in American peace-making efforts, I asked about his views on the exclusion of such a pivotal player in regional politics.[1] Indyk was outside of government at the time of the Madrid conference but remained close to the State Department team that organized it and served as a CNN commentator during the conference itself. What did he make of arguments, detailed in some historical accounts, that the Iranian leadership felt slighted by being excluded from Madrid?[2] Might that have played any role in Iran's subsequent attempts to sabotage the peace efforts? Indyk took a moment, expressing shock at the question. "Why on earth," he asked, "would Iran be invited to Madrid?"

1

Iran supported terrorism. Iran denied the right of Israel to exist. Iran wasn't an Arab state. What did Iran have to do with Arab-Israeli peacemaking?

His reaction was telling. Never mind that Iran's key Arab-state ally Syria was invited and agreed to attend. Or that Madrid and follow-on multilateral peace talks were designed to solve regional problems, many of which affected, and were affected by, Iran, particularly in the arms control and regional security arena. Even if Israel and a number of Arab states would have likely objected to Iranian participation, and Iranian leaders might have refused to join even if they had been invited, it is revealing that Iran's inclusion in such a large multilateral global forum would simply be incomprehensible to a senior American official.

Indeed, other former senior American policymakers who were actively involved in planning the Madrid conference acknowledge Iran was not the priority at the time. According to Dennis Ross, a key advisor in Baker's inner circle and well-known policy advisor to Democratic and Republican administrations, the prevailing view among the American team was that if Arab-Israeli peacemaking could restructure the Middle East, the United States could come back to deal with Iran later.[3] There would be no political upside for these American policymakers to fathom including Iran in their postwar plans.

A Country beyond the Pale

For many American officials at the apex of U.S. foreign policy, Iran has long been beyond the pale, distinct from other adversaries, an anomaly in American diplomacy. Henry Kissinger's oft-cited question as to whether Iran is a country or a cause resonates in Washington because Iran's revolutionary ideology and enmity toward the United States make it the ultimate "rogue" state, unbound by international law or conceptions of "normal" state behavior. Considering Iran to be anything else—to have its own strategic interests, objectives, and threat perceptions—is anathema to many of Washington's foreign policy elite.

This is not to say that U.S. officials have unified views on Iran. In nearly every administration, internal debates, at times at the very highest level, aired differences among policymakers about how to deal with Tehran. Every administration has contemplated negotiating with Iran, and in a number of cases direct and indirect diplomacy between Iranians and Americans did take place.

And yet, despite transformative global strategic shifts, changing leadership, and evolving domestic political contexts since the emergence of the Islamic Republic in 1979, U.S. policy toward Iran has remained remarkably, stubbornly consistent. There has been no "Nixon goes to China" moment in the U.S.–Iran relationship. Hostility, isolation, and containment have persisted as the prevailing policies of choice against a country that regularly ranks as among the top threats to U.S. regional interests in national security doctrines. On occasion U.S. policies have sought to lower the temperature, either in response to more pragmatic Iranian leaders or because of competing priorities at home. But such variations in policy are like bends in a river flowing largely in the same strategic direction.

Even the brief respite in U.S.–Iran tensions in the months leading up to and following the 2015 nuclear agreement (the Joint Comprehensive Plan of Action, or JCPOA) did not fundamentally alter U.S. views or longer term policies toward Iran. If anything, concerns about Iran's regional influence and activities only increased after the nuclear deal and subsequently after its unraveling caused by the first Trump administration's withdrawal in 2018. Despite the Biden administration's intention to rejoin the nuclear agreement, the JCPOA languished as U.S.–Iran tensions and even military escalation ensued. Animus toward Iran among American leaders may have reached its peak during the first Trump presidency, but the underlying anti-Iran stance has long been the default position in Washington.

Given the long and tortured history of U.S.–Iran relations, starting with the hostage crisis following the Islamic revolution, U.S. official hostility may seem unsurprising and eminently justifiable. Iran's arming, training, and funding of militant nonstate groups harmful to U.S. interests and personnel in the decades since have only reinforced prevalent views in Washington that Iran is the source of all the region's problems— the ringleader of the so-called resistance axis opposed to Israel and the U.S. presence in the Middle East.

Putting aside the fallacy of conflating a range of complex Middle East challenges with one return address, it is certainly the case that Iran is a dangerous adversary. But in comparison to global adversaries like Russia and China, or regional powers like North Korea, Iran's capabilities are considerably more limited, as is its ability to cause direct harm to the United States—though its threats to its neighbors and to U.S. personnel based in the region are of course far more serious. And yet, even in the midst of Russia's war against Ukraine and growing global competition with a more aggressive China, the United States has maintained diplomatic relations with both Russia and China.

Indeed, American policymakers have been able to overcome deeply rooted animosity toward other adversaries with far greater global reach and impact on U.S. interests to pursue a working relationship. The U.S. superpower rivalry with the Soviet Union during the Cold War is a good example of the ability of adversaries to maintain diplomatic relations even in the midst of ideological and, at times, armed confrontation, particularly among proxies. The United States was able to normalize relations with Vietnam after a bitter and humiliating war that cost more than fifty thousand American lives, indeed, even while many U.S. servicemen remained missing. Republican and Democratic administrations restored diplomatic relations with countries like Libya and Cuba, for decades prime examples of rogueness for Washington.

The United States maintains diplomatic relations with an array of repressive governments responsible for egregious human rights abuses, and some are even close American security partners. The United States supported Iraq in the Iran-Iraq War in the 1980s despite Saddam Hussein's use of chemical weapons, brutality at home, and support for terrorism abroad. The United States never broke diplomatic ties with Pakistan despite its links to terrorism and its development of a nuclear weapon and refusal to join the Nuclear Nonproliferation Treaty (NPT). Before the revolution, Iranian shah Mohammad Reza Pahlavi was among America's closest regional allies despite his repression at home. What has prevented the United States from pursuing a somewhat more normal, even if still adversarial, relationship with postrevolution Iran?

Iran has vast human capital with a well-educated population of 90 million people, many of whom have familial, business, and other affinities with the United States. It is one of the three most important non-Arab states in the region (along with Israel and Turkey). Iran sits on one of the most strategically and economically significant sea passages, the Strait of Hormuz, which accounts for a large share of global oil and trade shipments. Past tensions with Iran—including the Tanker War in the late 1980s, Iran's attacks on Saudi oil facilities following Trump's withdrawal from the nuclear agreement, and Iran-backed Houthi attacks in the Red Sea following the Gaza war—have disrupted global energy and financial markets.

U.S.-Iran hostility has also fueled nuclear and missile proliferation, as well as Iran's creation and backing of dangerous nonstate militia forces like Hezbollah in Lebanon, the Houthis in Yemen, Kata'ib Hizballah (KH) in Iraq, and extremist Palestinian groups in the West Bank and Gaza, including Palestinian Islamic Jihad and Hamas. Iranian-backed militias have killed U.S. military personnel. The risk of direct U.S. military confrontation with Iran is not hypothetical. Military clashes between the United States, Iran, and Israel only intensified and became more overt in the aftermath of the Gaza war.

There is no doubt that Iran deserves the condemnation it has received for this record of destructive activity. Iran engages in threatening and repressive activities, domestically, regionally, and globally. Iran regularly violates international law and norms through its support for terrorist organizations as well as its own hostage taking of civilians for political aims and other forms of transnational repression. But without understanding the driving forces underlying U.S. policy formation on Iran, and particularly the politics that shape the framing of the Iranian threat in Washington and the policy choices that are deemed possible, we lack the full picture about why U.S.–Iran relations have remained so consistently hostile.

The negative consequence of this hostility is not just an American-Iranian affair—it has touched every corner of the globe. American-Iranian enmity has at times harmed U.S. relationships with its closest European and Asian allies, and has provided opportunities to global rivals like Russia and China. Hostage takings, assassinations, terrorism, missile attacks, sabotage, sanctions, and energy crises are just some of the many ways this relationship has ricocheted within and beyond the Middle East. Foreign officials and scholars often ask me some version of the question, "Why is America so obsessed with Iran?"—because this hostile relationship has a direct impact on their own security.

Not only has American-Iranian hostility endured, but both sides—and the world—have had to endure it for nearly half a century. Given the stakes, why has there been nothing like a U.S.–Soviet détente moment in America's relations with Iran? Why, despite changing global imperatives and new administrations with differing foreign policy priorities, has U.S. hostility toward Iran remained a largely predictable feature in the Washington landscape?

It's Them, Not Us

The most popular response across the political spectrum in Washington is simple: "It's them, not us." *Iran* is the problem. *Iran* traumatized the United States by taking more than fifty U.S. diplomats hostage and holding them for 444 days following the turmoil of the Iranian revolution in 1979. It is not American stubbornness but the Islamic Republic's behavior—support for terrorism and proxy groups hostile to U.S. interests and partners, attempts to export its revolutionary Islamic ideology, its imprisonment of foreign and dual nationals, its repression at home—that explains why the United States views Iran as an abnormal state.

Iran is the country that established *velayat-e faqih* following the revolution, a system of government that gives its Shia clerical leaders authority to rule over the state, led by the Supreme Leader, or guardian of the state. Despite its hybrid system of institutions, with an elected president and parliament, the Supreme Leader holds ultimate authority. Unelected councils serve as gatekeepers vetting presidential candidates. The "republic" part of the Islamic Republic has failed to evolve in ways that allow for real democratic openings or even the ability of reformist or pragmatic leaders to steer the country away from its enduring hostility toward Washington.

If anything, hardline conservative factions within Iran, often called "principlists" because of their strict adherence to the Islamic principles underpinning the revolution, consolidated their rule over time. They successfully repressed multiple bouts of protests, including the widespread "Woman, Life, Freedom" movement in the fall of 2022. Such opposition is not likely to entirely dissipate, given the eroding legitimacy of the system across large segments of Iranian society and growing disenchantment with the possibility of change from within even when reformist presidents are elected.

So, yes, concerns about Iranian behavior *are* valid. Repressive, authoritarian, and corrupt leaders in Iran *do* pursue policies that destabilize the region and violate the rights of their own people. This book is not an effort to ignore the many reprehensible activities undertaken by the Islamic Republic of Iran. That Iran engages in destructive activities at home and abroad, and that it plays a meaningful role in U.S. policy and domestic perceptions, is a baseline assumption.

Some may argue that to understand U.S. policy toward Iran, one needs to understand the domestic workings of the country because this explains American positions. This is another version of an "it's them, not us" argument: that U.S. policy is largely responding to the anti-American foundations that drive Iran's foreign policies, even as Iranian domestic politics have fluctuated over the years. However, such assessments cannot fully account for strategic moments when Iranian leaders, despite the ideological underpinnings of a government inherently hostile to the West, have displayed pragmatism, including a willingness to engage in diplomacy with the United States. Even the hardline Supreme Leader Ali Khamenei made compromises—such as endorsing diplomacy with the United States through the JCPOA negotiations—that appear to work against the ideological orientation of a system that many believe cannot fundamentally accept relations with Washington.

Moreover, it is unclear whether American policymakers have been able to fully understand subtle domestic shifts within Iran. Limited interaction between American and Iranian leaders may only reinforce assumptions that Iranian behavior is largely unchanging. The complexity of the Iranian system poses serious challenges to outsiders genuinely interested in understanding domestic dynamics and potential openings. The absence of U.S. diplomats from the country does not make understanding Iran's confounding domestic politics any easier. As veteran American diplomat Ryan Crocker, who had considerable experience dealing directly with the Iranians during a lengthy State Department career, put it to me, it is "nonsensical" to think American policymakers have any idea about what motivates Iran.[4] Indeed, Iranian politics are extremely opaque even for the most astute analysts of the country who speak the language and are able to visit the country regularly.

Consequently, this is not a book that attempts to decipher Iran and what motivates Iranian leaders. It is not trying to settle longstanding debates about whether Iran is driven by ideology or national interests. Instead, this is a book about how American policymakers *perceive* Iran and how those beliefs inform the policies they have pursued toward Iran over time. This is ultimately a book about *U.S. foreign policy*. It seeks to illuminate why American policies toward Iran have remained relatively consistent, driven by deep animosity and political toxicity that seems to set Iran apart even from other difficult adversaries.

Looking Within

No policy is inevitable. Policymakers have agency. They are people influenced by the discourse and politics attached to specific issues, and by the way they have come to understand and discuss a particular policy over time. This book tells a story about the evolution of Iran policy in Washington. It is about American policymakers and their perceptions of Iran and the politics that have informed and constrained policy decisions on Iran. It is about the people who shaped these policies, the debates that emerged, and the policies that ultimately prevailed.

The account covers U.S. policies on Iran from the Reagan administration to the end of the Biden presidency, including through the 2024 presidential election of Donald Trump for a second term. It draws on U.S. archival material, oral histories of former senior U.S. government officials, memoirs of American presidents and other high-ranking policymakers, and congressional hearings spanning four decades, as well as many other historical and secondary sources—books, journal articles, and media accounts—focused on U.S.–Iran relations.

It also utilizes original author interviews with U.S. government officials who played direct roles in shaping U.S. Iran policy across administrations, as well as interviews with other policymakers and experts engaged with Iran policy in the United States, Europe, and Israel. My own experience participating in several dozen "track two" meetings related to Iran over the past twenty years provided additional insights.[5] Taken together, these resources provide a robust picture of U.S. policy formulation on Iran.

The book is not, however, a historical study attempting to include every detail in the back-and-forth of U.S.–Iran relations; other books cover this ground extensively already.[6] Many studies understandably concentrate on the momentous events that unfolded during the 1953 coup that ousted Iranian prime minister Mohammad Mossedegh and set the stage for the rule of Shah Mohammad Reza Pahlavi, the Islamic revolution, and the American hostage crisis.[7] The books that go beyond the revolutionary period provide detailed narratives by historians, former U.S. officials, journalists, and other political analysts. They often tell the story of missed opportunities for rapprochement because of poor understandings of the other side or bad timing, providing useful insights into domestic Iranian politics while doing so.[8]

Other studies draw on myth narratives to advance our understanding of the seemingly perpetual state of hostility between the United States and Iran since 1979. Hussein Banai, Malcolm Byrne, and the late John Tirman argue that both the United States and Iran have fallen into a narrative trap shaped by clashing myths that drive their respective policies.[9] For American policymakers, they argue that the frontier myth and the belief in American exceptionalism help explain U.S. dealings with Iran, including widely held views about "mad mullahs" and irrational, duplicitous leaders; the Iranians adhere to similarly unaccommodating myths that foster mistrust of outsiders and an elevation of Iranian culture over others.[10] While narratives are a useful frame to understand policy formation, they are also shaped by contemporary discourse, not just by longstanding political myths.

Some scholars have pursued a comparative perspective, examining how the concept of rogue states shaped broader U.S. strategy after the Cold War, to include other states like North Korea and Iraq.[11] Memoirs by American leaders provide additional, albeit selective, details about U.S. Iran policy. Such assessments can open insightful windows into policies at specific historical junctures but are not designed to provide the full arc of American policy evolution on Iran as presented in this book.

Analyses of U.S.–Iran relations by former U.S. military and intelligence officials have covered longer time frames and offer important details about the relationship at least up through the first Obama administration, but they often reflect an American viewpoint that largely places blame on Iran for the continued enmity between the two countries.[12] Some scholars offer more pointed critiques of U.S. policy, identifying Israel and the pro-Israel lobby in Washington as key factors shaping America's policies on Iran.[13] Other analysts have highlighted the risks emanating from the triangle of conflict between the United States, Iran, and Israel.[14]

There can be little doubt that Israel plays an important role in U.S. policy on Iran, and this book considers Israeli positions in every strategic era, given Israel's prominent position in Washington policy discourse on the Middle East. But Israel has not been the definitive driver for Iran policy, even if Israel factors into the thinking of American officials when it comes to Middle East policy to a greater than that of just about any other regional power. There are numerous examples in which Israeli preferences did not prevail—from the 1980s, when Israel sought more accommodating positions toward Iran than Washington, to Israel's strident opposition but ultimate failure to derail the JCPOA in the Obama administration.

Israel's impact on American policymakers is thus important but often inconclusive.

To fully capture what drives Iran policy, we must also look within. Looking within suggests examining the people, ideas, and framing that shape policy debates on Iran over time. That means a deep dive into how American policymakers see Iran and talk about Iran, and how they read strategic and domestic imperatives that feed into how they debate and consider policy choices.

We know from cognitive and political science research that the framing of issues can shape policy debates and outcomes. As George Lakoff argues, words matter; words have meaning and influence politics.[15] The words we use often define where we stand on critical political debates of the day. Frames reinforce worldviews, and worldviews impact policy, whether in the Supreme Court or the State Department. Indeed, elite framing is as applicable to foreign policy debates as it is to domestic politics. Iran is an excellent example of how a deeply rooted framing of a policy issue, using similar language repeatedly over time, has influenced worldviews, politically acceptable options, and ultimately policy results.

Specifically, the way in which American policymakers have framed Iran so consistently over the years—as an "outlaw," "abnormal," "rogue," "fanatical," "evil," or "malign" state—has impacted the domestic political space that might enable a more fundamental reconsideration of U.S. positions. Different types of language contribute to the framing of Iran as an abnormal state for different reasons. For example, seeing Iran as a "fanatical" regime led by the "crazy mullahs" evokes an Islamist and religious aspect, that Iran is not a normal state because it is driven by religious fanatics. Another framing, calling Iran a "malign" or "evil" state, suggests a moralistic underpinning to Iran's abnormality, feeding into an American inclination to see the world in Manichean terms, where the United States is the force for good leading the way against the "evil" actors promoting dangerous ideologies.[16] Seeing Iran as a "rogue" or "outlaw" state feeds into frames viewing Iran as an irrational, rule-breaking state, outside the bounds of international norms of how states are supposed to behave ("normal" states do not engage in terrorist acts or hostage taking).

These rationales combine to create an image of Iran as the quintessential abnormal state. Naturally, Iran has played into such framing with behavior that validates such labels. But even by the standards of other "abnormal" states, Iran stands out. Other adversarial states, such as North

Korea, Cuba, Venezuela, or more recently Russia under Vladimir Putin, are often described as "evil" and as "outlaws" breaking international rules, but not as "religious fanatics." In the case of Iran, we have a perfect storm of rogueness—an outlaw and a religious fundamentalist state all in one. This prevailing view of Iran stretches across the political spectrum and all segments of the foreign policy community. From the halls of Congress to the Defense Department to the foreign policy think tanks and media outlets shaping opinion in Washington, the notion that Iran is an abnormal state has become the mainstream and largely accepted frame.

There are exceptions, particularly within the intelligence community (including intelligence analysts at the State Department and Pentagon), that present accounts of Iranian motives and threat perceptions shorn of the typical Washington framing. Such accounts assume Iran is acting rationally to advance its interests, even if those interests are directly counter to America's (and in many cases to the well-being of the Iranian people). Pentagon reports to Congress, for example, regularly emphasize the defense-based and deterrence motivations of an Iranian leadership interested in survival, even as they catalog an array of Iranian capabilities of concern.[17] One of the most significant public intelligence documents on Iran's nuclear intentions and capabilities, the 2007 National Intelligence Estimate (NIE), attributed Iran's decision to halt its nuclear weapons program in 2003 to decisions "guided by a cost-benefit approach" that responded to both pressure and incentives.[18] This is hardly an assessment of an irrational state. But as this book demonstrates, policymakers arguing for a different way of looking at Iran—for a different frame—have rarely succeeded in impacting public debates and final policy decisions.

Indeed, the consistency and endurance of the American discourse hostile to Iran—made easier to sustain given Iran's own inability to change—might help explain why Iran's abnormal status sets it apart from even other dangerous adversaries. Some scholars argue that the United States selectively decides which adversaries are worthy of engagement and which are not based on realpolitik factors such as whether the stakes are too high, or the adversary is too powerful to ignore. But these scholars also point out that countries may base choices on domestic considerations. According to this reasoning, the United States is more likely to engage adversaries, even those labeled as rogue, when the chances of policymakers being accused of appeasement are lower.[19]

When a country has been so consistently framed as a pariah across the

political landscape for as long as Iran has, the political costs for American policymakers to contemplate more normalized ties become extremely
high. This is all the more so given Iran's Shia Islamic identity and the tendency in American policy circles to conflate political Islam with extremism. Policymakers are thus more likely to be concerned about accusations
of "caving in" or "looking weak" when it comes to Iran policy than with
just about any other national security issue.

Moreover, policymakers believe they can affect the calculations of
"normal" states because they are rational. But with abnormal, irrational
states, policy is unchangeable; they are destined to remain hostile. Why
expend political capital, particularly given that public views of the country
are already negative, to engage Iran in a new type of relationship if the
perception is that its leaders are not capable of change? The political costs
of compromising with such a state become significantly higher, particularly over time as grievances grow over Iranian actions that work against
U.S. interests and harm Americans and close American partners.

There is the added concern, distinct from political calculations, that
even if policymakers believe Iran is rational enough to respond to U.S.
pressure (or, less commonly, incentives), if Iran is ultimately a rogue state
willing to engage in illegal acts like terrorism, then compromise with such
a state will only lead to more rogue-like behavior. Consequently, American policymakers have more often than not believed that only military
and economic pressure will influence Iran's activities, and that a failure to
forcefully respond to Iran will only encourage more bad Iranian behavior.
Brian Hook, President Trump's Iran envoy in his first term, made exactly
these points in a congressional hearing on Iran in early 2024 in the context
of the Gaza war, arguing that the failure to keep up the pressure on Iran
was only emboldening Iran's bad behavior.[20] But as is so often the case
when it comes to Iran, these arguments were not new.

In a 1985 Intelligence Memorandum analyzing Middle East terrorism,
for example, CIA director William J. Casey pointed to a key conclusion of
the intelligence analysis: "If the US fails to respond to attacks by Iranian-
sponsored groups, Iranian terrorism will continue and very likely grow."[21]
The analysis even pointed to Tehran's release of American hostages (which
occurred just after Ronald Reagan was sworn in as president) as evidence
that Iran could moderate its behavior in response to "heavy pressure . . .
when its leaders believed a more aggressive US administration had been

elected."[22] Decades after Casey's assessment, American policymakers continued to hold similar assumptions about Iranian behavior.

In other words, America's Iran policy is not just responding to strategic imperatives, the influence of regional states, or Iran's own actions. It is at its core homegrown, shaped by the worldviews and predominant framing and assumptions about Iran among American policymakers. This account will provide insights into how worldviews become deeply rooted over time, reinforced by domestic pressures that make it politically difficult to change course. This domestic framework helps explain the relative consistency of America's Iran policy over time, even in moments when change seemed possible.

Dealing with the New Islamic Republic

Even in the earliest days of the Iranian revolution, during the Carter administration, domestic factors were at play. This is particularly apparent when examining how American policymakers debated whether to establish ties with and accept the new revolutionary rulers of Iran. This episode is an important prologue to the Iran debates that emerged in subsequent administrations, which the following chapters address.

U.S. officials held out hope for the early collapse of the Islamic Republic and wanted to continue backing the Shah. Before the Iranian revolution, successive administrations, Republican and Democratic, actively supported the Shah, an authoritarian, pro-American monarch and last ruler of the Pahlavi dynasty. U.S. leaders viewed him as one of the most important American allies in the region. By the Nixon administration, Iran had become a key pillar in U.S. regional policy to combat both communists and Arab nationalists hostile to America's presence in the Middle East.

In exchange, the United States largely turned a blind eye to human rights concerns, while selling billions of dollars' worth of advanced arms to the Shah's government. Even President Carter, who had come to office determined to elevate human rights concerns in U.S. foreign policy, continued America's close alignment and friendship with the Shah, including the sale of advanced U.S. weapons. In his last visit to Tehran, in December 1977, just before revolutionary protests began, Carter notoriously exclaimed during a toast at a dinner with the Shah that "Iran, because of the great leadership of the shah, is an island of stability in one of the more troubled areas of the world."[23]

The Shah's intimate relationship with Washington created resentment in many quarters in Tehran, including among the emergent class of revolutionaries. The question of what drove the Iranian revolution continues to spark endless controversy—and is not the subject of this book. Like any momentous and complex political event, it is likely that a number of external and domestic factors—including the Shah's own governing style—played a significant role in the revolution. But the legacy of the United States in supporting, along with the British, a coup to oust Iran's democratically elected nationalist prime minister Mohammad Mosaddegh in 1953 is hard to escape.

Analysts continue to debate whether the coup would have been possible without domestic support within the country, with some scholars challenging conventional views attributing the coup solely to workings of external powers and arguing that the overthrow was largely an Iranian affair.[24] Nonetheless, the perception that external meddling disrupted Iran's democratic government has endured. Such perceptions fueled significant mistrust of American intentions in the country and fed a deep well of animosity toward the United States among many of the Shah's domestic opponents, including the Islamic leaders who would come to consolidate power in Tehran after crushing the secular and communist supporters of the revolution. This historical context presented a significant barrier for any future American leader interested in normalized ties with a post-Shah Iran.

American diplomats in Tehran, supported by Secretary of State Cyrus Vance, nonetheless argued for early engagement with the new revolutionary leaders. After all, other Western governments were in dialogue with the Islamic leader of Iran's revolution, Ayatollah Ruhollah Khomeini. Khomeini was in fact exiled in France before returning to Iran in February 1979. Other European diplomats reached out to Iran's revolutionary leaders—why not the United States? American diplomats even warned about a severe backlash against U.S. interests should the United States demonstrate continued support for the Shah after he fled the country.

Indeed, the top U.S. diplomat in Tehran sent a cable to Washington in the summer of 1979 warning that giving refuge to the Shah would make it difficult to build a bilateral relationship with Iran's new leaders and "would almost certainly trigger demonstrations against our embassy. With luck, they may stop at that."[25] These arguments were ultimately overruled by

President's Carter's national security advisor, Zbigniew Brzezinski, who worried about the message the abandonment of the Shah would send to other allies, and the opening it might provide to the Soviets to increase their influence in the region—his overriding strategic concern.

Domestic political considerations were linked closely to such fears of undermining American credibility for Carter's close advisors. Exiles supporting the Shah and the Pahlavi dynasty had close relationships with top Nixon administration officials, such as Secretary of State Henry Kissinger, and prominent business leaders, such as David Rockefeller, who were also vocal supporters of the Shah. These influential voices supported a hard-line stance against the revolution, as Kissinger "mounted a vigorous public campaign accusing gutless liberals in the State Department of having 'lost Iran' . . . Newspaper editorials blasted Carter for 'desert[ing] the Shah and his regime at a time when he needed support' and allowing Iran to 'fall into the clutches of wild men.'"[26]

It is thus not surprising that in such a domestic climate Carter officials perceived a more accommodating approach to the new Iranian government as politically risky. Worrying that the Republicans might try to use Iran as a campaign issue, Carter's chief of staff Hamilton Jordan was reported to have remarked, at a White House discussion on whether to admit the Shah into the United States from Mexico for medical treatment, that "if the Shah dies in Mexico, can you imagine the field day Kissinger will have with that?"[27] In the end, Carter allowed the Shah to enter the United States in late October 1979. On November 4, 1979, the American hostage ordeal began as a group of Iranian students overran the U.S. Embassy compound amid large anti-American protests and took the diplomats who remained inside hostage, beginning what would become a 444-day crisis.

Concerns about American credibility that influenced these early debates were not unique to Iran. Fears about undermining American credibility became a regular feature in U.S. policymaking after World War II, when the United States assumed a global leadership role. But the particular way the policymakers at the time perceived the domestic pressures and the international consequences of the United States turning its back on the Shah set the stage for the framing of Iran policy for years to come. The hostage crisis, which became a dominant subject of public concern— blanketing the news and dominating the presidential election discourse— also cemented a proclivity to view the Islamic-ruled Iran as an abnormal state in the minds of American policymakers and indeed the public.

As Madeleine Albright, who at the time was a National Security Council (NSC) staffer working for Brzezinski, put it: "We became hostages to the hostages. The combination of that and Ted Koppel and *Nightline* was paralyzing. It overshadowed everything that was going on."[28] Another Carter administration NSC advisor, Gary Sick, told me he does not think it is possible to exaggerate the impact of the hostage crisis on Americans' perceptions of Iran. As he explained, it was reality TV; everyone in the United States saw this, and it was "444 days of scary mullahs."[29] Sick argues that Iran became an obsession for Americans and the hostage crisis left a permanent scar on the country's psyche. In his view, the hostage crisis is what differentiates Iran from Vietnam as it became the "prolonged humiliation of a superpower."[30] Sick recalls how talk radio covered the hostage crisis constantly, and he listened to coverage, every night on his way home from the White House, in which the "Iran is bad" messaging dominated.[31]

Senior officials did not see Iran's "fanatical" religious leadership as a state with which the United States could deal. In a memorandum just weeks after the hostage crisis began, Brzezinski flatly acknowledged this, assessing that "we are never going to be able to work with the Khomeini regime."[32] He called Khomeini his own worst enemy, who would eventually "destroy himself," arguing against a direct attempt to overthrow him because "we will probably not be able to bring it off." He believed that the effort would likely backfire and only strengthen Khomeini's appeal.[33] This would not be the last debate about the possibility of normalizing relations with the Islamic Republic of Iran, or changing its regime, but it was one of the first examples demonstrating just how difficult it would be for those arguing for a different approach.

Nonetheless, U.S. officials trying to secure the release of the American hostages thought Iran would rationally respond to diplomatic and economic pressure. The United States reacted to the hostage taking with sanctions, freezing of Iranian assets, and a global diplomatic push for opposition to the Islamic Republic's actions. Carter also authorized a military rescue mission of the hostages on April 24, 1980. Equipment failure and sandstorms forced the Americans to abort the mission; during the withdrawal one of the rescue helicopters collided with a refueling aircraft, killing eight U.S. servicemen. The failed mission only further tarnished the administration's image and added to the political toxicity of Iran for American policymakers.

Ultimately the Carter administration negotiated a settlement for the release of the American hostages that culminated in the Algiers Accords, signed on January 19, 1981, just a day ahead of the inauguration of Carter's successor, Ronald Reagan. The Accords established a tribunal between the United States and Iran—which still operates in The Hague—where claims between the governments and citizens of both countries could be settled. The Iran–U.S. Claims Tribunal has settled thousands of commercial and trade disputes between the United States and Iran, including approximately $2.5 billion in awards to American investors and businesses, which Iran paid, and hundreds of millions of dollars in settlements the United States paid to Iran arising, in part, from the end of the U.S.–Iran foreign military sales program in 1979.[34]

In the early days of the revolution, senior U.S. officials still believed that after the hostages were released, and as American pressure took its toll, U.S.–Iran relations could once again improve. As deputy secretary of state Warren Christopher, who negotiated the Algiers Accords, explained in a classified congressional hearing in May 1980 (since unclassified), "Our task in the weeks ahead will be to persuade the influential elements in Iran through the pressures of sanctions and through diplomatic means that a settlement of the hostage question is essential for Iran's future."[35] Christopher went on to argue that he expected Iran's leaders to respond to increased pressure for their own self-interest, and that by doing so the path for improved relations with the United States would be open again. As Christopher explained:

> As economic hardship within Iran grows, those Iranians most fervently committed to the revolution and to Iranian national independence must confront the hard truth that the hostage situation threatens both their independence and their revolution . . . the Iranian people must understand that the threat to their revolution does not come from the United States. We would like to see a strong, independent, stable Iran. If this situation is resolved without harm to our people, *the way will be open to develop a relationship that serves our mutual interests.* Clearly, it is not possible for us to do so as long as our people are endangered and illegally imprisoned.[36]

Former secretary of state Edmund Muskie similarly argued in a hearing just months after the release of the hostages in early 1981:

> The United States determined shortly after the success of the revolution to attempt to establish a new relationship . . . the judgment was made that our substantial interests in Iran warranted maintaining a presence

and attempting to build a new relationship . . . In the complex and fluid revolutionary environment, we sought to be open to contacts with all Iranians . . . Our posture was one of readiness to respond to Iranian initiatives and openness to any signs of Iranian desire to resolve the many commercial, military, and political problems that complicated our relationship . . . the United States wanted a relationship with Iran based on "mutual respect, equality and friendship."[37]

Muskie even relayed how the U.S. government understood the grievances Iranians felt over the practices of the former regime, and how the United States was prepared to unfreeze Iranian assets, facilitate "normal" commercial relations, and appoint a representative to discuss common concerns with Iranians over the Soviet invasion of Afghanistan.[38]

But Christopher and Muskie's framing of Iran as a rational actor, and hope for a more normalized relationship once the hostages were freed, became less common over time as the relationship grew more hostile and American policymakers had a difficult time finding leaders in Tehran who would be receptive to U.S. gestures. The times changed, but U.S. policies largely did not.

Changing Times, Unchanging Policies: Reagan to Biden

The best way to understand America's Iran policy, and the players who have shaped it, is to examine key debates and policy over time across different geostrategic contexts. This helps illustrate why, despite shifting global conditions and American priorities, Iran debates have looked astonishingly similar from the early years after the revolution to the present day. If anything, contemplating normalized diplomatic ties with Iran has only become more, not less, contentious within the American political system.

Consequently, the following chapters are organized around key strategic periods since the 1979 revolution, which to a large extent overlap with American presidencies. They are defined as follows: the Cold War (the 1980s during Reagan's two terms in office); the post–Cold War (the 1990s during the H. W. Bush and Clinton administrations); the global "war" on terrorism (the early to mid-2000s during the G. W. Bush administrations); and Great Power Competition (2009 to the present, covering the Obama, Trump, and Biden presidencies). In all eras we see a shift in the strategic environment and changes of American leadership that might have provided an opening for a more normalized relationship with Iran, and in fact most led to some engagement and testing of new policy positions. Internal U.S. debates and policy reviews about the direction of Iran policy occurred in each period. But despite these changing strategic imperatives, we see similar framing and domestic constraints driving Iran policy across the years.

As the following chapters demonstrate, Biden's policies on Iran looked similar to those he inherited from previous administrations, characterized by the dominance of military deterrence, economic pressure, and political isolation. The most visible and enduring change over the years was not the ephemeral nuclear deal but rather the hardening and growing sophistication of the U.S. sanctions regime, locking in years of hostility and only making further possibilities for change more elusive as Iran's own postures hardened.

A Window into American Foreign Policy

This book looks back at U.S. policy toward Iran to help us look ahead. It offers a window into debates beyond Iran policy about how the United States sees its adversaries, how foreign policy is constructed in Washington, and why it is so difficult to change. U.S. Middle East policy is particularly susceptible to deeply ingrained and static framing of adversaries, but the trends also speak to the way other foreign policies have evolved, or more accurately have not evolved, in the American system.

The so-called "blob" characterization of the policymaking community for American foreign policy, coined by Obama's deputy national security advisor Ben Rhodes, may cast its net too broadly in depicting a foreign policy consensus favoring an active, and often militaristic, American role in the world. The reality is far more complex, as multiple fissures divide Washington's foreign policy professionals and cannot fully account for the trend in recent years across the political spectrum to refocus attention at home. But the concept does capture the important point that there are certain boundaries and accepted narratives in Washington that may limit policy options and the testing of new approaches on some critical issues. U.S. Iran policy certainly has fallen victim to this dynamic.

I will explore some of these wider lessons in the conclusion, building on my own experience and observations of the policymaking world in Washington. The way Washington works creates an information environment and incentive structure that makes changing mindsets and policies extremely difficult, particularly on issues like Iran where the perceived risks, including to political careers, are high. Changing course would require more than a change of personnel; it would demand more fundamental perceptual shifts and transformations in the structure of American foreign policymaking itself.

ONE

The Elusive Search for Iranian Moderates

Early in 1986, after an eighteen-month leave to run a Berkeley-Stanford program on Soviet international behavior, Dennis Ross—who had previously served, in President Reagan's first term, at the Pentagon's Office of Net Assessment—returned to the National Security Council (NSC) to serve as the Reagan administration's senior director on the Middle East, working for deputy NSC advisor Donald Fortier. Ross was an expert on the Soviet Union and had written his dissertation on Soviet decision-making, but in later years he immersed himself in U.S. Middle East policymaking across Republican and Democratic administrations, becoming a foreign policy fixture for the next three decades.

To his admirers, Ross is a brilliant strategist who knows all the players—his advice still carries significant weight in many quarters in Washington. To his detractors, Ross's inclination to view the Middle East through the prism of Israel has distorted his assessments of regional dynamics and has led to U.S. policy failures time and again, whether on Arab-Israeli diplomacy or Iran policy. But Ross's career as one of the most influential American policymakers on the Middle East might not have happened had his boss Fortier told him the full story about what the Reagan administration was up to with Iran.

Fortier, a low-profile Republican foreign policy expert who had previously served at the State Department and on Capitol Hill, was closely involved with all the key figures in what would become one of the biggest scandals of the Reagan administration: the Iran-Contra affair. According to Ross, Fortier told him in December 1985—shortly before Ross returned to government—that "there's some things going on here that are a mistake . . . you'll have to help clean them up."[1] In Ross's view, had Fortier not died of liver cancer in August 1986 at age thirty-nine, he might have been able to control the damage. But given the scope of the affair while Fortier was still alive, and support from the very top, this seems unlikely.

The foundation of Iran-Contra was an idea held by several of Reagan's senior aides, including his then national security advisor, Robert "Bud" McFarlane, that they could work with Iranian moderates to help secure the release of American hostages held in Lebanon by militant nonstate groups aligned with Iran. The way to secure Iranian cooperation, the thinking went, would be through the transfer of American arms that the Iranians were desperately seeking in their years-long war with Iraq, particularly since Iran's military still relied on American weaponry acquired under the Shah.

But administration officials like McFarlane also believed the arms deals could lead to more than the release of American hostages. They saw the possibility for wider openings to Iran that could yield strategic benefits, particularly a central Cold War aim of minimizing Soviet influence in a critical oil-rich country sitting on key access points for the global supply of energy. Indeed, historical accounts suggest McFarlane demonstrated an interest in a diplomatic breakthrough with Iran early in the Reagan administration, along the lines of a "Nixon goes to China" moment.[2] That moment never came.

A Scandal instead of a Breakthrough

An advisor to McFarlane known for having close relationships in Israel, Michael Ledeen, worked with the Israelis to help hatch the plan that would become the Iran-Contra scandal. At the time the Israelis did not view Iran as the predominant regional threat; containing Saddam Hussein's Iraq was Israel's primary focus throughout the 1980s. The Israelis were especially concerned about the prospect of Iraq winning its war against Iran and supported better U.S. relations with Iran to maintain a balance. They saw an opportunity for alignment with Soviet-obsessed Reagan advisors amenable to Israeli arguments about the possibility of working with Iranian moderates within the regime. Working through the Israelis and a murky

Iranian arms dealer named Manucher Ghorbanifar, the administration began sending arms to Tehran.

The plan was mired in illegality and questionable conduct. It broke the U.S. arms embargo imposed by President Carter after the seizing of the U.S. Embassy. Adding to the scheme's illegality was the diversion of the profits from the Iranian arms deals to the Contras fighting the socialist government in Nicaragua—despite the congressional prohibition on such funding—carried out by Lieutenant Colonel Oliver North, an NSC advisor covering the Central America file. Publicly exposed in November 1986, the Iran-Contra affair led to dozens of convictions and indictments of administration officials, including Secretary of Defense Caspar Weinberger, all of whom were later pardoned in the final days of the George H. W. Bush administration (Bush was vice president at the time of the affair).

Uncertainty remains over the extent of President Reagan's direct knowledge of all aspects of the Iran-Contra episode. Nonetheless, the president publicly acknowledged U.S. arms sales to Iran, though he initially denied that the sales were an exchange for hostages. He later accepted responsibility for what a government review board characterized as a strategic opening that deteriorated into a trade of arms for hostages.[3] The president did not hide the fact that the arms sales took place, but he made a forceful case for why he backed the policy. In a speech shortly after the affair was exposed, he explained to the nation that he had authorized the secret engagement with Iran for "the simplest and best of reasons: to renew a relationship with the nation of Iran, to bring an honorable end to the bloody 6-year war between Iran and Iraq, to eliminate state-sponsored terrorism and subversion, and to effect the safe return of all hostages."[4]

Reflecting a realism that is rarely expressed publicly by senior U.S. officials, let alone American presidents, Reagan argued: "Without Iran's cooperation, we cannot bring an end to the Persian Gulf war; without Iran's concurrence, there can be no enduring peace in the Middle East."[5] He conceded, "During the course of our secret discussions, I authorized the transfer of small amounts of defensive weapons and spare parts for defensive systems to Iran. My purpose was to convince Tehran that our negotiators were acting with my authority, *to send the signal that the United States was prepared to replace animosity between us with a new relationship.*"[6]

By some accounts, Reagan genuinely believed in the possibility of a strategic opening that could help bring about a less antagonistic relationship. But he also was keenly focused on freeing American hostages in Lebanon. According to Bruce Riedel, a CIA analyst who served on the hostage task force under CIA director William Casey, Reagan asked about the hostages every day; for him, it was personal.[7] For Casey and others, the strategic rationale in restoring historic relations with Iran was central. Reagan officials became major proponents of the idea because, in Riedel's view, the Israelis "planted it" in their minds.[8] Opponents of the policy made the case that if you trade arms for hostages, Iran will take more hostages. But according to Riedel, Casey was "deluded" into believing the benefits of the policy.[9]

Because the Israelis were offering a plan to help the administration secure the release of hostages, they held significant sway over the thinking of the president and his key advisors. Dennis Ross argues that then Israeli prime minister Shimon Peres played a central role in convincing Reagan that there was an opening to moderate Iranians who could help secure the release of the Americans held in Lebanon. Reagan even famously sent his NSC advisor McFarlane to Tehran for a secret visit, with a personal copy of his Bible and a key-shaped cake, to demonstrate the seriousness of the president's interest in "opening the door" to a new U.S. relationship with Iran.[10]

Peres's counterterrorism advisor, Amiram Nir—who died in a plane crash in Mexico in 1988—worked with North to execute the plan. After Ross returned to government in early 1986 as the NSC head on the Middle East, he joined Vice President Bush on a Middle East trip to Israel, Egypt, and Jordan. In a conversation Ross found puzzling at the time, Nir asked Ross what he thought about covert action, remarking that not everyone is "cut out" for it, and told Ross that he was going to talk about it with the vice president. This got Ross "pissed off," as he thought he had a close relationship with Nir, and that Nir was being too aggressive in seeking a meeting with the vice president without him.[11] When Ross returned to Washington, he briefed his boss, national security advisor John Poindexter (who had replaced McFarlane in December 1985), and mentioned Nir's strange comments on covert action. In a move that Ross says "probably saved my career," Poindexter kept him out of the loop.[12]

Reflecting back on the affair, Ross was skeptical that a real strategic opening was in the offing. Why not just offer humanitarian assistance to Iran to test if Iranian leaders really were genuine about a different relationship with Washington, rather than selling arms? Ross's skepticism of

Iran's intentions is a theme that reemerged when he assumed more senior positions in future administrations. In later years, he also became a prominent voice in Washington advocating for a warmer relationship between Washington and Iran's primary regional adversary, Saudi Arabia.[13]

But at the time senior administration officials, including the president himself, believed a different relationship with Iran was possible and that Reagan could sell anything, even an opening to Iran. As Ross put it, there was a sense in the administration that, "yes, they're rogue, yes, they back terror, yes, they're behind the killing of the Marines [in a 1983 bombing in Beirut], but if you could turn them around, it would be a huge strategic shift."[14]

However, instead of a reset with Iran, the Reagan administration created a scandal. The press and the public viewed the scheme as an arms-for-hostages exchange, an embarrassing revelation for an administration that prided itself on presenting a tough stance toward adversaries and terrorist groups. Such exposure was scandalous enough in the psyche of the American policy community, where giving in to adversaries is a demonstration of weakness, to be avoided at all costs. But the added illegality of the episode—violating clear congressional proscriptions—cemented the Iran-Contra affair as a defining moment in the Reagan era, nearly bringing down a president and tainting officials at the highest levels.

The stigma of Iran-Contra also created a barrier for future diplomats and national security officials contemplating engagement with Iran. It reinforced the notion that the Iranians will burn you; that they cannot be trusted. Indeed, after the scandal was exposed, possibly by Iranians unhappy with the prospect of better relations with Washington, the administration's approach to Iran became tougher. And the legacy of the scandal lingered well beyond the Reagan administration. For example, Riedel, who continued working on Middle East policy through the Clinton administration, recalls Clinton's NSC advisor, Anthony Lake, being uninterested in back-channel talks with Iranians because of concerns, in a clear reference to Iran-Contra, that they "seduce you into bed and then turn the lights on at the most awkward moment."[15]

Interestingly, there was more willingness to explore engagement with Iran during the Reagan administration—too much willingness, as it turned out—than we see even in subsequent years when the hostage crisis was a more distant memory. But a review of the public debates and U.S. policy choices at the time—particularly toward the Iran-Iraq and Tanker

Wars—illustrates just how difficult it would be to put Iran policy on a different course, even when the most senior policymakers, and the president himself, had a number of reasons to move the relationship in a different direction.

Keeping the Iranians Out of the Soviet Orbit

As in strategic eras that would follow, there was a case to be made in the Cold War that a new relationship with Iran could benefit U.S. interests. A set of policymakers not only contemplated a different approach but actually acted on it—visiting Tehran and selling arms to the Islamic Republic. The president spoke publicly about the strategic rationale for a different relationship with Iran in ways that were more forward-leaning than those of future American leaders. Reagan was surely driven by his interest in securing the release of American hostages, but the strategic logic of the Cold War also supported engagement.

Concern about pivotal regional states like Iran, with its vast oil reserves, falling into the hands of the Soviets was a key Cold War consideration for U.S. Iran policy throughout the 1980s. Such strategic considerations led to considerable internal debate about reconsidering the American posture toward Iran, preparing in particular for new possibilities once Ayatollah Khomeini died (which American analysts believed was imminent in the mid-1980s, though Khomeini's death would not occur until 1989, after the Reagan presidency). Such considerations moved beyond internal debates into actual administration policies. The strategic logic supporting the arms sales policy was laid out in detail in a number of declassified U.S. government documents.

In a top-secret NSC action memo from Fortier to Poindexter in April 1985, the assumption was that the regime was in control and the opposition in disarray, but that there might be flexibility among some leaders within the inner circle, such as then Majlis [Iranian Parliament] speaker, Akbar Rafsanjani.[16] In thinking about U.S. interests in a post-Khomeini era, the memo highlighted restoring normal relations with Iran while preventing Soviet influence as among the most significant U.S. objectives.[17]

Fortier recommended that Poindexter circulate a draft National Security Decision Directive (NSDD) that he attached to his memo, which argues: "The war between Iraq and Iran, growing Iranian internal dissent, and the growing likelihood of Ayatollah Khomeini's death in the near future, combine to create potential opportunities for the United States to try to restore a position of influence in Iran."[18] The draft directive further called for "movement toward eventual normalization of U.S.–Iranian diplomatic consular and cultural relations, and bilateral trade/commercial activities" and recommended that, given the fluid environment within Iran, the United States should prepare to "restore a normal working relationship between Washington and Tehran," including "establishing links with clerical, Army and Bazaar leaders."[19]

Two months later, in June 1985, Fortier's boss, NSC director McFarlane, sent a memo to Secretary of State George Shultz and Secretary of Defense Weinberger on U.S. policy toward Iran.[20] McFarlane similarly suggested shifting U.S. policy toward a less escalatory posture to keep the Iranians out of the Soviet orbit and to leave the door open for improved relations. He referred to a CIA assessment suggesting the existence of accelerating instability in Iran, arguing that it could have "momentous consequences for U.S. strategic interests," making it sensible "to ask whether our current policy toward Iran is adequate to achieve our interests."[21] McFarlane included the draft NSDD to "stimulate our thinking on U.S. policy toward Iran," but noted that he was circulating the NSDD draft on an "eyes only basis" because of concerns about leakage should the president decide not to pursue a change in policy, underscoring the domestic sensitivity of the Iran file.[22]

The reactions were swift and forceful. Both Weinberger and Shultz vehemently opposed a policy shift. Weinberger thought McFarlane's ideas were "nonsense" because they assumed you could deal with Iran on a "rational basis."[23] Richard Armitage, then a Pentagon advisor, was even more blunt, calling McFarlane's ideas "bullshit."[24] Colin Powell, who was then a military assistant to Weinberger at the Defense Department, said he read through the directive and perceived it as McFarlane making a bid for "Kissingerian immortality," referring to historic achievements like Nixon's opening to China.[25] Viewing Iran as a terrorist state linked to the Marine barracks attack in Lebanon, Powell asked, "Could anything be more audacious?"[26] Weinberger wrote a message across a memo Powell sent him registering his agreement, commenting: "This is almost too absurd to comment on . . . It's like asking Qaddafi to Washington for a cozy chat."[27] When McFarlane asked for a meeting to make the pitch that the United States could win over Iranian moderates and get back into Iran, Weinberger answered that "the only moderates in Iran are in a cemetery" and that Khomeini was "equaled in evil" only by the Soviets.[28]

Despite this opposition from top advisors, many of the strategic points Reagan would later make publicly echoed the contents of this draft directive, even if the president's primary motivation was to secure the release of American hostages.[29] Meanwhile, other senior officials, most notably CIA director Casey, backed McFarlane's approach. According to David Crist, a former Marine whose father headed U.S. Central Command (CENTCOM) during the 1980s, Casey did not see Iran as "an intrinsic threat" and downplayed the Islamic aspects of the regime, seeing Iran instead through the Cold War prism.[30] Casey believed the United States could find moderates to work with to keep Iran away from the Soviets. He was left unconvinced by expert analysis at the CIA and State Department expressing skepticism that Iran would be vulnerable to Soviet influence, given its difficult history with the Russians.[31]

It is thus not surprising that the draft NSDD document provided a clear Cold War strategic rationale for rethinking U.S. policy on Iran. The assessment expressed concern that "the Soviet Union is better positioned than the U.S. to exploit and benefit from any power struggle that results in changes in the Iranian regime" and that increased Soviet influence in Iran would change the "strategic balance in the area."[32] It clearly stated that "our primary short-term challenge must be to block Moscow's efforts to increase Soviet influence (now and after the death of Khomeini) . . . We must improve our ability to protect our interests during the struggle for succession."[33] Even though the U.S. government assessment acknowledged Iran's antagonism to Moscow and communism, American policymakers still thought Iranian leaders would be open to improved ties with the Soviets and worried that Moscow would increase its economic and technical assistance to Iran.

To blunt such perceived risks of increased Soviet influence, American policymakers saw an opportunity in a post-Khomeini Iran for a conservative, though still Islamic, regime to emerge that "might lessen the emphasis on revolution and terrorism and could move cautiously toward a more correct relationship with the U.S."[34] The NSDD suggested policy adjustments to prevent Iran from falling into the Soviet camp, including encouraging Western allies to help Iran meet import requirements to offset Soviet assistance and trade offers. The directive also recommended that the administration be ready to communicate with Iran through allies and begin "discreetly communicating our desire for correct relations to potentially receptive Iranian leaders" and avoid "actions which could alienate groups potentially receptive to improved U.S.–Iranian relations."[35]

Reagan publicly defended his decision to authorize arms transfers to the Iranians based on strategic concerns. In a 1986 address, he argued:

> But why, you might ask, is any relationship with Iran important to the United States? Iran encompasses some of the most critical geography in the world. It lies between the Soviet Union and access to the warm waters of the Indian Ocean. Geography explains why the Soviet Union has sent an army into Afghanistan to dominate that country and, if they could, Iran and Pakistan. Iran's geography gives it a critical position from which adversaries could interfere with oil flows from the Arab States that border the Persian Gulf. Apart from geography, Iran's oil deposits are important to the long-term health of the world economy. For these reasons, it is in our national interest to watch for changes within Iran that might offer hope for an improved relationship.[36]

While acknowledging the "bitter and enduring disagreements" with Iran, its sponsorship of terrorism, and Iran's efforts to rid the region of Western influence, Reagan accepted that "the Iranian revolution is a fact of history, *but between American and Iranian basic national interests there need be no permanent conflict.*"[37]

Even after Iran-Contra, some of Reagan's advisors continued to emphasize Iran's strategic significance and the risks of siding with Iraq against Iran in the Iran-Iraq War because of continued concerns about Soviet influence. In a State Department memo of February 4, 1987, considering a shift in U.S. policy to allow the sale of weapons of U.S. origin from third parties to Iraq, assistant secretary of state for Near East affairs Richard Murphy argued, "We believe that such a change in policy would be inadvisable and counterproductive."[38] In addition to arguments based on feasibility problems—such as the compatibility of U.S. equipment with Iraq's largely Soviet- and French-supplied military and the assessment that U.S. arms wouldn't make considerable difference in Iraq's poor military performance—Murphy's memo argued against arms to Iraq for Iran-related reasons. In his assessment, "assistance for Iraq would set back even further any prospects for normalization of relations with Iran and would be used by those Iranians seeking better relations with the USSR to our detriment . . . Aid to Iraq would increase the risk of Iranian and Shia terrorist actions against the U.S."[39]

In short, there was a compelling strategic rationale in the 1980s, driven in large part by the Cold War imperative to blunt Soviet influence, for improved U.S. ties with Iran. There were senior policymakers advocating such a shift. The president himself backed the policy. And yet, by the end of Reagan's second term, U.S. relations with Iran remained hostile. Not only that, relations even worsened with direct American military intervention when the U.S. Navy led a mission to protect commercial shipping in the Persian Gulf, starting in July 1987, in what became known as the Tanker War.

Reflecting a pattern that would repeat in the years ahead, strategic considerations favoring a better relationship with Iran ultimately did not win the day. The opposite view prevailed—that changing course with Iran was unthinkable and dangerous, that any alternative, even support for a repressive autocratic tyrant like Saddam Hussein, was preferable to changing policy directions with Iran.

Not a Country You Can Deal with

Despite the secret arms deals, the administration's public stance and policy actions throughout the 1980s backed Iran's adversaries, namely Iraq, and maintained a largely hostile stance toward the Islamic Republic, culminating in direct American-Iranian conflict toward the end of the decade during the Tanker War. This was also the first decade of the Islamic Republic, when the Iranian leadership most aggressively sought to export its revolution to the wider region. Consequently, it is far from certain that even if the United States had succeeded in implementing a new policy toward Iran, rather than an arms for hostages scandal, it would have found an accommodating partner. But the way in which Iran was perceived and discussed among American policymakers made such a genuine testing of a new relationship moot. In the American discourse, Iran was simply not a country with which the United States could or should deal. This helps explains why the administration attempted to keep its dealings with Iran secret and, even apart from the scandal's illegal aspects, why their exposure so disgraced top officials.

VIEWS OF IRAN DURING THE IRAN-IRAQ WAR

An early example of the stigma associated with Iran was the U.S. decision to favor Iraq—then under the iron rule of Saddam Hussein, whom the United States would later overthrow in the 2003 Iraq War—in its nearly decade-long conflict with Iran in the 1980s. The war began with Iraq's invasion of Iran in September 1980, just as the new Islamic leaders in Tehran were consolidating power at home. But the Iraqis failed to secure a swift victory, and the war turned into a protracted stalemate. By 1982 Iran launched a counter-offensive. It was at this time (which also coincided with Iran's creation of Hezbollah as a pro-Iranian Shia force in Lebanon) that the United States shifted its policy from staying out of the war to favoring the Iraqis, including the sharing of military intelligence.[40]

American policymakers worried about a "doomsday" scenario whereby Iran would dominate the entire Middle East, take over its oil, and destroy Israel; the United States was even willing to share intelligence with Saddam Hussein to target Iranians despite believing that Iraq possessed chemical weapons and would use them.[41] American policymakers were persuaded by Iraqi arguments that the Iranians were too fanatical to be "dealt with in a rational fashion."[42] In the prevailing American assessment, preventing an Iranian victory, a victory by "fanatics" poised to take over the region, was more important than Iraq's possible use of chemical weapons.[43]

There were some U.S. officials who opposed the tilt toward Iraq, such as the State Department's Near East Affairs (NEA) director for regional affairs, Philip Wilcox, and deputy assistant secretary of state (DAS) James Placke. Such officials did not believe the United States should take actions that might close the door to normalization with Iran. Other U.S. officials at the Pentagon, such as Paul Wolfowitz and Richard Perle, also opposed favoring Iraq because they believed Saddam Hussein posed a grave danger to the region, a view associated with the Israeli positions in that era.[44] But senior Reagan officials largely ignored such concerns and supported the U.S. tilt toward Iraq. A former senior American diplomat in the Middle East, Richard Murphy, explained the seemingly puzzling U.S. decision to favor Iraq as follows:

> The view was, here is that wild-eyed religious fanatic, Khomeini, who was taking the children of Iran and marching them straight into the minefields to clear the way for his army. In return, Khomeini offered

these kids the promise of a weird sort of Islamic paradise. I want to emphasize that this was not only the image of Mr. and Mrs. America, who had tied all those yellow ribbons around the trees until the fanatics let our hostages go free. Images like this were very bright, very vivid in Washington, too, even among people who you would have thought had a more nuanced and balanced view of the situation. You could even bring up the incredibly inhumane way the Iraqis treated their own soldiers— you know, like "But Saddam cuts off the ears of deserters." "Yeah, sure," would be the reply, "he's not a nice man, that's true." But many peo- ple—as I say, many people in Washington in those days—were unmoved by facts like these. No matter what was said, the reply was, "Oh, the Iranians are much worse; in fact, the Iranians are crazy zealots."[45]

Murphy's observations illuminate the early inclination to frame Iran as an outlaw state like none other. This view, in Murphy's telling, led to a tendency among policymakers to find evidence to support such view- points. For example, U.S. officials suspected Iran was also using chemical weapons in its war with Iraq. Even though the evidence was not yet clear, Murphy noted a distinction in how American policymakers viewed Iran in comparison to Iraq: "the point at the time wasn't that the Iranians were much *less* guilty of CW [chemical weapons] use than the Iraqis, if I may put it that way, but that the Iranians were simply *guilty*. Period. There was palpable joy in some quarters over this. The feeling expressed was, 'Oh boy, this is great news. Now there is no need to even consider harsh measures to condemn or cut off the CW capability of Iraqis. Let's put our energy into finding some evidence of Iranian use.'"[46]

It is also important to note that while Israeli views were influential among several Reagan advisors associated with Iran-Contra, U.S. policy ultimately went against Israeli preferences that favored a softer stance toward Iran in this period. Israel viewed Saddam Hussein's Iraq as a major regional threat and did not let the new clerical rulers in Tehran get in the way of their realpolitik concerns about Iraq winning the war, leading Israel to support arms transfers to Iran. But most U.S. officials, including the military leadership, opposed such arms transfers.

In a September 1981 memorandum, Lt. General Paul Gorman, assis- tant to the chairman of the Joint Chiefs of Staff, argued against a shift in U.S. policy to allow for arms shipments to Iran. He believed that a shift in policy would be "perceived by the moderate Arab states as an action directly counter to their interests" and that it would intensify the war.[47]

Gorman was particularly concerned that Israeli policies favoring arms transfers to Iran was complicating U.S. relationships with Arab states vital for U.S. access in the region, noting that Iraq already considered the United States responsible for arms "transferred to Iran by Israel since, in Iraq's view, those transfers were possible only because U.S. arms supplies to Israel are more than actually needed for Israel's defense."[48]

Indeed, Crist's account suggests that Weinberger specifically established CENTCOM to help embrace "pro-Western Arabs," a move he viewed as necessary for countering Soviet influence.[49] These Reagan policies were not well received in Israel; Israelis at the time viewed CENTCOM as favoring Arab states at the expense of Israeli interests. President Reagan and his first secretary of state, Alexander Haig, wanted Israel to be part of CENTCOM, but the Joint Chiefs and Pentagon civilian officials opposed such an invitation; they argued that Israel was too far from the Persian Gulf and that if Israel joined CENTCOM it could jeopardize U.S. relations with Arab states.[50]

Such postures raise questions about Israel as a key driver of U.S. Iran policy despite Israel's strong influence and access to top American policy-makers. Indeed, even with Israeli involvement in the Iran-Contra scandal, Israeli preferences ultimately did not prevail when it came to U.S. policies throughout the Reagan years, which remained largely hostile to Iran and actively backed Iran's primary regional adversary, Iraq.

VIEWS OF IRAN DURING THE TANKER WAR

By the late 1980s, the American anti-Iranian stance only became more pronounced. We see this in U.S. policy actions and debates over the U.S. role in the Tanker War, when U.S. reflagging of oil tankers put the United States in direct military conflict with Iran. The United States viewed Iran as the predominant threat to the freedom of navigation in the Persian Gulf, even at times blaming Iran for Iraqi actions. For example, in May 1987 an Iraqi missile attacked a U.S. ship, killing several dozen Americans; Reagan nonetheless blamed Iran for creating the dangerous situation in the Gulf that led to the incident.[51]

U.S.–Iran naval confrontation escalated throughout 1987–1988, leading to tragic incidents that unintentionally killed civilians. Among the worst was when, in July 1988, the U.S. carrier *Vincennes* shot down a civilian Iranian airliner, killing 290 people, creating particular resentment on the

Iranian side, especially as the United States did not apologize for the incident. Instead, the United States reached a settlement years later through the claims tribunal in The Hague where it agreed to an ex gratia payment to the family members of victims which allowed it to avoid accepting legal responsibility for the shootdown. In addition to their lingering anger from this traumatic incident, Iranians also resented the inability of American policymakers to see Iran as the target of devastating Iraqi attacks during the war, including heavy missile strikes on Iranian cities and the Iraqi use of chemical weapons.

The prevailing view in Washington continued to see Iran as the main aggressor in the Persian Gulf. Reagan told American media outlets that he would not let a "barbaric country" like Iran close down shipping routes for oil, defending the administration's decision to deploy American warships to escort oil tankers under a U.S. flag to defend against Iranian attacks.[52] There were some exceptions to such views, such as Cold War hawks at the Defense Department who worried that confrontation with Iran in the Tanker War would benefit the Soviets.[53] And some debate emerged over the wisdom of direct U.S. military involvement to protect the oil tankers. But a hostile stance toward Iran nonetheless dominated the domestic policy discourse.

Congressional debates on the conflict throughout 1987 and 1988 illuminate the growing enmity.[54] Senators and administration officials alike saw the escalation of the Tanker War as a direct consequence of the blunders made by the Reagan administration in violating the U.S. arms embargo on Iran. The general consensus was that Reagan's olive branch to Tehran, in the form of U.S.-made anti-tank and anti-aircraft missiles, had shaken the trust of American regional partners like Kuwait. Members of the Senate Foreign Relations Committee (SFRC) believed that those countries now needed bold new assurances from the United States that they would be protected from Iran or else they would turn to the Soviets.

The three objectives of the United States during this phase of the Iran-Iraq War were aptly summed up in the testimony of assistant secretary of state Murphy. In his words, the United States sought "to galvanize the international community to press for a just end to the Iran-Iraq War; to motivate the Iranian leadership to cease its aggressive posture and rejoin the ranks of peaceful nations; and to prevent a strategic gain by the Soviet Union in the region."[55] While such goals were widely accepted, members of Congress and administration officials debated whether or not reflagging tankers served American interests or posed an inordinate risk of escalation.

The camp in favor of giving American protection to shipping transiting the Gulf was led by Secretary Weinberger. Despite his earlier characterizations of Iran as too irrational to deal with, in this instance Weinberger believed that Iran was rational enough to be deterred from attacking the United States. He argued that "while the Iranian leadership is certainly fanatical and irrational on many things, I think they do weigh costs and they do weigh choices."[56] Weinberger was backed by his administration colleagues Richard Armitage, assistant secretary of defense for international security affairs, and assistant secretary of state Murphy, who testified that the Iranian regime needed to be contained and that the United States had "an immediate need to deter Iran from making cheap gains through intimidation and blockage of shipping in the Gulf."[57]

On the congressional side, the reflagging camp was led by Republican senator Larry Pressler who favored a U.S. presence in the Gulf because American forces were "keeping Iran and the Soviet from controlling that 'lake,' and that is what our policy should be."[58] This camp was generally hawkish but also made clear that the United States did not need to escalate tensions with Iran. They feared Soviet influence and the spread of the Iranian revolution, but they recognized the Iranian revolution as "a fact of history," and they did not seek regime change.[59]

Democratic senators who opposed the administration's reflagging scheme warned that it would lead to an inevitable clash between the United States and Iran. Senators Joe Biden, Alan Cranston, and committee chairman Claiborne Pell all warned that such a move could lead to war between the United States and Iran. As then Senator Biden argued, "Instead of building United States credibility throughout the world, the reflagging policy threatens to undermine our ultimate objective of ending the Iran-Iraq conflict and could slowly drag us into a full-fledged war."[60] These senators and other former officials and experts opposing the reflagging effort feared that Iran might not be deterred and argued that U.S. interests were poorly served by inviting war with Iran. These voices also were wary of siding with Saddam Hussein's Iraq.

But despite these differing assessments over the risks of the American role in reflagging shipping in the Persian Gulf, there was no fundamental questioning of the need to counter Iran or consider a different relationship with what was widely viewed as an abnormal state. Indeed, congressional rhetoric during the Tanker War hearings took a more belligerent tone. Assertions by members of Congress that Iran was "insane" and therefore could not be treated like a normal nation typified the common framing of Iran among American policymakers. In an emblematic example of the rhetoric on the Hill, Democratic representative Charles Bennet argued:

> The President apparently reasons that the Iranians would not fire at our ships or tankers because to do so would be insane. But driving a truck bomb into the Beirut Marine barracks was also insane, and Defense Secretary Weinberger told our Armed Forces Committee last week that the Iranian leadership was "a bunch of lunatics"—and I am quoting precisely from him—and it would probably be only a short time before our ships would be hit.[61]

Pell, meanwhile, accused Iran of "international banditry."[62]

Counterintuitively, harsher rhetoric against Iran was employed by members of Congress *opposed* to U.S. intervention in the Persian Gulf. Policymakers supporting American intervention tended to justify their position by reminding their colleagues that Iran was still rational enough that it would respond to such tried-and-true methods as deterrence and sanctions. Therefore, they argued, the United States need not fear escalation with Iran. Meanwhile, members of Congress opposed to an active American role in the Persian Gulf warned that Iran was a uniquely irrational state that sought to provoke conflict. Few, if any, voices in the public debate, or even within internal policy deliberations, returned to the logic espoused before the Iran-Contra affair that suggested an opening to Iran was possible and could serve U.S. interests.

Talk of leaving the door open to reconciliation with Iran largely fell out of policy debates by the end of the Reagan presidency, and actual U.S. policies only hardened as the United States and Iran engaged in direct military confrontation in the Persian Gulf. The framing of Iran as an irrational state, beyond the bounds of international norms and run by fanatical leaders, was becoming firmly settled in the American discourse.

Hope of Openings to Hardening Hostility

Rather surprisingly, openness to the possibility of a less hostile U.S. relationship with Iran was more prevalent early in the decade after the Iranian revolution, even with the traumatic hostage crisis fresh on the minds of American policymakers, than was the case in later decades. President Reagan himself made a forceful, public case to the American people that a different U.S. relationship with Iran could benefit American interests. This was partly, or perhaps largely, due to the perceived Cold War imperatives of reducing Soviet influence that dominated the thinking of the Reagan era and by the president's fervent desire to secure the release of American hostages in Lebanon.

During this decade Israel favored engagement with Iran, viewing Iraq under Saddam Hussein as its larger concern. U.S. officials sympathetic to Israeli views and fierce ideological opponents of communism similarly saw value in a strategic opening to Iran to thwart Soviet influence and protect its oil. These officials did not just contemplate an opening. As recounted earlier, a former U.S. national security advisor actually flew to Iran with symbolic gifts to express an American interest in an opening to Iran. But instead of cutting that key-shaped cake, they cut secret arms deals in exchange for the release of American hostages in what became known as the Iran-Contra affair.

Yet it was not just scandal that hindered a strategic breakthrough in U.S. relations with Iran during the Cold War. Domestic politics and perceptions of Iran as an abnormal state, not a country that could be dealt with in a rational manner, decreased the appetite for testing openings. The idea that the United States could deal with a country like Iran was not accepted as a viable policy option. Iran's track record—starting with hostage taking of American diplomats and continuing with its backing of devastating terror attacks killing hundreds of American servicemen—only reinforced views of Iran as a fanatical state that could not be engaged.

Such views help explain why many policymakers saw Iran as a more problematic and dangerous country than even Saddam Hussein's Iraq, which also broke international law and norms. The attempt to find Iranian moderates was likely an unrealistic aspiration among a small circle of Reagan advisors, particularly during the early years of the Islamic revolution. But the notion that Iran itself was not a normal country further limited the ability to pursue strategic opportunities, with the political costs of doing so only increasing after the Iran-Contra scandal.

Indeed, the legacy of Iran-Contra created a chill for future policymakers because the episode, in many officials' thinking, demonstrated the unacceptably high political cost of dealing with Iran. It also reinforced a common view among American policymakers that the Islamic Republic was not a government the United States could trust, and therefore any overtures to Iranian leaders would be strategically unproductive on top of being politically costly. Such prevailing assumptions only became more deeply entrenched among American policymakers in the years to follow, when the hostile track record of U.S.–Iran relations only worsened.

TWO

From Sidelining to Containment

Richard Haass, who served in President George H. W. Bush's administration as the senior director of Near East and South Asian affairs at the National Security Council, once had a passing encounter with Iranian diplomat Javad Zarif at the United Nations. Zarif jokingly referred to Haass as "Mr. goodwill begets goodwill," referencing a phrase President Bush had included in his January 1989 inaugural address that was widely viewed as a positive gesture to Iran. But Haass had no idea how the phrase made it into the speech. He certainly did not put it there. In fact, he was surprised by the language, thinking it "came out of nowhere."[1]

From Haass's vantage point, Iran's penchant for kidnapping and terrorism made the country too difficult for the administration to spend time on, and he saw very little evidence of Iranian actions that would justify engagement, particularly given other global priorities as the Cold War was coming to an end. And yet, even in Haass's own telling, President Bush remained intrigued by "doing something on Iran."[2] Like Reagan, he wanted Iranian assistance with freeing American hostages and sensed that Iranian pragmatists could help. As Bush put it in his inaugural speech, "There are today Americans who are held against their will in foreign lands and Americans unaccounted for. Assistance can be shown here and will be long remembered. *Good will begets goodwill*. Good faith can be a spiral that endlessly moves on."[3]

Regardless of who convinced Bush to include this statement, or whether it was the president himself who wanted to test the waters with Iran, the incident ultimately demonstrated a repeated pattern—initial interest by high-level U.S. officials, including American presidents, to turn the page with Iran, followed by unmet expectations and ultimately little change in the contentious nature of the relationship, leading to a hardening rather than softening of views.

Between uncertainty about whether the Iranians could deliver and an administration more focused on Arab-Israeli peacemaking and building partnerships with Gulf Arab partners, Haass observed that the Iran issue simply "got lost with a million other things" on the administration's agenda.[4] But what made it easier to sideline the Iran file in the midst of other pressing issues was the domestic reality that policymakers perceived little upside in dealing with the Islamic Republic.

A decade after serving first as Bush's CIA director and then as secretary of defense, Robert Gates shared a revealing sentiment that illustrates some of the domestic considerations hovering over U.S. Iran policy. When asked in an oral history interview what his recollection of U.S. policy toward Iran was in response to the death of Ayatollah Ruhollah Khomeini in June 1989, Gates responded:

> Well, we really didn't pay much attention to Iran, to tell you the truth, as a policy issue, because there was nothing to be done. We paid attention to it as an intelligence problem, as a source of terrorism and we monitored sort of internal affairs and what was going on and so on, but I don't think there were, in contrast to when Mao died or other long-term leaders had died, there wasn't this great rush of enthusiasm in Washington that gee, maybe things will change for the better now that the old man's gone . . . *There was really not much interest in having anything to do with Iran. One of the things I think you have to remember is all these players from the President on down had been on the edges of Iran-Contra, and Iran essentially was the third rail of foreign policy.* I like to remind people that since 1976 there had been two covert actions not communicated to Congress, one by Jimmy Carter and one by Ronald Reagan. They both had to do with Iran and they both led to all kinds of hell breaking lose. So maybe somebody will finally learn. But there really wasn't much interest in anybody's part in pursing any policy initiatives with respect to Iran.[5]

Gates was not the only senior Bush administration official to observe the domestic toxicity of Iran for policymakers who had experienced the Iran hostage crisis and the Iran-Contra scandal. As the politically attuned secretary of state James Baker put it, "As the electoral beneficiaries of this unhappy period in American diplomacy, and having witnessed the unfortunate consequences of the Iran-Contra scandal in 1986, we were all too well aware of the Ayatollah's destructive capacities in terms of domestic politics."[6]

The Clinton administration would pick up Iran policy where the Bush administration left it. President Bush essentially shifted from largely sidelining Iran toward a stiffening of the American posture toward Iran by the end of his single term in office. While the term "containment" was not yet in vogue, it was the de facto policy already in place by the time Bill Clinton came to office in January 1993. Unlike President Bush, however, Clinton did not initially contemplate the possibility of better relations. His innovation was the containment not just of one adversary but of two. Iraq, like Iran, would now also face American containment measures, particularly the ever tightening U.S. sanctions regime.

This "dual containment" policy aimed to isolate Iran and Iraq at the same time rather than choosing the lesser of the two evils, as was the case with the American tilt toward Iraq in the 1980s. Saddam Hussein's invasion of Kuwait in August 1990, successfully repelled through a U.S.–led international coalition, put Iraq squarely in the outlaw camp. And in a new era of American primacy following the collapse of the Soviet Union, U.S. policymakers viewed the United States as the power responsible for reining in the world's rogue states.[7] That Iran was included in the list of rogues came as no surprise, given that the country was already viewed as a well-established outlaw. But the "rogue" framing that became so popular over the course of the 1990s only bolstered the American inclination to view Iran as an unchangeably hostile pariah.

It was not until Clinton's second term, particularly after the election of reformist Iranian president Mohammad Khatami in 1997, that his administration pursued openings to Iran. These outreach efforts ultimately failed, and Iran policy reverted to its normal course of animosity as America's era of primacy moved into a counterterrorism footing by the start of the twenty-first century. Meanwhile, the public discourse over Iran policy became increasingly antagonistic, further reinforcing deeply held frames of Iran as an abnormal adversary where, as Gates put it, "nothing could be done." Iran's continued backing of terrorism throughout this decade only further bolstered the enduring hostility, making it difficult for American policymakers to significantly change course.

An Opportune Moment for New Thinking on Iran

Three pivotal events unfolded within a short time span early in the Bush administration: the death of the Islamic Republic's first Supreme Leader, Ayatollah Khomeini, in the year following the end of the Iran-Iraq War; the fall of the Berlin Wall in November 1989 that triggered the end of the Cold War; and the first Persian Gulf War in 1990–1991. These events created new strategic conditions that would come to shape the post–Cold War era and arguably might have opened the door for new thinking on Iran. These shifts also marked the onset of an era marked by American predominance, where a "unipolar" order replaced the decades-long bipolarity of the U.S.–Soviet Cold War rivalry.

In the aftermath of the Iran-Iraq War, President Bush called for a national security review of U.S. policy toward the Persian Gulf, including U.S. policy toward Iran.[8] The response to the review from the National Intelligence Council assessed that "a new regional order has emerged in the Persian Gulf that will reduce the likelihood of regional hostilities . . . no Persian Gulf State can dominate the region . . . This new order will serve the key interests of the United States by lessening the likelihood of an oil supply disruption and reducing the need for direct US military involvement in the Persian Gulf."[9]

National Security Directive (NSD) 26, dated October 2, 1989, was a culmination of the review and further reflected the diminished sense of threat from the region. The president supported the decision to reduce the U.S. naval presence and expressed the importance for the United States to "continue to nurture the mutually beneficial and enduring cooperative security relationships with the GCC [Gulf Cooperation Council] states that grew out of the Iran/Iraq war."[10] The president called on the Defense Department to maintain and even increase "its peacetime and contingency access to friendly regional states, and to broaden the scope of security cooperation through military exercises, prepositioning arrangements and contingency planning."[11] In other words, the administration expected strategic benefits from the conclusion of the Iran-Iraq War, arguably creating more conducive conditions for outreach to Iran based on a position of strength.

When it came to the question of how to handle Iran in the aftermath of the war, NSD 26 argued that the United States "should continue to be prepared for a normal relationship with Iran on the basis of strict reciprocity." Reciprocity in the U.S. view would be linked to Iranian actions to help obtain the release of American hostages and to cease its support for international terrorism, among other demands related to its activities in the region and its human rights practices. The possibility of normalizing ties was presented at the highest level as the president directed the State Department to handle all contacts with Iran to avoid the mistakes of the Iran-Contra era when U.S. Iran policy was conducted through unreliable back channels.

The death of the stridently anti-American Ayatollah Khomeini and the election of the more pragmatically inclined Iranian president Rafsanjani in 1989 created further hope for a reset in U.S.–Iran relations in some quarters, even if questions remained about the influence of Iranian presidents in a system that favored the authority of the Supreme Leader. According to some assessments, Rafsanjani wanted to relax the hardline positions of Iran's religious theocracy that emerged in the decade after its revolution, including extreme practices like hostage taking and assassinations (interestingly, European policymakers maintained diplomatic relations with the Islamic Republic following the revolution despite these practices that violated diplomatic protocols).[12] Rafsanjani's motivation for relaxing Iran's revolutionary posture was to improve its business climate and thus its international image, which was necessary to reconstruct the country after the decade-long war with Iraq. President Bush appeared interested in exploring this opportunity, as his "goodwill begets goodwill" offering indicated.

Building on these already favorable regional shifts from an American perspective, the geostrategic global landscape altered even more dramatically with the fall of the Berlin Wall, essentially ending the Cold War and leading to the collapse of the Soviet Union by the end of 1991. The United States emerged as the remaining global superpower, bolstering perceptions among American policymakers that the United States held unparalleled global power and the ability to shape the world in directions more aligned with its interests and values.

In the Middle East, the first test of this newfound power was the U.S. response to Iraqi president Saddam Hussein's invasion of Kuwait in August 1990. Bush saw confronting an invasion that violated state sovereignty as a critical imperative in a post–Cold War era and believed the United States had "an obligation to lead" the effort.[13] The administration subsequently built an international coalition and, with the approval of the U.N. Security

Council, launched a military campaign to roll back Iraq's invasion and lib-
erate Kuwait. Given that Iraq under Saddam Hussein was Iran's primary
regional adversary, the war essentially put the United States and Iran on
the same side. Saddam Hussein's minority Sunni leadership repressively
ruled over a Shia majority population and the bitter legacy of the Iran-
Iraq War of the 1980s generated significant Iranian animus toward Iraq.
Iran condemned the invasion and welcomed the targeting of its greatest
regional rival, even if its greatest global adversary was heading the effort.

European leaders like German chancellor Helmut Kohl assessed that
Iranian leaders might be interested in improved relations with the United
States once the "dust settle[d]"; and relayed to the White House that Iranian foreign minister Ali Akbar Velayati told him that after the war, "all
relevant countries have to play a role, including the U.S."[14] Other accounts
suggest that the Iranians were also interested in playing a larger role in
support of the U.S.–led coalition forces. But when this proposition was
put to Secretary Gates years later, Gates responded, "No, there was never
any serious discussion of involving Iran in the war. There was no interest
in that. We figured that Iran's attitude was, this is great, our two worst
enemies going to war with each other."[15] Senior U.S. officials were also
mindful of not reducing Iraq's military power so significantly that it would
be unable to balance Iran following the conflict.[16]

If the United States did not want Iran involved in supporting its military campaign against Iraq, it was just as uninterested in having Iran play
any role in the region's security architecture following the war. Indeed,
rather than capitalize on the war as an opportunity to reconsider U.S.
policy toward Iran, the Bush administration largely ignored Iran as it
turned its attention to Arab-Israeli peacemaking and the convening of
the Madrid peace conference in October 1991. The Clinton administration
continued on this path, albeit with some brief detours, viewing American
primacy as an opportunity to confront the world's rogue states, including
Iran, and transform the world order into one of America's making.

The monumental regional and global strategic shifts that reduced the
saliency of Iran in American decision-making and arguably put the United
States in an advantageous position did little to change the U.S. posture
toward Iran. Favorable strategic conditions ultimately did not steer U.S.–
Iran relations in a different direction.

Domestic Considerations

NOT MUCH INTEREST IN IRAN

By some accounts President Bush intentionally excluded Iran from the Madrid peace conference in the aftermath of the first Persian Gulf War in order to limit Iranian influence in the region.[17] But according to policymakers who shaped decisions in this period, Iran was less intentionally excluded than it was largely ignored when it came to administration's priorities. The administration's focus was mostly directed toward containing Iraq after galvanizing a large international coalition to roll back Saddam Hussein's invasion of Kuwait and leveraging the 1990–1991 Gulf War for Arab-Israeli peacemaking.

According to Dennis Ross, who then headed the policy planning bureau at the State Department and was a close aide to Secretary of State James Baker, a Middle East expert on his team wrote a paper in November 1990 exploring the possibility of an opening to Iran in the aftermath of the war, but "there was no interest."[18] Iran was viewed as a "complicating factor" in building the coalition against Iraq, given that America's Arab partners preferred to keep Iran distant, and as a result there was very little communication on Iran during the war. Even when the administration worked on a joint statement with the Soviets, according to Ross, Iran was not discussed. Nor did Iran make it onto the agenda when Ross went on a trip to NATO, Turkey, and other regional stops in the buildup to the war to forge an international coalition. As he explains, events were so overwhelming that "Iran just didn't make the list."[19]

Given this context, Ross acknowledges he did not push hard on his staffer's memo on how to open to Iran, since he just did not think Iran was key or that there was any serious opportunity with Iran. He did not see "a win" there, or a potential to change Iran's anti-American posture.[20] The prevailing view of the American team was, if you can restructure the Middle East, starting with an Arab-Israeli peace, then you can come back to Iran later.

The Madrid peace process was largely focused on advancing Arab-Israeli peace, but also created a parallel multilateral peace process to address regional issues of common concern, establishing working groups on water, the environment, refugees, economic development, and arms control and regional security (or ACRS).[21] Iran was relevant to discussions in the ACRS working group given widespread regional threat perceptions of Iran's missile capabilities and emerging concerns about its nuclear intentions. But Ross does not recall much pushback about putting Iran aside even on regional security discussions in internal deliberations about Madrid. While Ross explained that he is normally a proponent of testing possibilities in diplomacy, he recognized that "Iran was still a symbol" that evoked negative reactions within the American system, and that the team would not be applauded for including Iran—there was no political benefit for doing so and the effort would only generate pushback that might detract from the wider effort.[22]

TESTING THE WATERS FOR A HOSTAGE DEAL

Despite the skepticism of key advisors and the low priority of Iran for the incoming administration, President Bush did initially appear interested in testing the waters, as his "goodwill begets goodwill" inaugural speech indicated, at the very least to address the protracted issue of American hostages in Lebanon. A telephone conversation with Sultan Qaboos bin Said Al Said of Oman demonstrated that the president had the welfare of hostages on his mind, particularly as the conversation took place following reports that a pro-Iranian Lebanese terrorist group killed U.S. Marine Lt. Colonel William Higgins.[23] Higgins had been heading an observer group of a UN truce-monitoring force in Lebanon before his abduction. The president sought Oman's help in securing the release of the remaining American hostages, given Muscat's good relationship with Iran.

As a White House memorandum of the conversation between the two leaders detailed, President Bush told Sultan Qaboos that the United States "had reports that the Iranians were trying to be helpful in seeing there were no more killing[s] of American hostages. The President said he knew Oman had some contacts with Iran and that the Foreign Minister was quite forward-looking in his dealings with them."[24] Bush was also conscious of handling the hostage situation in ways that might not foreclose opportunities to explore other openings with Rafsanjani in power. According to the memorandum, the president said that "Rafsanjani might turn out to be more reasonable, but he had some radicals in the government . . . who might make things difficult. There might be a ray of hope, and we didn't want to mishandle our affairs if there might be change in Iran."[25] Bush worried that if more American hostages were killed, he "may have problems explaining that [Rafsanjani might be more moderate] to many from our side."[26]

The administration drew on the mediation of a U.N. envoy, Giandomenico Picco, to explore whether the Iranians would assist with the release of hostages and what they might want in return. The Iranians were interested in the U.S. release of frozen Iranian assets dating from the 1979 embassy takeover, as well as compensation for the victims of the Iranian civilian aircraft the United Sates had shot down in 1988, among other demands.[27] Senior U.S. officials like Secretary of State Baker were concerned about rewarding Iran for actions they believed it should be taking in any case.[28]

According to former CIA analyst Bruce Riedel, Scowcroft and Baker's enthusiasm for engagement was more tepid than the president's; Bush even took what turned out to be a prank call by an Iranian whom he thought was Rafsanjani, demonstrating the limited understanding of Iranian personalities within the American system.[29] Scowcroft in particular was hesitant; he did not believe the Iranians were serious about a dialogue with the United States, as they no longer needed hostages for leverage since they had already taken "over a country [Lebanon]."[30]

Nonetheless, Picco attempted to secure a deal. Building on the momentum of the Persian Gulf War, Rafsanjani successfully helped obtain the release of all remaining American hostages from Lebanon by the end of 1991. But the Bush administration did not reciprocate as the Iranians expected, frustrating Picco, who years later wrote about the incident in his memoir:

> Scowcroft had intimated at our first two meetings that the United States might have difficulty living up to its "promise" of three years earlier. Even so, I held out hope that the administration would give me *something* I could take to the Iranians . . . Scowcroft made it official in April [1992] . . . there would be no gesture toward Iran anytime soon. Was it the upcoming presidential election? Perhaps. After all, could the incumbent risk looking soft on a country that still tarred America as "the Great Satan"? Could he appear to pay off a government that had essentially taken over the U.S. Embassy in Tehran . . . Whatever the reasons, a three-year operation in Beirut built on a foundation of trust had suddenly turned to sand. Unwittingly—naively, as it turned out—I had misled an entire government.[31]

The administration did support a U.N. resolution ending the Iran-Iraq War that placed blame on Iraq for initiating the conflict, and in November 1991 paid several hundred million dollars in compensation for Iranian material confiscated after the revolution as a settlement at the claims tribunal in The Hague.[32] The United States also allowed an Iran interests section to open in the Pakistani embassy in Washington, D.C. But other anticipated measures, such as the release of frozen Iranian assets and increased sanctions relief, never came.[33] U.S. officials viewed the political costs of compensating Iran as too high to be worth it, given the backdrop of continued assassinations of dissidents in Europe, and during an election year no less. American analyst Kenneth Pollack blames Iran for the failure to capitalize on the post–Gulf War outreach, arguing that the administration could not have pursued rapprochement after Iran murdered the last Iranian prime minster under the Shah, Shapour Bakhtiar, in August 1991—that would amount to dealing with terrorists.[34]

But other Iran observers argue that the failure of the Bush administration to reciprocate was a big blow to Iranian pragmatists like Rafsanjani, who had lobbied hardliners within Iran to free the hostages.[35] Yet with concerns about how dealing with Iran would play domestically and other regional priorities—including staying on the good side of Arab partners whom the administration viewed as critical for Arab-Israeli peacemaking—it was never clear that the administration was going to meet Iranian expectations.

Indeed, a June 1992 report in *The New York Times* suggested that a policy review on Iran earlier that year had found that any sanctions lifting that might withstand domestic resistance would not likely be enough for Iran, and that anything that might be enough for Iran would not be domestically possible within the United States.[36] When asked about this review in an oral history interview, Richard Haass said that it "sounds right," but he could not remember the details.[37]

Some scholars hold that Israeli influence may have played a key role in shaping American calculations toward Iran after the war, arguing that the Israelis began portraying Iran, not Arab states, as their main adversary in Washington policy circles and argued against Iran's inclusion in the Madrid conference.[38] But even if this was the case, American policymakers had their own reasons for sidelining Iran, as discussed earlier. Iran was simply not a priority, and thus the Israelis would be arguing for a policy that was already de facto in place.

Indeed, other scholars argue that Israel's influence on U.S. policy toward the end of the Bush administration and into the transition to the Clinton administration was negligible.[39] Although Israeli prime minister Yitzhak Rabin was more focused on Iran than his predecessor Yitzhak Shamir had been, President Bush had already moved toward policies of isolation and containment by the end of his administration, including restrictions on the export of dual-use technology and the enactment of the Iran-Iraq Arms Non-Proliferation Act, which he signed in October 1992. Arguably, Rabin's heightened concern over Iran reflected a desire to align Israel with existing U.S. policy rather than an instance of Israel lobbying Washington for that policy.[40]

Moreover, the revelation following the Gulf War that Iraq was able to advance its nuclear program despite international inspections was likely to impact thinking in Washington about Iran's nuclear ambitions as nuclear nonproliferation emerged as a higher priority following the end of the Cold War. Indeed, as head of the CIA in March 1992, Gates stated publicly the U.S. government judgment that Iran was seeking a nuclear capability.[41]

At the same time that U.S. policy moved in more confrontational directions toward Iran, European countries pursued a "critical dialogue" with the Islamic Republic during the 1990s despite assassinations of Iranian dissidents in Europe, demonstrating that other policy paths were possible. It was thus not inevitable that the only way to respond to Iran's emerging nuclear activities was continued economic pressure and political isolation. The United States might have considered pursuing diplomacy as an option to thwart Iran's nuclear program at this early stage, as it did in later years. That American policymakers did not consider such options, and largely dismissed or resented European outreach, illustrates the limited policy discourse in Washington when it came to Iran and the narrow range of options. Israel was part of this domestic discourse, but not its primary driver.

DUAL CONTAINMENT AND THE INDYK FATWA

Unlike Presidents Reagan and Bush, Clinton did not contemplate an opening to Iran at the outset of his administration, nor did he order a review of existing policy, which by the time he came to office had largely solidified into a containment approach.[42] Though by many accounts President Clinton had an inclination for dialogue even with difficult world leaders, such proclivities were "counteracted by his desire to demonstrate his toughness as President."[43]

Clinton's Middle East team also largely viewed policy in the region through the lens of the Arab-Israeli peace process. Madeleine Albright—who served as Clinton's ambassador to the United Nations and as secretary of state in his second term—could not remember any debates on Iran policy early in Clinton's first administration, noting that the team's focus was on the Arab-Israeli conflict.[44] As Albright put it in a 2006 oral history interview, "Dennis [Ross] and his team would be in the Middle East a lot of the time. I would go a lot. The President would meet people in different places; I would meet people in different places. It [Israeli-Arab peace negotiations] was probably the central theme of everything we did."[45]

Central personnel serving in a variety of high-level roles throughout both Clinton administrations, including Martin Indyk, also had deep familiarity with Israel. Twenty years before entering the Clinton administration in 1992 as a special assistant for the Middle East in the NSC, Indyk was a student at Hebrew University in Jerusalem "caught up in the Yom Kippur War," which he called a "defining moment" that led him to become "obsessed" with the American role in promoting Arab-Israeli peace.[46] Indyk, whose "dual containment" speech became the hallmark of the Clinton administration's Iran policy, confirmed in an interview with me that his focus before he entered the U.S. government was on Arab-Israeli issues and that at the time he had limited knowledge about Iran, even though he was tasked to cover the entire region.[47]

Indyk reiterated that the Clinton team viewed the Arab-Israeli peace process as the engine for the Middle East, and that "everything was seen through this lens."[48] Indyk explained that there was no one in the administration who was arguing for engagement in interagency discussions, though some of his colleagues were arguing that Rafsanjani wanted to improve relations. But Indyk saw no evidence to suggest that Rafsanjani wanted to moderate Iran's policies—he was "part and parcel" of the regime [and its backing of terrorism] and "was as bad as the rest of them."[49] He supported then deputy national security advisor Sandy Berger's view that there were no moderates with whom the administration could work.[50] NSC advisor Anthony Lake also opposed engaging Iran, believing that Republicans had wasted time looking for Iranian moderates in both the Reagan and Bush administrations.

Indyk also noted that, in "those days, there was a real sense of vulnerability" and risk of "looking weak" by talking to enemies, but in any case Iran was not on their radar as a priority. And since engagement was viewed as unrealistic and military options as too dangerous, sanctions and isolation (essentially containment) emerged as the only "logical" policy option.[51]

It is thus unsurprising that Indyk wrote and presented the signature dual containment speech. While the speech is often viewed as conflating the Iraqi and Iranian threats as equal menaces to regional stability, Indyk insisted that the administration viewed each country differently. Saddam Hussein was considered "beyond the pale" and in a "league of his own," and the plan was to back efforts to overthrow him.[52] In essence, the administration's policy for Iraq was regime change, not containment, even if it used the "dual containment" framing.

With Iran, engagement was off the table, but the administration was not seeking the regime's overthrow. As Indyk stated in the speech, "I should emphasize that the Clinton administration is not opposed to Islamic government in Iran . . . Rather, we are firmly opposed to these specific aspects of the Iranian regime's behavior . . . We do not seek a confrontation but we will not normalize relations with Iran until and unless Iran's policies change, across the board."[53] Indyk argued that containment did not rule out talking to Iran later if its behavior changed; administration officials, in his telling, did not view Iran as beyond the pale, or think that Iranians were "psychopaths."[54] And over time Clinton's team believed Iran's revolution would subside and that they might be able to engage Iran.

The Iranians evidently did not interpret the dual containment strategy this way. According to Indyk, he was not supposed to give the speech; he wrote it for one of his bosses at the NSC to deliver. But Tony Lake and Sandy Berger were busy that day. Indyk delivered it on May 18, 1993, at a symposium for an Israel-friendly research institute that he used to head. In an incident that Indyk said was not widely known—certainly not known as the famous fatwa against renowned author Salman Rushdie for his book *The Satanic Verses*—he claimed that the Iranian government issued a fatwa against him in response to the speech.[55] Indyk told me that there was an active threat on his life that required him to obtain secret service protection, and when he moved to Israel to become the U.S. ambassador in the spring of 1995, the fatwa was transferred to other high-ranking officials in Washington.[56] Regardless of the veracity of Indyk's fatwa claim,[57] it is nonetheless clear that Iran did not take well to being put in the "rogue" and "backlash" category along with Saddam Hussein's Iraq. And Iran's targeting of U.S. officials no doubt affected their views of Iran. As Indyk put it, "This is not moderation."[58]

During this period, the Israeli approach similarly favored more pressure on Iran, in contrast with its stance of the 1980s. Israeli leaders like Yitzhak Rabin shared the Clinton team's view that Arab-Israeli peace could diminish Iranian influence, though Rabin's assassination in 1995 significantly dimmed the prospects for peace instead. What the Clinton team did not anticipate was that Iran would respond to its Israel-centered strategy by seeking to sabotage the peace process, which it did quite successfully through a series of terrorist attacks by Iranian-aligned groups throughout the late 1990s. Such attacks rattled Israelis, helping to usher in hardline Israeli leaders like Benjamin Netanyahu and marginalized pro-peace leaders like Shimon Peres.

Dennis Ross similarly points out that every time the Americans were making progress on Israeli-Palestinian peacemaking, there was a new bombing, with intelligence showing active Iranian involvement.[59] These terrorist incidents not only helped derail the peace process, but also fed the skepticism of policymakers like Ross and Indyk about subsequent engagement efforts after Khatami came to power because U.S. officials "didn't want to be played."[60] These American policymakers did not need Israeli lobbying to convince them to pursue a hardline stance on Iran; they already viewed Iran's actions as a direct challenge to American interests.

THE EMBARGO AND ILSA: ANTI-IRAN POLICIES INTENSIFY

Despite the hardening of a containment strategy toward Iran, contradictions emerged in its implementation. By 1994 the United States was the largest importer of Iranian crude oil, and in 1995 American oil company Conoco was awarded a $1 billion contract in Iran. But the domestic political climate was tilting in the opposite direction. The Republican-controlled Congress used the Conoco deal to highlight how the United States was still dealing with Iran despite Clinton's dual containment policies, and passed legislation to shut down all trade with Iran, which at the time still amounted to more than $4 billion annually.

Clinton's secretary of state, Warren Christopher, viewed the Conoco deal as a way to support Iran's terrorism, not as a goodwill gesture by Rafsanjani to signal interest in engagement.[61] Meanwhile, European allies were pursuing a different strategy toward Iran that favored dialogue, not sanctions, to the great frustration of many U.S. officials. Clinton subsequently stepped up pressure and vetoed the Conoco deal with an executive order banning American investment in Iran's oil sector. On April 30, 1995, Clinton announced a total U.S. embargo against Iran.

While Clinton framed the decision as a means to stop Iran from supporting terrorism, a *New York Times* report noted that the announcement "was also suffused with domestic politics" following growing anti-Iran sentiment in Congress.[62] That Clinton chose to give the speech at a World Jewish Congress dinner attended by Israeli foreign minister Shimon Peres and honoring a Bronfman family member (the Bronfmans were major shareholders of Conoco's parent company and opposed the oil deal with Iran) added to the "political symbolism and appeal" of the decision.[63] The move was "met with fierce opposition from senior officials at the Defense, Commerce, Treasury, and Energy Departments, who argued that curbing American trade would have little effect on Iran and could hurt American companies instead."[64]

But Israel's concerns about the Iranian threat were growing, leading to "intense lobbying activity on Capitol Hill."[65] Indeed, the embargo generated significant congressional debate over Iran during this period, and ultimately the passage of the Iran Libya Sanctions Act (ILSA) in 1996, which placed secondary sanctions on non-American companies investing over $40 million in Iran. The legislation created considerable friction with European allies given their continued trade with Iran.

Indyk argued that the administration tried to stop ILSA because of the complications it created with Europe.[66] It was widely known that the American Israel Public Affairs Committee (AIPAC), the pro-Israel lobby in Washington, was behind the legislation, but Indyk emphasized that the administration was "not in cahoots with them."[67] Howard Berman, the Democratic chair of the House Foreign Affairs Committee, confirmed in an interview that it is "absolutely true" that AIPAC drafted and lobbied for the ILSA legislation.[68] Despite the administration's concerns, ILSA proved to be extremely popular on Capitol Hill, passing nearly unanimously in the House and Senate.

But Berman, who did not focus on Iran until the mid-1990s when its nuclear advances attracted more attention (his focus before that was largely on the Iraq threat), says that ultimately ILSA proved to be "totally worthless" because many European companies continued dealing with Iran.[69] President Clinton waived sanctions enforcement because of concerns about targeting European allies. Consequently, the bill "had no teeth."[70] When Khatami came to power in 1997, Berman did not oppose Albright's outreach; he believed that some elements within Iran seemed to be more reasonable and wanted to reduce tensions, so why not help the moderate forces, particularly given that a lot of business was at stake when it came to Iran.[71]

Indeed, congressional views on Iran were not uniform, and did not always track with Israeli preferences. Even during the congressional debates over ILSA, while there was unanimous agreement that sanctions were needed against Iran, members were split over how effective various executive and congressional proposals would be at bringing Iran to heel. Republican representative Toby Roth led the opposition to Clinton's embargo. Roth argued that the embargo would do more damage to American companies than to the Iranian government. He asserted that the United States could not act unilaterally against Iran, and that any actions that lacked international support would be futile and self-destructive. Instead, Roth called for an international sanctions regime in order to punish Iran. A number of expert testimonies from Washington think tanks were also critical of Clinton's unilateral actions.[72]

Despite such concerns about going it alone, the ILSA hearings generated strong support for further pressure and represented a sharp escalation of rhetoric toward Iran, especially compared to the discourse of the 1980s. Gone are any nascent overtures to Iran for cooperation, compassion for the Iranian people, or hopes for moderation. Instead, members of Congress from both parties repeatedly framed Iran as a rogue and outlaw state.[73]

Statements by representatives like Democrat Sam Gejdenson illustrated typical congressional discourse on Iran across the aisle:

> The United States considers Iran to be an outlaw and is simply unwilling to make believe that Iran is among the family of civilized nations . . . There are countries, even those with which we have significant differences, where a constructive dialogue could serve to further our objectives. Iran is clearly not among those nations. It is a rogue regime that is intent upon fomenting unrest in the region and determined to acquire weapons of mass destruction to terrorize their neighbors and the rest of the world.[74]

Republican members of Congress, such as Benjamin Gilman, compared Iran's leaders to Hitler, warning that "as we celebrate the 50th anniversary of the defeat of Nazism and Hitlerism, let not the seeds be sown for more acts of terrorism and threat of a nuclear-armed Iran."[75] Nearly every member of the House Foreign Affairs Committee echoed this hostile rhetoric in one form or another. Iran was accused of being the greatest threat to American security, an uncivilized nation, the chief factor destabilizing the Middle East, a threat to the Israeli-Palestinian peace process, a mass human rights violator, and an irrational rogue state. While members acknowledged that the United States faced other threats and that other countries around the world supported terrorism, the consensus held that, in the words of Representative Gejdenson, "if there is a threat to the United States today of a military and political nature, it is Iran."[76]

TESTING ENGAGEMENT

Indyk argues that Clinton's dual containment strategy still left the door open for engagement if Iran "changed its tune," and the election of President Khatami during Clinton's second term seemed to indicate such a shift, given his reform and anticorruption platform. Consequently, Indyk, who at this stage was the assistant secretary of state for Near East affairs, says he did not resist Secretary of State Madeleine Albright's efforts to reach out to Iran.[77] In his assessment, the engagement developed not just because of Khatami's election, but also because Iraq policy was running its course, and some in the administration thought that an opening to Iran could help weaken and balance Saddam Hussein, so it was worth at least exploring on strategic grounds. But Indyk remained skeptical that Iran's hardliners would reciprocate and was concerned "that our own Republican hardliners could accuse Clinton of coddling a rogue regime."[78]

Nonetheless, Albright supported a number of steps to test engagement, including cultural, academic, and athletic exchanges, as well as the lifting of U.S. sanctions on symbolic items like carpets, caviar, and pistachios.[79] The United States also designated an exiled Iranian opposition group, the Mujahedin-e Khalq (MEK), a foreign terrorist organization in October 1997. Albright called Khatami an "avowed reformer," noting his January 1998 interview with CNN journalist Christiane Amanpour where he called for a "dialogue of civilizations" (at the time Amanpour was engaged to James Rubin, a senior aide to Albright).[80]

In Albright's assessment, the time was ripe to move beyond dual containment. Even Iran's stance on the Middle East peace process appeared to be softening. According to Albright, Palestinian leader Yasser Arafat showed U.S. officials a letter from Khatami in January 1998 that backed Palestinian participation in the peace process, acknowledged Israel's legitimacy, and supported a regional peace if the Palestinians established a state.[81] But thawing U.S.–Iran relations was not easy given the high levels of suspicion on all sides. Even sports diplomacy was difficult. The FBI objected to bringing the Iranian soccer team to the United States, for instance, because of concerns that Iranian spies or possibly terrorists would be sent with them; President Clinton had to overrule Attorney General Janet Reno to enable one such visit.[82]

Some embarrassing incidents also occurred. In one ministerial meeting of the so-called "Six Plus Two" forum to discuss Afghanistan, a U.N.-backed grouping that included both the United States and Iran, Albright thought she would have the opportunity to meet Iranian foreign minister Kamal Kharrazi. Afghanistan was a challenge where the United States and Iran had some overlapping interests, including a desire to end the civil war and counter narcotics trafficking. At one point in the meeting, she thought she was speaking to Kharrazi but noticed that he looked different and sensed something was off. She passed a note to her advisors asking if it was him, and they answered that they didn't know.[83] When the chair answered the Iranian as "Mr. Deputy Iranian Foreign Minister," it became clear that Iran's Supreme Leader was restricting high-level contact with senior U.S. officials. It also underscored the still limited understanding within the U.S. government of Iran's internal workings.

President Clinton even attempted direct outreach to President Khatami in a letter delivered through the Omanis in June 1999, which included an oral message to express Clinton's desire for better relations to "offset the sharp tone of the letter . . . which demands justice from Iran for the Khobar bombing, and which the White House feels is required to fend off domestic pressures to be tough with Iran."[84] The 1996 bombing of the military barracks at Khobar Towers in Saudi Arabia, killing nineteen Americans, was a particularly sensitive incident given the high number of American casualties and the subsequent U.S. determination that Iran's Revolutionary Guards played a role in it (the Islamic Revolutionary Guard Corps [IRGC] is the powerful military force operating independently of Iran's conventional armed services). This was not an attack the administration could ignore, even if it took place before Khatami was elected.

Diplomatic openings nonetheless ensued. Albright gave speeches pushing for an opening to Iran, including a so-called "apology" address in which she acknowledged an American role in the overthrow of Iranian prime minister Mohammed Mossadegh in 1953 and argued that the coup was a "setback for Iran's political development."[85] In that speech she also pointed to the election of Khatami as an opportunity for the United States to "adjust the lens through which we viewed Iran," while also urging Iranians to broaden their lens of the United States; she believed that "the possibility of a more normal and mutually productive relationship is there."[86]

During our interview Albright read parts of that speech to me for emphasis, to demonstrate how serious the administration had been about a new relationship. But she told me the reaction of the Iranian American community, while not monolithic, was largely negative. She met with a number of Iranian American groups during this time, calling some of these groups a "complicating factor" for the administration's outreach.[87] She said the pressure from the Iranian American diaspora was real, which was disappointing to her as someone who understood diaspora communities as the daughter of a Czech diplomat.

She saw some generational change and different views among the community (which chapter 5 explores in more depth), but understood that Iranian Americans "had their own version of history," which in her view made "signal catching" from Iranian leaders who wanted to test openings harder.[88] A former senior State Department official observed that while Albright "entertained a lot of ideas," the political risks for engagement were only "magnified" in a Democratic administration because "they struggle with how to be tough" in foreign policy, and Albright was certainly sensitive to such pressures.[89]

And on the Iranian side, the leadership, particularly hardliners who were not enthusiastic about Khatami's outreach, were irritated by a particular phrase in Albright's speech that referred to "unelected" leaders. Albright argued that Iranian leaders were not picking up on the positive signals the administration was sending, or, in the case of the Supreme Leader, may not have wanted to.[90]

Still, Presidents Khatami and Clinton remained in the UN General Assembly Hall to listen to each other's speeches at the fall 2000 meeting, which was not the norm in previous U.N. sessions. Clinton wanted to meet Khatami in person, but this never happened. According to Bruce Riedel, the CIA analyst who served as Clinton's senior director for the Middle East at the NSC, President Clinton was eager for a deal with Iran after the election of Khatami and viewed an American Embassy in Tehran as the "silver grail," second only to the "holy grail" of an Israeli-Palestinian peace.[91] Riedel likens Clinton's attempt to meet Khatami at the General Assembly meeting to "seventeen-year-old guys chasing seventeen-year-old girls" and thought Clinton would "spill coffee" on the Iranian president if that was what it took to get a meeting.[92]

Riedel was relieved that the meeting attempts did not work, because he believed it was clear the Revolutionary Guards would not go along with a rapprochement, and that Khatami basically "told us that."[93] Moreover, although Clinton found Khobar frustrating, he wanted to put the incident in the past, but senior U.S. officials like Sandy Berger opposed doing so, arguing that the administration could not be seen as "holding Iran's hand when this comes out."[94]

American policymakers believed the United States had already made significant gestures to Iran. There was little appetite for offering more, including concrete actions like the sanctions relief that was Iran's highest priority. As Indyk explains, "there were big debates about what to do to Iran for Khobar . . . Now you expect the United States to make a bold move? . . . You have to be kidding. We were already pushing the envelope."[95] The reality of the U.S. domestic context meant that the idea of taking bigger steps just "wasn't on the menu" because the administration "couldn't get into bed with Iranians without some sense of accountability."[96]

No Political Upside to Changing Course

The strategic conditions in the early 1990s were arguably as favorable as they might ever be for a rethink of the American approach to Iran. President Bush himself was interested in testing an opening. Policy reviews considered different strategies in the aftermath of the Iran-Iraq War, the end of the Cold War, and then following the first Persian Gulf War. President Clinton was personally interested in a deal with Iran even as his administration hardened U.S. containment policies, and Secretary of State Albright engaged in a number of high-profile gestures in Clinton's second term, after a reform-minded Iranian president was elected.

But in the end, U.S. containment policies and the hostile nature of the U.S.–Iran relationship remained firmly in place at the end of the decade. There is little doubt that a variety of Iran's activities—particularly support for terrorist groups—contributed to this outcome. Yet the "it's them, not us" explanation does not fully capture why American policymakers responded to Iran's actions in the way they did, both when the policies were dangerous and when they were more accommodating. Without looking into the domestic dynamics within Washington, it is difficult to understand why American policy outcomes on Iran tended to land in the same position regardless of the strategic context or levels of animosity coming from Tehran.

Even when there appeared to be openings and interest among American policymakers, other priorities overtook the Iran file. It was not inevitable that policymakers had to sideline Iran in their deliberations about American engagement in the post–Cold War era or the future regional architecture in the aftermath of the first Persian Gulf war. Iran was repeatedly sidelined because policymakers understood that Iran was not worth expending political capital, especially when the predominant thinking among key policy elites was skepticism that Iran could deliver or deliver enough that would be sufficient cover to sell domestically.

By the time the Clinton team came around to considering openings to Iran in the second administration, the hostile framing of Iran was well entrenched within Washington, backed by unprecedented Iran sanctions legislation. Few other policy issues in the U.S. system generate this level of bipartisan support—animus toward Iran is always the safer political bet.

It may be the case that Iranian hardliners never supported reaching out to the United States, even explicitly opposed it internally, and therefore normalization efforts were doomed to fail. But such explanations too easily dismiss resistance within American policy circles to normalized ties, and the underlying political context, which often limits diplomatic outreach. As a number of scholars have observed, the "rogue" framing of Iran—a framing that was accentuated during an era of American primacy—limited the political space for officials like Albright to respond in ways that could have fully capitalized on the moment when Iranian leaders, even if constrained, were signaling an interest in a different type of relationship.[97]

In other words, how American policymakers reacted to Iranian actions was not a foregone conclusion and was shaped and constrained by the discourse and politics in the American system. The labeling of Iran as a "rogue" and "outlaw" state in public discourse had an impact, increasing the political vulnerability of any policymaker thinking about exploring policies other than isolation and containment. Combine such pressures with competing global priorities for both the Bush and Clinton administrations, and the result was the continuation of status quo policies over two decades after the Islamic revolution, and just as the United States was about to enter a more tumultuous era fighting nonstate terrorism from extremist groups also opposed to Iran, and as the aura of American primacy faded.

THREE

Parallel Universes

When Stephen Hadley saw the draft, he knew it could mean trouble. Hadley, who served as President George W. Bush's first-term deputy national security advisor and his second-term national security advisor, had in front of him the text of Bush's first State of the Union address since the September 11, 2001, terror attacks on the United States, set to be delivered in January 2002. The language, as contained in the final speech, asserted that Iran "aggressively pursues these weapons [of mass destruction] and exports terror, while an unelected few repress the Iranian people's hope for freedom . . . States like these, and their terrorist allies, constitute an axis of evil, arming to threaten the peace of the world."[1]

"Axis of evil," a phrase that came to be associated so closely, even notoriously, with the Bush administration and its approach to Iran, also applied to two other U.S. adversaries, Iraq and North Korea. Hadley called the president to make the case against including the language. Though he did not think the phrasing impeded future engagement or that it would "scupper a breakthrough," he was concerned with its inclusion in the speech at the time.[2] This was just months after the trauma of the September 11 (9/11) attacks that came to define a new era in America's approach to the world for the coming decade. If President George H. W. Bush surprised many of his advisors by including conciliatory language toward Iran in his own State of the Union address, his successor and son took a determinedly different tack.

The president, of course, included the controversial line in the final

61

draft of the speech. In later years Bush argued that the speech was misunderstood—that he was not suggesting the three countries were forming an alliance against the West, but that they each rose to the highest level of threat because of their employment of terror in conjunction with efforts to acquire weapons of mass destruction.[3] In her memoir, Condoleezza Rice, Bush's first-term national security advisor and second-term secretary of state, called the line one of the most "overdramatized phrases of his time in office" and said she does not "remember a great deal of focus on the phrase during the speechwriting process," though she acknowledges discussing with Hadley whether the word "evil" sounded too dire.[4] Still, she wrote, the speech was reviewed in the Pentagon and at the State Department, "and no one raised even a yellow flag."[5]

Given the history of U.S.–Iran relations, it is not particularly surprising that many U.S. officials didn't bat an eye when seeing Iran referred to as "evil." But the timing was peculiar. America had just been attacked by a Sunni Islamic extremist group, Al Qaeda, that operated through the sanctuary of Taliban-controlled Afghanistan. Iran, a Shia majority country, similarly viewed the Taliban as an adversary and supported the American overthrow of the Taliban in Afghanistan following the 9/11 attacks. Iranian and American officials had even participated in multiparty talks on Afghanistan before 9/11, and both supported the main opposition group to the Taliban, the Northern Alliance.

Iranian people expressed sympathy with America after the attacks, with large crowds holding candlelight vigils and thousands observing a moment of silence at a soccer match. The Iranian government, while not shedding its official anti-American stance, even offered assistance during the U.S. campaign to oust the Taliban. To be sure, Iran had a vested interest in the overthrow of the Taliban regime—it was not going out of its way to do any favors for Washington. But the gestures and tone of the Iranian government toward the United States were considerably less hostile after 9/11.

The State Department sent U.S. diplomat Ryan Crocker to lead the U.S. delegation for talks on Afghanistan, with Crocker speaking to his Iranian counterparts directly at his first meeting in Geneva just weeks after 9/11.[6] The idea was to find common ground with the Iranians on Afghanistan, which Crocker says "wasn't hard at that time."[7] It is in this context that the president's "axis of evil" speech was jarring to diplomats involved in these talks; Crocker believes the speech undermined his diplomacy.[8] While the diplomatic channel on Afghanistan continued, Crocker observed that after the State of the Union address the Iranians changed their entire team, downgrading from IRGC-linked operatives with significant influence to diplomats who had little authority to negotiate with Washington. In Crocker's assessment, the United States "lost the window that had opened."[9]

Nonetheless, the administration continued to engage the Iranians on multiple occasions throughout President Bush's two terms in office. Some of this engagement flowed from common interests. In addition to the Crocker channel, senior diplomats like James Dobbins worked closely with their Iranian counterparts in multilateral negotiations in Bonn to establish a post-Taliban government in Afghanistan. In other instances, the talks resulted from necessity, because of Iran's role in supporting nonstate militia groups targeting and killing American forces that occupied Iraq after the 2003 U.S. invasion of the country.

Yet, in a repeat of past debates, those favoring engagement to explore improved relations met either skepticism or fierce resistance from high-level cabinet members and other political appointees in the administration. Civilians in the Defense Department and the vice president's inner circle were particularly convinced that Iran was ripe for overthrow; the predominant view in this camp was that the United States would confront Iran after Iraq.

The administration did not take seriously Iran's "grand bargain" offer in 2003 through Swiss intermediaries. Senior U.S. officials viewed the offer as "freelancing by a Swiss diplomat hoping to be the one to make peace between Iran and the United States."[10] Whether the offer was genuine is up for debate, as so many initiatives are when it comes to Iran and its complex domestic power dynamics. That the United States did not test the offer, or other potential openings during Bush's first term, puzzled some of the diplomats who dealt with the Iranians at the time.

President Bush's "freedom agenda" only reinforced pressure policies toward Iran, including continued sanctions and an information campaign designed to highlight Iran's nefarious regional and domestic activities, seeking to drive a wedge between the Iranian government and its people. Such policies are not unusual in American policymaking, and there is a strong case to be made that distinguishing the objectionable policies of an adversary from the aspirations of its people can serve American interests over the longer term. But when such advocacy emerges within the context of economic pressure campaigns and hostile rhetoric—and not-so-subtle suggestions that Iranian leaders might follow Saddam Hussein's fate—it is not difficult to see why Iranian officials might have viewed American policies as an effort to topple them.

The administration's confrontational stance toward Iran intensified with the 2006 National Security Strategy, which supported preemptive action against "rogue" states. Attacks on U.S. forces in Iraq by Iranian-aligned groups did nothing to soften U.S. positions. Meanwhile, the nuclear challenge only worsened during President Bush's tenure, with his "carrots and sticks" approach leading to some promising multilateral diplomacy to curb Iran's program but with ultimately disappointing results. A former Bush administration official characterized the Iranian threat as "a manageable one" in the 2002–2003 period.[11] But by the time President Obama entered office in January 2009 the Iranian challenge worsened on every front. In short, the early promise of cooperation and new dialogue channels ended with active confrontation and a growing proliferation challenge by the end of the Bush presidency.

Strategic Conditions Again Favor Openings

U.S.–Iran relations were not destined to remain frozen, or even to worsen, in the first decade of the twenty-first century. Geostrategic drivers were arguably pointing in a different direction. In the first months of the Bush administration, some officials were interested in exploring whether there was any possibility of building on the outreach that had accelerated in Clinton's second term after the election of the reformist Iranian president, Mohammad Khatami.[12] Yet, as in previous administrations, engagement gestures did not garner wider support across the government. Senior political appointees in the Department of Defense, for instance, rejected the Joint Staff's assessment that recommended continuing outreach to Khatami.[13]

Nonetheless, after the 9/11 attacks, the case for improved relations with Iran strengthened. Nonstate terrorist groups like Al Qaeda, with their fundamentalist agendas, shocked and alarmed Washington and indeed the world as the twin towers crashed down on that fateful day. While Iran was also long associated with terrorism and maintained an ambiguous relationship with groups like Al Qaeda, it was nonetheless a state actor with which the international community could work. Indeed, Washington and its European allies cooperated with Iran during and following the over-throw of the Taliban in Afghanistan. The Iranians reportedly even shared Taliban troop locations with the Americans in some of the first direct U.S.–Iran talks since the 1980s, as discussed further in this chapter.[14]

Ryan Crocker developed a "productive bilateral dialogue" with his Ira-nian counterparts; direct bilateral engagement was actually the Iranians' idea, according to Crocker, with the Iranians "cornering him" at their first multilateral meeting in Geneva to invite him for coffee at their hotel.[15] When compared to nonstate terrorist groups like Al Qaeda, Iran arguably presented itself as a more rational, if still dangerous, actor on the world stage.

Zalmay Khalilzad, who served through both Bush administrations as the U.S. ambassador to Afghanistan, Iraq, and the United Nations, argued in his memoir that "despite Iran's long record of sponsoring terrorism, the atmosphere between Washington and Tehran had actually improved since 9/11."[16] As a consequence, Khalilzad thought "it would be worthwhile to engage Iranian diplomats, who tended to be among the more moderate elements of the regime . . . the United States could benefit from their ex-perience, knowledge, and insights related to Afghanistan."[17]

Even on Capitol Hill, Iran received a more favorable look and was even praised for hosting Afghan refugees fleeing the Taliban. But such favorable consideration faded quickly. Despite the strategic logic pointing toward a potential shift, American policymakers largely continued to view Iran as a global outlier, making the case for a new approach far more dif-ficult. Rice viewed Iran as more dangerous than other "axis of evil" states like North Korea, seeing Kim Jong-Il as "crazy but not suicidal."[18] At the same time, she acknowledged that the rest of the world, even close U.S. partners in Europe, did not see Iran as Americans did, nor did they share the Americans' "political antipathy toward Iran."[19]

In other words, there was nothing preordained about how American policymakers approached Iran in the early 2000s. America's closest part-ners in Europe, and Asian allies like Japan, did not see Iran the same way that many American policymakers did. Global developments led to overlapping interests and even direct engagement between American and Iranian officials. And yet, the predominant hostile framing and policies toward Iran ultimately prevailed.

Two "Parallel Universes"

COMPETING CAMPS

William Burns, the head of the Near East Affairs Bureau at the State Department during President Bush's first term, characterized Middle East policy in the Bush administration as competing camps that were "two parallel bureaucratic and conceptual universes."[20] On one side, there was Vice President Richard Cheney and his "activist staff," along with the civilian leadership at the Department of Defense and most of the National Security staff. On the other side stood Secretary of State Colin Powell and career diplomats. Elliott Abrams, a senior neoconservative political appointee overseeing Middle East policy and democracy promotion at the White House throughout both Bush administrations, similarly observed that the fissures largely reflected friction between State Department officials like Powell, Armitage, and Burns, and political appointees at the White House and Pentagon.[21]

Fissures between these camps were especially notable when it came to Iraq, with State Department officials like Burns, as well as analysts in the intelligence agencies, skeptical of the case for the Iraq war, which Burns calls the "original sin."[22] Other officials at the State Department, such as Richard Haass, who served as head of policy planning, did not see invading Iraq as an opportunity, but Haass acknowledges he was "not on the same frequency" as the administration on this issue and did not have influence in what he described as the "bleachers" of the State Department.[23] But such divisions also emerged when it came to Iran policy, especially on the question of whether to capitalize on engagement following the wars in Afghanistan and Iraq.

TOP DIPLOMATS FORGE AHEAD DESPITE PUSHBACK

As noted above, Ryan Crocker, who served as Burns's deputy at the State Department and later as the U.S. ambassador to Iraq, was among the first U.S. diplomats to engage the Iranians directly after 9/11. Although a common view is that the Crocker channel was clandestine, Crocker himself notes that the talks were not secret, just low profile, and did not attract the attention of the media, which was just as well from his perspective.[24]

In fact, Crocker went out of his way to ensure that the talks stayed off the radar in Washington, particularly given that "half the administration hated the idea of direct conversations" with the Iranians.[25] To make sure the talks remained discreet, Crocker would fly out of Washington on Friday nights to Paris or Geneva, spend the rest of the following day and night with his Iranian counterparts, and fly back to Washington on Sunday so he would be back in the office on Monday morning.[26] He was careful to avoid leaving any paper trail of the meetings, only briefing Burns on secure calls; according to Crocker, he did not produce a "single piece of paper" on the talks.[27] Aware of opposition within the administration, Crocker ignored this camp, went ahead with direct talks, and was careful not to tell "any of these guys" anything about what was happening.[28]

Though Burns backed his engagement, Crocker understood that he worked in an administration with longstanding Iran hawks who opposed his efforts, including Pentagon political appointees like William Luti and Douglas Feith. At one point during his months of talks with the Iranians on Afghanistan, Feith knew Crocker was about to get on a flight to a meeting in Geneva and remarked, "Give our love to your Iranian friends."[29] This type of jabbing was common among the administration's warring camps, but in Crocker's assessment, these officials were not able to derail the talks until the State of the Union address.

Indeed, between Crocker's first meeting in Geneva in September 2001 and the "axis of evil" speech in January 2002, the Americans and Iranians made significant progress. The U.S. goal was to prevent Iran from interfering in the American military campaign against the Taliban. But it turned out that the Iranians were willing to do more. Crocker found it easy to work with his main Iranian interlocutor, Mohammed Taherian, who later served as Iran's ambassador to Afghanistan and Pakistan, and was believed to have links to the IRGC. The Iranians, according to Crocker, were fairly transparent about their interest and support for the United States attacking the Taliban.

At one of the multilateral meetings a week before the U.S. military attack on Afghanistan started, Crocker observed that Taherian was getting "very edgy." U.N. diplomat Lakhdar Brahimi was chairing the meeting, and the group was "blue-skying" what a future Afghanistan would look like. Taherian finally stood up, slammed his papers on the table, and asserted that if someone did not do something on the ground soon, "all this crap won't mean anything."[30]

The Iranians had agreed to assist if American aircraft were shot down during the mission, and even offered overflight assistance, which Crocker viewed as "going too far." Nonetheless, Taherian did show a map to Crocker identifying Taliban targets, suggesting where the United States should strike.[31] The United States also later accepted intelligence from the Iranians on an Al Qaeda operative in Afghanistan whom they helped turn over to Afghan leaders.[32]

Even Qassem Soleimani, the infamous IRGC head whom President Trump ordered killed nearly twenty years later, was apparently open to "rethinking things" with the United States.[33] Taherian convinced Soleimani to join (under an assumed name) the Iranian delegation at one of the multilateral economic ministerial meetings on Afghanistan in the fall of 2001, with Soleimani shaking hands with all the Americans, who had no idea who he was at the time.[34] But in Crocker's assessment, little progress was made after President Bush's State of the Union address, when the Iranians downgraded their team. In his view, had this channel continued, the United States might have succeeded in targeting more Al Qaeda operatives, which might have saved lives.

James Dobbins, another distinguished career foreign service diplomat who served across multiple administrations, revealed one of the best documented stories of engagement with Iranian counterparts on stabilizing a post-Taliban Afghanistan, and the resistance he encountered from within the administration's anti-engagement camp. In Dobbins's view, the United States had spent thirty years talking to the Soviets, so why not talk to the Iranians?[35] His views of Iran departed from the conventional Washington frame; in his reading, Iran was not just an irrational theocracy ideologically opposed to any engagement with the United States, but a country, like any other, that the United States could work with when interests overlapped. As he put it, "Iran wasn't Switzerland, but at that point [after the 9/11 attacks] it was more democratic than Egypt and less fundamentalist than Saudi Arabia, two of the United States' most important allies in the region."[36]

Ryan Crocker came to see Dobbins before his first trip to handle the post-Taliban file in early November 2001. Illustrating the sensitivity even among State Department officials who supported talks with the Iranians, Crocker was "remarkably uncommunicative" with Dobbins, saying little more than that he had conversations with Iranians and no one else was allowed to speak with them.[37] Burns also warned Dobbins that direct contact with Iran was forbidden.[38] But Dobbins was not asking for permission; he already had the green light from Secretary Powell, with Rice and Hadley's blessing, as long as he stuck to the Afghanistan file.[39]

As the State Department's point person in multiple hot spots—Haiti, Somalia, Kosovo, Bosnia—Dobbins had considerable experience in post-conflict stabilization and was willing to talk to any relevant actor to get the job done. He knew he would need to work with Iran to shape a new government, along with all the other external actors in the conflict—which, before the American overthrow of the Taliban, was essentially a proxy war between Pakistan (backing the Taliban), on one side, and Iran, India, and Russia backing the Northern Alliance, on the other. In preparation for the Bonn conference that established a post-Taliban government, Dobbins participated in "Six plus Two" meetings involving a group of states bordering Afghanistan plus the United States and Russia. At one of these multilateral sessions, Iran's foreign minister said that Iran stood with the United States against terrorism and Secretary Powell shook the minister's hand at the end of the meeting, signaling nascent possibilities for a more normalized relationship.[40]

On the eve of the 2001 Bonn conference, the warming continued as the Iranian delegation extended an invitation to Dobbins to meet at their hotel. Dobbins asked Khalilzad, who then served as a special presidential envoy to Afghanistan, to join him but rebuffed requests from William Luti to participate. As noted earlier, Luti opposed dealings with Iran, along with other civilian political appointees at the Defense Department (Luti was also a former assistant to Republican representative Newt Gingrich, who reflected the traditionally hostile views of Iran pervasive in Congress). Luti told Dobbins the Iranians were bad and "two-faced."[41] At one previous dinner in Rome, Luti had protested talking with the Iranians so loudly that he disturbed other patrons and Dobbins had to change the subject.[42]

Despite such pushback from within the administration, Dobbins and Khalilzad met with Mohammed Taherian (Iran's ambassador to the Northern Alliance who also served as Crocker's interlocutor) and with Mohammad Javad Zarif (the Iranian representative to the talks, who also served as Iran's ambassador to the United Nations and in later years as the Iranian foreign minister). Khalilzad believes this initial meeting set the stage for "amicable and productive relations between the American and Iranian delegations throughout the [Bonn] conference."[43]

When Dobbins went to brief the American delegation about the meeting, Luti and his Pentagon colleague Harold Rhode "grumbled" and left the next day.[44] Dobbins learned six years later—from CIA director George Tenet's memoir—that Luti and Rhode did not go back to the United States but instead traveled to Rome to meet with regime opponents to discuss Pentagon funding for overthrowing the regime. According to Tenet, Michael Ledeen, who had been active in the Iran-Contra affair, was also involved in the secret meetings in Europe.[45] Tenet received reports that Ledeen and other likeminded Pentagon officials were discussing a "twenty-five-million-dollar program to support Iranians who opposed the Tehran regime . . . what we were hearing sounded like an off-the-books covert-action program trying to destabilize the Iranian government . . . This started to give the appearance of being 'Son of Iran-Contra.'"[46]

Tenet called Hadley to complain about the scheme, telling Hadley that "this whole operation smells," while Secretary of State Powell "hit the roof" when he found out about it.[47] Hadley ultimately ordered Ledeen to shut down the effort after complaints from Tenet and Powell, and according to Tenet, the Pentagon opened an investigation into the secret contacts between its staff and what the CIA deemed as untrustworthy Iranian dissidents.[48] As Tenet notes, "the Ledeen follies on Iran were a distraction from the administration's main focus: Iraq."[49] Abrams also asserts that "no one trusted Ledeen," and there was no active cultivation of the Iranian opposition.[50]

Meanwhile, the pro-engagement diplomatic track was moving forward successfully in Bonn. According to Dobbins's account, Zarif played a critical role in getting the Northern Alliance envoy to make the final concessions on the makeup of the new Afghan government that paved the way for the final Bonn Declaration.[51] Hadley corroborated Dobbins's story and acknowledged, "The Iranian team was pivotal in convincing the Afghan opposition to support the U.S.–backed candidate for president, Hamid Karzai."[52]

Iran offered additional assistance on Afghanistan in the months following Bonn. In a meeting in Geneva in March 2002 involving governments that wanted to help the Afghan security sector, the Iranians asked Dobbins for a private meeting, where he was introduced to an IRGC general in the hotel lobby. The Iranians said they would back a U.S.–led program to support the new Afghan army, offering to house, clothe, arm, and train

up to twenty thousand troops. Dobbins recognized that some aspects of
the offer were likely not genuine, but thought the proposition was worth
testing. He reported the proposal to Secretary Powell back in Washington,
who thought it was "very interesting" but told Dobbins he needed "to see
Condi [Rice]" about it.[53] Rice also found the offer "very interesting" and
set up an NSC meeting where Dobbins briefed Cabinet heads. According
to Dobbins, Defense Secretary Donald Rumsfeld shuffled papers and did
not look up or ask questions; no one else spoke or asked questions; and Rice
moved on to the next agenda item. As Dobbins noted, Iran "never got a
response."[54]

In Dobbins's assessment, Powell and other senior officials, such as
Deputy Secretary of State Armitage, were not willing to push too far on
Iran. Armitage did not think Iranian overtures were genuine and was
skeptical as to whether the officials Dobbins was engaging with had the
necessary authority within their own government, though Dobbins still
wondered why the administration did not at least probe the offer.[55] Armitage told Iran analyst Barbara Slavin that in his view even if the United
States had engaged with Iran more seriously, "the demands on the US
side, because of the divisions in the [Bush] administration, were so exces-
sive that I don't think we would have been able to make the compromises
necessary [to improve relations]."[56]

Richard Haass also does not recall much debate about engaging Iran
after the Bonn conference; the issue just "didn't excite people."[57] The administration was focused on Iraq, so in Haass's view it was not surprising
there was little traction on engagement ideas with Iran or an official U.S.
response to its gestures.[58] The neoconservative camp thought Iran would
be dealt with as an extension of Iraq—that once Saddam fell, Iran would
follow naturally through a demonstration effect.[59] Pro-engagement voices
were consequently either resisted or ignored.

Another potential opening emerged in May 2003 through a Swiss
channel. The Swiss ambassador in Tehran, Tim Guldimann, met with
Burns's deputy, Jim Larocco, to present a short paper drafted with the Iranian ambassador in Paris (who was also the nephew of the Iranian foreign
minister).[60] The Swiss emissary believed the document was approved by
the highest levels in Iran and was offering a wide-ranging dialogue with
the United States, or what many accounts describe as a "grand bargain,"
to address the full array of issues dividing the United States and Iran. But

Burns believed Guldimann was "too vague" for Larocco, and they were not convinced that Iran's leaders endorsed the document, given their history of poor messages.[61]

Burns nonetheless conveyed the Swiss document to Powell and Armitage, and despite his doubts, still recommended they explore the offer. But, according to Burns, while Powell and Armitage supported following up on the outreach, there was little White House interest, in the aftermath of the Iraq war. Administration officials were concerned that a response would look like a reward for bad behavior. As Burns explains, Cheney and other "hardliners" in the administration wanted the Iranians to "stew a little" after the American invasion of Iraq.[62]

As it turned out, Iraq offered another arena for potential U.S.–Iran engagement. In the first half of 2003 Khalilzad and Crocker held talks with Iranian diplomats to discuss Iraq's future, with Zarif again heading the Iranian team.[63] Khalilzad held two meetings with Zarif before the war and told the Iranians that the United States intended to overthrow Saddam Hussein, not the Iranian regime, and expected Iranian cooperation, given that Saddam Hussein was also Iran's top regional adversary.[64] Specifically, the administration wanted Iranian commitments that it would not fire at American aircraft if they flew over Iran. Zarif agreed.[65]

According to Khalilzad, Zarif told him that Iran opposed an American occupation of Iraq and warned about instability after the war, warnings Khalilzad wished the Americans had taken more seriously.[66] But Khalilzad's channel with Iran broke off after a truck bomb in Riyadh killed eight Americans and was linked to Al Qaeda militants based in Iran. U.S. engagement with Iranians on Iraq continued through the second Bush administration, with common concerns about the Sunni insurgency that was destabilizing the country. But Iranian-backed militant groups responsible for killing thousands of American personnel in Iraq undermined such efforts and only further narrowed the political space for engaging Iran.

Crocker supported the Iraq talks, but he did not expect much to result from this track, in contrast to his talks with the Iranians on Afghanistan, because the Iranians were far more invested in Iraq. There was "no Taherian" in these talks, nor was there any freelancing on the Iranian side; the Iranians would stop the conversation every ten minutes to call Soleimani for instructions.[67] That said, Crocker believes that if there had not been an "axis of evil" speech and the Afghanistan channel had continued constructively, the United States might have been able to "tame" Iran's anti-American actions "a little," even if it would not have been possible to completely stop Iran's support for Iraqi militias attacking American forces. In his view, Iran wanted some instability in Iraq to ensure that Iraq would never be capable of attacking Iran again, but it was not looking for "total chaos."[68]

A FREEDOM AGENDA OR REGIME CHANGE?

In the midst of these difficult outreach efforts, the Bush administration also pursued a "freedom agenda" that sought to promote democracy and human rights across the Middle East. Distinguishing between the Iranian people and the Iranian regime is widely supported across the political spectrum in Washington and makes strategic sense. But President Bush's "freedom agenda" evolved in ways that caused it to be widely perceived as a "regime change agenda," particularly given the hawkish personnel who populated senior positions in the administration.

In his memoir, President Bush argued that, although Iran was a leading sponsor of global terrorism, the country was also "a relatively modern society with a budding freedom movement."[69] Bush viewed the Iran challenge as two "ticking clocks": Iran's progress toward a nuclear bomb, on the one hand, and the ability of reformers to instigate change, on the other. The administration's goal was to slow the first clock and "speed the second."[70] The president opposed direct negotiations with Iran because of concerns that such talks could "dispirit Iran's freedom movement."[71] Though President Bush expressed regret that he ended his presidency without resolving the nuclear issue, he believed that the "success" of Iraq would "inspire Iranian dissidents and help catalyze change."[72]

Neoconservative voices that dominated the administration's foreign policies were more direct about their ambitions. They viewed the Afghanistan and Iraq wars as a way to bring regime change to Iran in what they thought would be a domino effect. For example, William Kristol, a former official in the elder Bush's administration and then the editor of the conservative *Weekly Standard*, argued that overthrowing the regimes in Iraq and Afghanistan would "show that dictatorship is not the inevitable way in the Middle East or in the Arab world" and "put pressure on Iran for serious regime change."[73] Former senior military officials similarly argued that "Iran will take care of itself once Iraq goes."[74]

Such beliefs were supported through concrete policy actions. In 2002 the administration increased the "flow of news and information into Iran" and established a Persian News Network through Voice of America (VOA) as well as Radio Farda.[75] Senior officials Elliott Abrams and Liz Cheney developed an "Iran Action Plan," which President Bush signed in late 2005, and which included an information campaign to promote freedom in Iran.[76] Abrams insists, however, that the administration's prodemocracy initiatives were not about regime change by force but instead focused on improving human rights within the country and "using human rights as a weapon against the regime."[77] But distinguishing such human rights and democracy initiatives from the desire among many in the administration to encourage the downfall of the government was difficult in practice, and most critically, it was likely not how the Iranians viewed such efforts.

RENEWED ATTEMPTS FOR OUTREACH

Despite the continued influence of neoconservative voices within the administration harboring hopes for regime change—as well as growing tensions between the United States and Iran in the Iraqi theater—some senior U.S. officials continued to contemplate outreach to Iran throughout President Bush's second term in office. Such positions were strengthened by the high-profile bipartisan Iraq Study Group (ISG), led by former secretary of state James Baker and former congressional representative Lee Hamilton, which recommended direct exchanges between the United States and Iran to build on overlapping interests in Iraq. Former U.S. diplomat Edward Djerejian served as a senior advisor for the ISG and met with Iranian diplomat Zarif in New York in 2006, finding the Iranians ready to cooperate and interested in a "working relationship" with the United States," though he noted that such engagement would be difficult because "in dealing with the Iranians, you always have to keep one hand on your wallet."[78] Such sentiments reflected common perceptions in Washington, even among the pro-engagement camp, that the Iranians were duplicitous. Nonetheless, such engagement countered prevalent beliefs among experts and officials in Washington that the Iranians were not willing to deal with the United States.

Within the administration, William Burns, as the head of the Near East Affairs bureau at the State Department, and other officials continued to argue for engagement but made little headway toward renewing direct dialogue. Efforts that bypassed the Iranian government proved more successful, such as programs to train American diplomats with Persian-language skills and station them in posts in Iran's neighborhood to follow developments within Iran more closely.

Indeed, gaps in knowledge on Iran among American diplomats were widely acknowledged, underscoring the need for improved expertise on Iran within the U.S. government. Until 2005 there was no Iran affairs office at the State Department; before this time the Iran file was handled by just two desk officers within the Gulf Arab affairs unit.[79] The State Department had also created a formal "Iran watcher" position in Dubai in 2002, assigning a fluent Persian-speaking career diplomat, Alan Eyre, to the position.

Secretary of State Rice saw value in such efforts but believed the focus on Iran needed to increase. The administration established a separate Iranian affairs office at the State Department, as well as an Iran Regional Presence Office (IRPO) in Dubai in 2006, appointing career diplomat Jillian Burns as its first office director.[80] The intention of the Dubai office was to better understand the political, economic, and social dynamics within Iran and increase American access to Iranian people.[81] In addition to contributing to policies that reflected a more "sophisticated understanding of Iran," the office was also established with the intention to "develop a new cadre of Iran experts and Farsi speakers to prepare for the day when we would reopen our embassy in Tehran."[82]

Toward these ends, the administration also considered initiatives to put American diplomats back in Iran itself. In a memo drafted for Secretary Rice in May 2008, titled "Reimagining the Strategic Initiative on Iran," Burns proposed steps to gain "tactical advantage," including staffing an interest section in Tehran with a few American diplomats (though he did not expect Iran's Supreme Leader to accept the idea).[83] Rice supported Burns's suggestion, noting that even without normalized relations, the United States had such a lower level presence in hostile countries like Cuba.[84]

Rice believed an American presence within Iran would be helpful to gain firsthand knowledge of the country. Given that American diplomats had been out of Iran for nearly thirty years by that time, Rice argued that "we had no eyes and ears on the ground" and that by relying on others, like the Swiss, to report on the domestic situation, "we were making policy toward Iran with one hand tied behind our back."[85] While the Dubai office issued visas to Iranian citizens and offered better access to Iranian people, in her view it was no substitute for an actual presence in the country.

Comparing such an initiative to Cuba, Rice argued that an interest office "might even give us a platform from which to get to know and
engage dissidents in the country."[86] Elliott Abrams reiterated that such
discussions about creating a physical U.S. diplomatic presence in Iran were
serious because Rice wanted to "do something to change the frozen relationship."[87] Even President Bush recognized the need for more information about Iran, often making a point to meet with European ambassadors
stationed in Iran when they passed through Washington.[88]

But Rice acknowledged to her Russian counterpart, Sergei Lavrov, that
establishing a diplomatic presence in Iran would be a tough sell at home: "I
explained that I had a lot of work to do at home if we were going to move
in that direction. 'Sergei, this can't be seen as a favor to the Iranians . . .'"[89]
In the end, the moment to open an interest section "never came"; Iranian policies on the nuclear issue and the harassment of U.S ships caused
officials to scuttle the plan, according to Rice.[90] A former senior State
Department official who participated in the brainstorming sessions with
Rice—including ideas like establishing an American diplomatic presence
in Tehran—says the initiatives ultimately didn't go anywhere because administration officials "just didn't think it would work."[91] Abrams called
the interest section proposal "complicated" because of security concerns,
with U.S. officials worried that if the facility "was overrun, the president
would look like an idiot."[92] Some experts suggest that additional political sensitivities worked against the proposal, including concerns that the
effort could harm Republican presidential candidate Sen. John McCain
because he could not afford the political cost of the administration opening to Iran during a tough campaign.[93]

Moving such initiatives forward within the American system would
prove difficult, given the long legacy of hostility and the more recent experience of Iranian attacks on Americans in Iraq. The Iranian leadership
was also unlikely to accept such a presence, not only because of ideological
opposition to normalizing ties with the United States, but also because
Iranian leaders no doubt feared that such an American presence would be
a cover for efforts to undermine the regime itself. Given the backdrop of
the administration's freedom agenda and the not-so-subtle arguments for
regime change in Iran among neoconservative voices who remained influential even in President Bush's second term, Iranian fears may not have
been totally unfounded.

SYMPATHY WITH ISRAEL BUT LIMITED INFLUENCE

Given the strong neoconservative presence in the Bush administration among officials widely viewed as strong supporters of Israel, the question of Israeli influence on Iran policies again emerges. For instance, in the lead-up to the 2003 Iraq War, Michael Ledeen was based at the neoconservative-dominated think tank, American Enterprise Institute, and was long associated with back-channel dealings with dubious Iranian dissidents with links to Israel, including the secret meetings in Europe discussed earlier. Fellow neoconservative Elliott Abrams, who served as the top Middle East expert at the NSC in the run-up to the Iraq War, was another former Reagan official who had been entangled in the Iran-Contra scandal backed by the Israelis. Other senior administration officials were considered friendly to Israel within the Washington establishment and in the region itself, including Paul Wolfowitz and Douglas Feith.

But with some exceptions, the focus of this group was overthrowing Saddam Hussein in Iraq, not attacking Iran, as the Israelis preferred (as noted earlier, the assumption was that the Iranian regime's demise would logically follow the fall of Iraq). A conservative analyst advocating for regime change in Iraq summarized what he coined as the "Ledeen Doctrine": "Every ten years or so, the United States needs to pick up some small crappy little country and throw it against the wall, just to show the world we mean business."[94]

Some Pentagon staffers were unhappy with the Iraq focus. Larry Franklin, who worked for Under Secretary of Defense Feith and participated in the secret meeting with Iranian dissidents that Dobbins learned about years later,[95] was charged with passing classified information to pro-Israel lobbyists and Israeli officials.[96] In an interview with a Jewish news outlet several years after the trial, Franklin accused the U.S. intelligence community of an anti-Israel, even antisemitic, bias. In his telling, he "had grown frustrated with decisions made by his Pentagon bosses on Iraq and Iran, believing that regime change in Iran was the course America should have pursued."[97]

The Israelis agreed. They thought Iraq was a distraction from Iran, which by that time they viewed as their most pressing regional threat. Richard Haass recalled that the Israelis often approached him because they knew he was one of the few senior officials who was not supportive of the Iraq war within the administration. As they put it to him, "there are two countries that start with I, and you're invading the wrong one."[98] On research trips to Israel to discuss the Iraq war, I heard similar sentiments from multiple Israeli defense analysts—that Israel had not been pushing for a U.S. invasion of Iraq and worried the war would distract from Iran. Indeed, a number of Israeli analysts viewed the U.S. invasion of Iraq as a strategic mistake that only amplified Iranian power and regional influence.[99]

As Haass put it, the Israelis thought the United States was "using up calories" by focusing on Iraq when it should be turning its sights on Iran.[100] But according to Haass, the Israelis were cautious about publicly opposing administration officials who were determined to go to war with Iraq but were otherwise friendly to Israel. The Israelis did not want to "piss off" the president and influential advisors because they knew the administration was going ahead with the war regardless of what the Israelis said, so why waste political capital getting into that fight?[101]

In the end, the United States went to war with Iraq, not Iran, despite Israeli preferences. Attempts to scuttle engagement with Iranians in the lead-up to and aftermath of the American campaign in Afghanistan similarly failed, as pro-diplomacy officials gained the upper hand, for a time at least. The notion that the Israelis, or the pro-Israel lobby, were calling the shots is a simplistic framing of how U.S. policy is shaped and is not supported by policy outcomes and the accounts of those who were shaping U.S. policy at the time.[102] That said, the growing Israeli focus on Iran's nuclear capabilities did increase attention to the issue in Washington, particularly on Capitol Hill where sensitivity to Israeli security concerns was particularly strong.

INCREASING ATTENTION ON NUCLEAR PROLIFERATION

Even with the focus on terrorism and Al Qaeda after 9/11, concern about Iran's nuclear program continued to draw more attention. The Senate Foreign Relations Committee held hearings on the threat posed by Russian assistance to Iran's nuclear program. U.S. senators from across the aisle expressed alarm at the possibility of a member of the "axis of evil" becoming capable of nuclear warfare. They argued that such capabilities would make Iran a threat not only to Israel and the Middle East but to the United States itself.[103]

Concern about Iran's nuclear activity increased later in 2002 after an

Iranian exile group revealed that Iran had built a secret uranium enrichment facility at Natanz.[104] Though the focus in Washington shifted to
Iraq, administration officials believed that its war effort there did more
to influence the Iranians to suspend their program in 2003 than did the
European economic incentives that were offered to halt the program. As
a partly declassified Bush NSC transition memo argues: "It was sometime
during 2003, around the build-up to the Iraq war and the quick removal
of Saddam Hussein from power, that we believe Iran decided to halt, or
perhaps suspend, its nuclear weaponization efforts."[105]

That said, former senior U.S. officials argue that the administration
signaled to the Europeans that the United States did not intend to attack
Iran after Iraq, and attempted to show flexibility with limited gestures like
removing objections to Iranian membership in the World Trade Organization (WTO) and offering spare parts for civilian aircraft.[106] Their logic
was that if the United States took "modest measures to support European
diplomacy," they could toughen and unify policies against Iran's nuclear
program, a strategy the administration believed worked, as multilateral
pressure increased and the nuclear file moved to the U.N. Security Council.[107]

But as EU foreign policy chief Javier Solana told Rice, the strongest
incentive for Iranian compliance was American participation in the talks
with Iran: "They want America. That's all they want—America."[108] The
administration, however, was not prepared to enter into talks with Iran
unconditionally, and would only consider doing so in exchange for Iran's
suspension of uranium enrichment and reprocessing. Even then, Rice
thought getting domestic support for nuclear talks with Iran would be
a tough sell, acknowledging that a "U.S. policy shift of this magnitude
would not be easy. I wasn't even sure that I could get the President to that
point."[109] Indeed, British former foreign secretary Jack Straw blamed the
United States for the failure to reach a nuclear deal with Iran in 2005 when
Hassan Rouhani was a national security advisor to Iranian president Mohammed Khatami. As Straw argues, "a deal was close. It only failed when
hardliners in the Bush administration refused any concessions over issues
such as spare parts for Iran's ageing civil airline fleet."[110]

Rice nonetheless wrote a policy paper in the spring of 2006 outlining a possible policy shift with an offer to join nuclear negotiations, but
the president was not "immediately convinced."[111] According to Rice, she
went back and forth with the president six times on this point, trying to

address his concerns that the Iranians would drag out negotiations while the Europeans and Russians would not come through with sanctions. The president and other NSC officials also worried that the gesture would look like rewarding Iran while the Iranians were killing American personnel in Iraq.[112] Frustrated that the president was wavering on the decision to join multilateral talks, Rice was reassured by national security advisor Stephen Hadley, "He just considers it a big deal . . . I think he'll get there."[113]

In the end, the administration offered to join negotiations with Iran alongside European partners if Iran verifiably suspended enrichment and reprocessing, and on condition that all issues would be on the table, not just the nuclear file. The United States announced the offer on May 31, 2006, with what Rice characterizes as a tough statement because it had to protect "our right flank at home."[114] In a revealing reflection for how the domestic political climate impacted the space for diplomatic overtures on Iran, Rice acknowledged that she would at times bring in Fox News personalities for off-the-record sessions to get a political read on policy ideas and to help her defend administration policies.[115] While there was some skepticism on the Iran offer, there were "no accusations of having gone soft," given that the group understood that the United States did not have the capacity to confront Iran alone with the difficult situation it was facing in Iraq.[116]

Still, the offer had to be couched in tough terms in Rice's view, so the Iranians did not perceive they had the upper hand. While the administration was not seeking regime change, Rice believed that if Iran actually took the "carrot," it would be a "very different regime in any case."[117] If the Iranians did not, the United States would employ the "stick" of more sanctions and isolation. Predictably, the Iranians reacted negatively, while the Russians similarly complained about the undiplomatic tone of the offer. The "carrot and stick" strategy ultimately failed as additional sanctions were placed on Iran, including designations of Iranian state-owned banks and the IRGC and the Qods force in what was the first targeting of government institutions in Iran. U.S. Treasury officials warned European executives and firms about the dangers of doing business in Iran.

In an incident illuminating some of the domestic rifts on Iran policy within the U.S. government, administration officials felt blindsided by the November 2007 National Intelligence Estimate (NIE) on the Iranian nuclear program that concluded with "high confidence" that Iran had halted its suspected nuclear weapons program in fall 2003, which in the view of administration officials downplayed Iran's continued enrichment activities. The administration debated for several weeks how to respond to the NIE; because they were vulnerable when it came to intelligence assessments, given what turned out to be the erroneous claims concerning Iraqi weapons of mass destruction (WMD), Bush's national security team did not believe they could simply reject the estimate. Ultimately, the president released the findings. But administration officials believed that the NIE estimate undermined their multilateral diplomacy to curb Iran's nuclear program and tied the president's hands on a military option. As President Bush put it to the Saudis when he met with the Saudi king in January 2008, "I am as angry about it as you are," reflecting that the NIE finding had a "big impact—and not a good one."[118]

The Bush NSC transition memo for the Obama administration noted a last-ditch effort by the administration to offer a "refreshed" P5 + 1 (the permanent members of the U.N. Security Council plus Germany)[119] incentives package to Iran in June 2008, offering economic aid and energy cooperation in exchange for Iranian nuclear rollbacks.[120] The administration even sent Under Secretary of State Burns to participate in a P5 + 1 meeting with Iran in Geneva in July 2008 to demonstrate the unity of the international community and that the administration was serious about the offer. But as administration officials saw it, the Iranians gave an unclear response and were "playing for more time."[121]

Historians like John Ghazvinian disagree, arguing that the Bush administration's policies failed because the "carrots and sticks" approach was largely a narrow and coercive policy that treated Iran as "problem to solve" rather than as a country with legitimate aspirations and security concerns.[122] Regardless of explanations for diplomacy's failure, the reality was that by the end of the Bush presidency, the Iranian nuclear challenge had increased exponentially.

Bush Leaves Iran Policy Largely How He Found It

The beginning of the twenty-first century presented yet another strategic moment when new thinking on Iran policy might have been possible. Opportunities to chart a new course were not hypothetical. The Bush administration engaged in constructive cooperation with Iran on Afghanistan. A Bush administration NSC transition memo acknowledged that despite Iran's support for militant groups seeking to "bleed the United States," and an ambivalent relationship with Al Qaeda, Iran's "efforts in Afghanistan have not been all bad," noting cooperative positions on counternarcotics as well as development support for Afghan reconstruction.[123]

Indeed, at a donors' conference in January 2002, Iran pledged $540 million in assistance to Afghanistan, the largest amount of a non-OECD country.[124] The United States was also forced to deal with Iran in Iraq after the U.S. invasion, though talks to stabilize Iraq were less successful than the Afghanistan experience.[125] The United States and Iran were at times fighting the same enemy, and Iranian and American diplomats began talking to each other directly and regularly. But ultimately, very little changed in U.S.–Iran relations by the end of the Bush presidency, while the challenges stemming from Iran, particularly on the nuclear front, worsened.

To be sure, Iran continued to engage in activities that appeared to pose insuperable barriers to further openings, especially its backing of armed militia groups responsible for the deaths of American military personnel in Iraq. Iran's advancing nuclear program also continued to present a stumbling block to a broader thaw in relations, though multilateral diplomacy gained some traction after 2003. The emergence of the hardline Iranian president Mahmoud Ahmadinejad in 2005 and his "wipe Israel off the map" rhetoric only made contemplating improved relations more difficult.

But it is too easy to pin the continuation of U.S. policies of containment and coercion solely on Iran's bad behavior. From the start, the administration was skeptical of Clinton's diplomatic outreach. And many neo-conservative voices in the administration were outright hostile to dealing with Iran, believing the regime was on the brink of collapse and would follow Saddam Hussein's downfall. Some policy options were not tested, especially in Bush's first term, before Iraq deteriorated into another bloody battleground for U.S.–Iran confrontation and while the nuclear issue was still relatively contained (and before Ahmadinejad's rise).

The framing of Iran as an "axis of evil" state early in the administration narrowed the political space for gestures and risk-taking in later years. The "freedom agenda" was widely perceived as synonymous with regime change ambitions. Even diplomacy favored by Secretary of State Rice was viewed skeptically, as intended more to close the gap with Europe and increase prospects for greater international pressure than to pave the way for a genuine diplomatic settlement. European former diplomats blamed the United States in subsequent years for the failure to reach a nuclear deal when Iranian president Khatami was in power and Iran's nuclear program was significantly smaller. Basic diplomatic norms, such as sitting at the same table with Iran alongside other international partners, were viewed as major gestures that were expected to meet steep domestic resistance. Policymakers supporting engagement were conscious of not looking weak or pursuing policies that would be viewed as doing favors for Iran, reflecting how difficult it is to move the needle on Iran policy in Washington.

At the end of the Bush administration officials warned the incoming Obama administration that even in the relatively less contentious Afghanistan arena, Iran's "strategic intentions remain murky, and the trendlines are enough to elicit caution."[126] A section in the NSC Iran transition memo focused on the question of "To Talk or Not to Talk" concluded that previous attempts at talks had all been disappointing.[127] The memo spent more time outlining how to pressure Tehran more effectively than on how to improve the prospects for diplomacy. A postscript from Michael Singh, who served as the Bush administration's NSC director for the Middle East, emphasized the futility of diplomacy, noting that the Bush administration inherited "what it regarded as a fruitless campaign of engagement with the reform-minded but disempowered President Mohammad Khatami . . . Viewing Iran as the foremost state sponsor of terrorism, the Bush administration saw little value in continuing that effort—and indeed little prospect that the path to better U.S.–Iran relations lay in talks with regime officials of any stripe."[128]

Despite efforts by some U.S. diplomats to change course and capitalize on an altered geostrategic landscape in the early 2000s, the Bush administration left Iran policy largely as it found it. The enmity toward Iran in American discourse—across the political aisle—worsened in the era of countering terrorism, increasing the political costs for any substantive policy shifts that might depart from longstanding American postures.

FOUR

The Obamacare of Foreign Policy

Just after the election of Barack Obama in the fall of 2008, the chair of the House Foreign Affairs Committee, Howard Berman, got a call from a well-connected foreign policy luminary. The former U.S. diplomat asked whether Berman might be interested in the possibility of meeting with the head of Iran's Majlis (Parliament) during a high-level regional forum in Manama sponsored by a British think tank. A meeting between an Iranian parliamentarian and a senior member of Congress who had sponsored sanctions legislation against Iran would have demonstrated the potential for diplomacy just as a new American president was coming into office after campaigning on the necessity of talking to adversaries.

Based on previous experience, Berman thought the Iranians would back down. Indeed, this was not the first Iranian attempt to reach out to him. In the early 2000s he had received a request from the Iranian ambassador to the United Nations, Javad Zarif (later to become foreign minister), to meet with him in New York. Upon the advice of an Iran expert in Los Angeles, Berman told Zarif's office that he was willing to meet, but that Zarif would have to come to Washington. Berman even secured a travel waiver from the State Department that would have allowed Zarif to make the trip—the United States normally restricts the movement of Iranian officials assigned to the U.N. or attending U.N. meetings to a small area within New York City. Zarif did not come.

Berman acknowledges that he was not among the school that thought there was a diplomatic way to work everything out with Iran. He believed the reason to engage Iran was not because Iran would respond positively, but because by doing so the United States would stand a better chance of convincing American allies to support tougher sanctions.[1] Nonetheless, Berman bought his ticket to Manama. He held multiple calls with the think tank organizing the meeting, where he was assured the Iranians wanted to move forward. Just as Berman was about to leave for Manama, however, the Iranians backed out; he was told the "time was not right."[2]

The incident confirmed Berman's doubts about engaging Iran, a view shared by many senior U.S. officials joining the new administration in Washington. And yet, President Obama came to office determined to reset relations with Tehran. He saw the Middle East as weighing down the United States, distracting attention from engagement in Asia to address a rising China. He sent a letter to the Supreme Leader, recognizing him as the real power broker in the country. He recorded a friendly Nowruz message to the Iranian people and its leaders voicing a desire for greater engagement. He used revolutionary Iran's official name, the Islamic Republic of Iran, making it clear he was not after regime change and favored diplomacy.

This promising start did not last long. Obama's early personnel choices were telling, as top advisors in his first term were engagement skeptics, offering diplomacy with Iran in order, by some accounts, to place the blame on Iran for failure rather than as a genuine path to improving relations.[3] Ben Rhodes, an Obama speechwriter and his deputy national security advisor, argues that Obama was "pushing the envelope in setting a new tone" with Iran, but that his words "didn't align with the personnel [in his first administration]."[4] According to Rhodes, appointments like that of Dennis Ross, who first served as a special advisor on Iran to Secretary of State Hillary Clinton and then as a special assistant to President Obama and a National Security Council senior director for the Central Region, "ran counter to this messaging," as the wider foreign policy team was "built for a pressure campaign."[5] While some of Obama's national security advisors, such as Dennis McDonough, wanted to "preserve space for diplomacy," other senior advisors, including Secretary of State Hillary Clinton, Defense Secretary Bill Gates, CIA Director Leon Panetta, and Chief of Staff Rahm Emanuel (who, Rhodes notes, had a long relationship with both Clinton and Ross), reflected the "momentum of democratic politics and policy" and the "internal habits of how Democrats looked at Iran."[6]

Developments within Iran did not help, particularly the government's harsh crackdown on the Green movement protests that contested hard-liner Mahmoud Ahmadinejad's win over reformist leader Mir Hossein Mousavi in Iran's June 2009 presidential election.[7] Iran's nuclear efforts also advanced, leading the administration to shift to a pressure track and sanctions in 2010, backed by multilateral support, with the passing of U.N. Security Council Resolution 1929. Rhodes maintains that Obama's "reasonableness" helped him gain such international support for more pressure on Iran.[8] Very quickly the "reset" seemed more like a "resume."

The Stuxnet cyberattack on Iran's nuclear program, uncovered in 2010, was reported to be a joint American-Israeli operation that used malware to disrupt the functioning of Iranian nuclear enrichment centrifuges. Obama's overtures rapidly shifted to increased economic sanctions and war preparation, signaling the resumption of the past administration's approach.[9] Despite an administration determined to "pivot to Asia" and focus on great power competition, the constraints in Washington added to predictable obstacles from Tehran, making a course correction on Iran extremely difficult even under an American president inclined to do things differently.

The pattern finally broke with the success of the Iran nuclear agreement in 2015 in Obama's second term, after a new set of advisors came on the scene with a different outlook on diplomacy. Secretary of State John Kerry's appointment in particular strengthened pro-engagement voices within the administration; the former senator and chair of the Senate Foreign Relations Committee (SFRC) had a reputation for favoring diplomatic outreach to adversaries and had previously met with Iranian counterparts through organizers of track two dialogues.[10] The election of Hasan Rouhani as president of Iran in 2013, the leader of what was widely perceived as a more pragmatic faction within the Iranian system, built on the momentum of the new pro-diplomacy personnel on Obama's second term team.

And yet, while some analysts hailed the nuclear deal as a final chapter ending decades of American-Iranian confrontation,[11] debates resurfaced about how far the United States could go in transforming the relationship beyond the nuclear file. Even those favoring the agreement pushed back on using it for a wider opening, favoring continued pressure on Iran in other arenas. It is unclear whether U.S. Iran policy would have fundamentally changed had Hillary Clinton won the 2016 presidential election. But that possibility was never tested, with the arrival of Donald Trump and the unprecedented upheavals of his presidency. Indeed, instead of a nuclear deal leading to a transformed American-Iranian relationship, Trump's disruptive policies in his first administration would quickly come to set the relationship back to its normal antagonistic course.

The Strategic Case for a New Chapter with Iran

When discussing the global outlook of the incoming Obama administration, a former senior U.S. official reflected that, as America entered a strategic era of great power competition with a focus on peer competitors like China—combined with changes in energy markets making the United States less reliant on Middle East oil—it became hard to "objectively argue that Iran was in the top ten priorities" for American interests, particularly if its nuclear program could be contained.[12] Indeed, American policymakers across the political spectrum were tired of Middle East wars after more than a decade of costly interventions in Afghanistan and Iraq, and were eager to turn their sights elsewhere.

Obama's campaign speeches reflected such sentiments. In a foreign policy address in the summer of 2008, Obama lamented the Bush administration's response to 9/11, particularly in Iraq where the United States lost "thousands of American lives, spent nearly a trillion dollars, alienated allies and neglected emerging threats—all in the cause of fighting a war for well over five years in a country that had absolutely nothing to do with the 9/11 attacks."[13] He further asserted that the war "distracts us from every threat that we face and so many opportunities we could seize."[14] Obama wanted to end the war in Iraq so the United States could focus on other areas, including containing the spread of nuclear weapons and rebuilding alliances to meet twenty-first-century challenges.

This strategic outlook was conducive to improving ties with adversaries like Iran in efforts to de-escalate regional conflicts and contain proliferation threats that distracted attention from the administration's wider global priorities and challenges at home. In one of his earliest major addresses on the Middle East, at the University of Cairo, Obama expressed his desire to turn the page with Iran: "For many years, Iran has defined itself in part by its opposition to my country, and there is in fact a tumultuous history between us . . . Rather than remain trapped in the past, I've made it clear to Iran's leaders and people that my country is prepared to move forward."[15]

The administration's highest priority was shifting the American focus to Asia. In a prominent speech to the Australian Parliament in November 2011, President Obama most clearly outlined his desire to pivot away from the Middle East:

> After a decade in which we fought two wars that cost us dearly, in blood
> and treasure, the United States is turning our attention to the vast poten-
> tial of the Asia Pacific region . . . Our new focus on this region reflects
> a fundamental truth—the United States has been, and always will be,
> a Pacific nation . . . Here, we see the future . . . As President, I have,
> therefore, made a deliberate and strategic decision—as a Pacific nation,
> the United States will play a larger and long-term role in shaping this
> region and its future.[16]

For Obama, his desired pivot to Asia underscored the urgency of a diplomatic solution to contain Iran's nuclear program. Such strategic realities
would require more engagement with Iran, as would the rise of the Islamic
State terrorist threat in his second administration when the United States
and Iran faced a common adversary, similar to the situation in Afghanistan after the 9/11 attacks.

The nuclear breakthrough in Obama's second term thus in part reflected the logic of coming to terms with Iran at a strategic moment where
other global challenges were more pressing. But at the end of the day, there
was no transformative moment in U.S.–Iran relations as candidate Obama
had envisioned. A strategic environment favorable to rapprochement can
only go so far when ultimately domestic drivers within Tehran and Washington put on the brakes.

New Beginnings?

OBAMA'S "EXTENDED HAND"

As a presidential candidate, Obama regularly argued for unconditional
dialogue with adversaries as part of his critique of President Bush's policies
in the Middle East and to draw a contrast with his more hawkish Democratic primary contender, Hillary Clinton, the former first lady and soon
to become President Obama's first secretary of state. Once elected, Obama
sought to make good on his campaign promises. In his inaugural address,
Obama spoke of a "new way forward" with the Muslim world based on
"mutual interest and respect," and even a willingness to "extend a hand" to
adversaries if they are "willing to unclench" their fists.[17] In his first inter-

view after taking office, to an Arab satellite television outlet, the president repeated his offer that, "if countries like Iran are willing to unclench their fist, they will find an extended hand from us."[18]

He followed up that spring with a Nowruz (Iranian New Year) message emphasizing a desire for engagement and, most notably, an openness to accepting the leaders of the Islamic Republic, even using its formal name in his message to signal American acceptance of the Iranian government, avoiding rhetoric that might be construed as harboring regime change ambitions:

> For nearly three decades relations between our nations have been strained. But at this holiday we are reminded of the common humanity that binds us together . . . So in this season of new beginnings I would like to speak clearly to Iran's leaders. We have serious differences that have grown over time. My administration is now committed to diplomacy that addresses the full range of issues before us . . . This process will not be advanced by threats. We seek instead engagement that is honest and grounded in mutual respect . . . The United States wants the Islamic Republic of Iran to take its rightful place in the community of nations. You have that right—but it comes with real responsibilities, and that place cannot be reached through terror or arms, but rather through peaceful actions that demonstrate the true greatness of the Iranian people and civilization . . . I want you, the people and leaders of Iran, to understand the future that we seek. It's a future with renewed exchanges among our people, and greater opportunities for partnership and commerce. It's a future where the old divisions are overcome, where you and all of your neighbors and the wider world can live in greater security and greater peace.[19]

Senior officials at the State Department translated the president's aspirations into policy recommendations for how to shift course with Iran. William Burns, who also played a significant role in shaping Iran policy during the final stages of the Bush administration, served in Obama's first term as undersecretary of state for political affairs and then as the deputy secretary of state, before retiring from the foreign service in 2014. In the first weeks of the Obama administration in 2009, Burns sent the new secretary of state, Hillary Clinton, a memo entitled, "A New Strategy toward Iran."[20]

In the memo, Burns argued for a "comprehensive approach" that sought "a long-term basis for coexisting with Iranian influence while limiting Iranian excesses, to change Iran's behavior but not its regime." He recognized that such an approach would take patience, given Iran's own suspicions of U.S. motives and factional disputes among its leadership that is "prone to false starts and deceit," and the reality that for the Supreme Leader and the "hard men around him, animus toward the United States was the core organizing principle."[21] Burns also acknowledged that the administration would face pushback from Israel and Arab partners wary of American engagement with Iran, and that "we'd have a big challenge managing Congress and its widespread aversion to serious engagement with Iran."[22]

Nonetheless, the president went ahead with his public Nowruz message as well as with a "long secret letter" to the Supreme Leader in which he "reinforced the broad points of the Nowruz message."[23] According to Burns, the letter was direct about Obama's determination to prevent Iran from acquiring nuclear weapons while accepting that Iran had the right to a peaceful civilian nuclear program; Obama also wrote that he was not trying to change the regime and was open to dialogue.[24]

The Supreme Leader replied a few weeks later with what Burns calls a "rambling" message, but one that nevertheless indicated a "willingness to engage"; Obama then proposed a "discreet bilateral channel for talks," naming Burns and senior NSC staffer Puneet Talwar as the key contacts.[25] Ben Rhodes also recalls that the Supreme Leader's approximately one-and-a-half-page response to Obama included the "normal Iranian points," but did not "preclude future negotiations."[26] But in Burns's account, the momentum for talks was abruptly halted when the "Iranian presidential elections in June turned into a bloodbath."[27]

The regime cracked down violently on the largest mass protests to emerge in Iran since the revolution. What became known as the Green movement protests, backing opposition leader Mousavi, contested the reelection of incumbent Ahmadinejad, accusing the regime of vote rigging. The Supreme Leader backed Ahmadinejad's win and accused foreign powers of fomenting the domestic unrest, which was violently suppressed as the Green movement's political leadership was forced into house arrest.

Critics of Obama's Iran policies faulted the administration for not backing the Green movement more forcefully when protests erupted in June 2009. The administration, for its part, was concerned about tainting the opposition and feeding into the regime's conspiracy theories about external meddling, particularly given widespread perceptions of previous American intervention in Iranian domestic affairs. Administration officials also argued that opposition leaders preferred that the U.S. government keep its distance from their movement. Nonetheless, by the end of 2009 President Obama expressed support for the opposition, commenting on the unrest in Iran: "Along with all free nations, the United States stands with those who seek their universal rights."[28] Congressional legislation showcased more overt support for the opposition, as Congress passed a number of resolutions condemning the violence and calling for the sanctioning of regime officials linked to the repression; some legislation went even further in calling for the regime's overthrow.[29]

Years later, President Obama expressed some regret about refraining from more active support for the Iranian opposition. He reflected in a podcast with former officials in his administration: "When I think back to 2009, 2010, you guys will recall there was a big debate inside the White House about whether I should publicly affirm what was going on with the Green movement, because a lot of the activists were being accused of being tools of the West and there was some thought that we were somehow gonna be undermining their street cred[ibility] in Iran if I supported what they were doing . . . And in retrospect, I think that was a mistake."[30]

Despite the challenge of engaging Iran after such a violent domestic crackdown, the administration still pursued initiatives to curtail Iran's advancing nuclear program through the P5 + 1 multilateral format, including an initiative to supply fuel for the Tehran Research Reactor (TRR) that would not be susceptible to being used for enrichment with a weapons-grade potential. While such initiatives ultimately failed, they demonstrated a sincere interest even in Obama's first term to tackle the Iranian nuclear challenge through diplomacy.

DIFFERENT ADVISORS, DIFFERENT LENSES ON IRAN

However, not everyone in the incoming Obama administration viewed Iran through the same lens as the president. Such divisions may not have been as pronounced as the competing camps in the previous administration, but they existed and influenced policy outcomes. As one former senior official explains, Obama saw Iran as a dangerous actor but viewed the conflict as one driven by a security dilemma whereby Iran had reasons to fear the United States. The United States had supported regime change in the past, labeled Iran part of an "axis of evil," and militarily encircled Iran in the region—and Obama understood that.[31] In essence, the former official characterized Obama as a defensive realist, whereby if you could correct misperceptions and mistrust, you could move adversaries into more accommodating positions.

That was the president's "baseline view of Iran," and it was why Obama was ultimately willing to accept face-saving measures on issues like domestic nuclear enrichment, though not until his second term when Middle East advisors like Philip Gordon and Robert Malley became more influential and similarly saw Iran through this security dilemma prism. Deputy national security advisor Ben Rhodes was also in this camp, as was the senior director on the Middle East, Puneet Talwar.

But, as noted earlier, other senior advisors had different views. Defense Secretary Gates, a holdover from the Bush administration, was not a strong advocate for engaging Iran, given his negative experiences in prior administrations.[32] Secretary of State Clinton was also viewed as more hawkish and was wary of looking "soft" on Iran; even Obama characterized Clinton's instincts as "hawkish" on national security issues.[33] As a former senior administration official put it, the "views on Iran were more Clintonian coming in" to Obama's first term.[34]

This camp viewed military force as essential to deter Iran's bad behavior; their model was deterrence, not a risky spiraling of conflict as implied by the security dilemma. They also held low expectations for diplomacy changing Iran's behavior, on the nuclear file or regionally. Dennis Ross, who as previous chapters have illustrated played key roles on U.S. Middle East policy in prior administrations, was the most notable senior advisor in Obama's first term representing this viewpoint.

Ross was a strong advocate for a dual track approach, maintaining economic and military pressure while testing diplomacy. Administration allies of the pressure track included Stuart Levy at the Treasury Department, who played a leading role throughout the Bush and Obama administrations in devising an elaborate network of sanctions against Iran. A number of scholars view Ross's writings and influence during this period as illustrating skepticism for engagement and an expectation that diplomacy would fail.[35] They observe an "innate distrust" of Iran among key administration officials that led them to disregard diplomatic initiatives because they saw no political benefit.[36] Other analysts characterize Ross's approach as "a charade," and argue that it was "designed to fail."[37] Former officials in the Obama administration echoed such views in a number of conversations, with one former official agreeing Ross's position was that "cynical engagement would work."[38]

But Ross was not the only skeptic of engagement with Iran. In my conversation with Ross about this period, he recalled a meeting in March 2009 in which Secretary Clinton asked him to give a presentation on Iran to President Obama.[39] Ross argued that Iran was not a regime that would change, but that it would make tactical adjustments when pressured, drawing on a number of historical examples to make the case: when Iran accepted the "poison chalice" and ended its war with Iraq in the 1980s; when it stopped assassinations when worried about sanctions in the 1990s; or after the 2003 Iraq War when the Iranians offered a proposal to the Swiss because they thought they would be the next American target after Saddam Hussein.

Ross said that Clinton's response to his presentation among a small group of advisors meeting with the president was doubtful, arguing that there was no more than a 10 percent chance that diplomacy would work. President Obama put the odds at 25 percent. At that point in the meeting, Ross observed that the principals were competing against each other to demonstrate that they were not soft on Iran. Still, Ross made the case that it was worth testing Iran because engagement could be a form of pressure that could help get the rest of the world to support U.S. policies. Obama agreed.

Indeed, even though Obama was a strong advocate for engagement in public, he acknowledges in his memoir that he was not expecting outreach to Iran to work. Obama's secret letter to Iran's Supreme Leader tried to avoid the mistakes of previous administrations that engaged Iranian presidents and Foreign Ministry officials who were not necessarily Iran's main power brokers. Obama offered to open a dialogue on a range of issues, including the nuclear file. But Obama says that the Supreme Leader never answered him, indicating in his view that Iran had no interest in direct talks.[40] As Obama explains, "the truth was, none of us in the White House had expected a positive response. I'd sent the letter anyway because I wanted to establish that the impediment to diplomacy was not America's intransigence—it was Iran's."[41]

However, as noted earlier, both William Burns and Ben Rhodes assert that Khamenei *did* respond and left the door open to diplomacy. It is a striking omission by Obama, one that illustrates how the "it's them, not

us" narrative persists, even among leaders who maintain a more nuanced
view of Iran and believe that security dilemmas may in part drive adversaries to do the bad things they do. Nonetheless, there still might have
been more space for diplomacy during this earlier period, but the domestic
environment in Washington did not allow a long leash to pursue it.

THE PRESSURE TRACK WINS OUT

Representative Berman acknowledges he "slow walked" sanctions in the
first half of 2009 to allow the new administration some time for diplomacy.[42] In early 2009, Berman was working with AIPAC to prepare new
sanctions on Iran, assisted by a congressional staffer, Brad Gordon, who
previously had served as a political analyst with the CIA working on the
Iran desk and who went on to work for AIPAC as its director for policy
and government affairs (in that capacity he was later a vocal opponent of
the 2015 Iran nuclear deal).[43] Berman told AIPAC that he was not going
to enact sanctions legislation during Obama's first year because he wanted
sanctions to be multilateral, which required getting the Europeans on
board by demonstrating that the United States was flexible and had ex-
hausted diplomacy.[44]

When Berman first introduced sanctions legislation, in June 2009,
Treasury Department officials Stuart Levy and David Cohen, whom
Obama also kept on from the previous administration, came to see him
and argued that the sanctions legislation should shift to targeting financial
institutions to increase the pressure on Iran. Berman rewrote the bill based
on this input, moving the legislation through the House with the Senate
passing it in the fall of 2009. But Berman and his Senate counterparts
held off on conference committee action until the spring of 2010 to allow
the administration time to persuade European and Asian governments
to also impose sanctions to more effectively put pressure on the Iranian
government. Berman understood that without getting Europeans, the
Chinese, and the Russians in the game, sanctions would not be useful in
halting Iran's nuclear efforts, arguing that the entire U.N. sanctions effort
throughout 2010 was less about diplomacy and more "about effective sanctions and how to squeeze them [Iran]."[45]

The 2009 repression of the Green movement further decreased the appetite for diplomacy. Nonetheless, the urgency of addressing the nuclear
file increased following the exposure of a secret Iranian enrichment fa-

cility at Fordow, at the Group of 20 (G20) summit in September 2009. Diplomacy focused on a proposal for a fuel swap at the Tehran Research Reactor (TRR), a civilian nuclear facility largely used to produce medical treatments for diseases like cancer, but which had previously raised proliferation concerns because of undeclared activities at the facility.

The proposal, negotiated in October 2009, would have required Iran to ship out most of its 3.5 percent low enriched uranium (LEU) stockpile in exchange for external actors, notably Russia (with French involvement), further enriching the material for use at the TRR. The package was seen as a "win-win" opportunity, removing the majority of Iran's LEU stockpile and any justification for Iran to enrich to higher levels that could increase proliferation risks, while allowing Iran to maintain its principle of domestic enrichment capabilities.[46] American negotiators also viewed the proposal as a way to probe Iran's nuclear intentions and as a confidence-building measure that could lead to more comprehensive negotiations to curtail Iran's nuclear program.[47]

In a shift from the Bush administration's preference to deal with the Iranian nuclear file within a multilateral framework, the Obama administration agreed to engage the Iranians directly. Under Secretary of State William Burns led the initial TRR talks for the United States, meeting with the head of Iran's team, the secretary of Iran's Supreme Council for National Security, Saeed Jalili. Some viewed the high-level representation of the American team during the technical stage of the talks—including Deputy Secretary of Energy Daniel Poneman and respected arms control experts such as Robert Einhorn, the State Department's special advisor for nonproliferation and arms control—as demonstrating that the administration was serious about reaching a deal.

But reflecting longstanding mistrust of Iran, U.S. negotiators had their doubts about whether the Iranians were sincere in wanting to strike an agreement, and acknowledge that skepticism about the talks grew quickly in Washington as policymakers were concerned Iran was "playing for time."[48] Tough rhetoric from Washington, particularly remarks from Secretary Clinton, also did not help to build trust during the negotiations, with even U.S. officials expressing concerns that hardline remarks from Washington could lead the Iranians to "low-ball" the talks by not sending serious negotiators.[49]

Accounts by former U.S. negotiators acknowledge that rhetoric by U.S. officials that portrayed Iran as having capitulated under pressure "appeared to play some role in influencing the debate within Iran and thereby the chances of consensus" in favor of the deal.[50] The former U.S. negotiators observe that "rhetoric that 'spikes the ball' too hard regarding Iran's relative position of weakness or its concessions typically results in Khamenei hardening his public and potentially private position."[51]

Ultimately, former U.S. officials attribute the collapse of the TRR to Iranian domestic politics and a lack of consensus among rival political factions leading the Supreme Leader to oppose the arrangement. Burns recounts how Iranian president Ahmadinejad was the "biggest booster" of the TRR deal, seeing the agreement as a success by recognizing Iran's right to domestic enrichment, but his rivals did not want Ahmadinejad to get credit for a deal.[52] According to another former U.S. official, the view in Washington was that all Iranian factions sank the initiative—the reformers did not want Ahmadinejad to get credit, and hardliners did not want a deal and did not trust the West, in addition to despising Ahmadinejad.[53]

Regardless of whether hardline rhetoric from Washington fueled the internal fissures within Iran on nuclear diplomacy, Iran's rejection of the fuel swap proposal provided the opportunity for the administration to shift tracks, culminating in increased economic pressure through U.N. Security Council Resolution 1929 in June 2010. Gary Samore, the White House coordinator for arms control and weapons of mass destruction during the TRR negotiations, characterized the American reaction to Iran's rejection of the fuel swap deal as "frustration and anger . . . Rather than appreciating the complicated and convoluted internal politics of Iran, the view was, 'these people are impossible to deal with.'"[54]

Less than a month before Resolution 1929 was passed, there was a last-ditch effort by Turkey and Brazil to save the TRR deal and prevent U.N. sanctions on Iran. Turkey and Brazil announced that the Iranians agreed to ship LEU out of the country in exchange for TRR fuel. But in Burns's assessment, shared by other U.S. negotiators, the Turkish-Brazilian proposal was "too little, too late"[55] as it would have left Iran with too much LEU, particularly because Iran had already started enriching to 20 percent levels that went far beyond civilian nuclear needs. As Einhorn put it, "The deal's 'sell by' date has expired."[56] France and Russia also raised concerns about the proposal.

Moreover, the United States had invested so much effort in getting Russia and China to support Resolution 1929 that in Burns's assessment it would have been "foolish" to turn back and accept the Turkish-Brazilian compromise unless Iran made a "spectacular" move.[57] Another former U.S. official argues that the administration could have taken the TRR deal even if it would have only bought time. But sanctions momentum "took on a life of its own" and became hard to stop.[58] At that point, the situation with Iran moved into the more familiar "world of sanctions" for the next two years, along with continued talk, and genuine American concerns, about Israeli military options.[59]

THE ISRAEL FACTOR

Israel's role in influencing U.S. policy on Iran features prominently in some accounts of Obama's first term. One scholar argues that congressional pressure on the president, with AIPAC-supported sanctions in force and talk of an Israeli war with Iran, closed the door on opportunities for diplomacy.[60] Indeed, with little prospect for diplomacy by mid-2010, and Iran policy moving fully into the sanctions (and sabotage) direction, discussion about the possibility of Israeli military strikes on Iran's nuclear program became more prominent in the U.S. discourse.

Journalist Jeffrey Goldberg wrote an influential cover story for *The Atlantic* in September 2010 about the possibility of an Israeli military strike on Iran, arguing that a consensus had emerged among American and Israeli officials that "there is a better than 50 percent chance that Israel will launch a strike by next July."[61] Israeli journalist Ronen Bergman wrote another high-profile piece in *The New York Times Magazine* provocatively titled, "Will Israel Attack Iran?" further amplifying the case that Israel was serious about a military option and concluding: "After speaking with many senior Israeli leaders and chiefs of the military and the intelligence, I have come to believe that Israel will indeed strike Iran in 2012."[62]

Israel's prime minister Benjamin Netanyahu further messaged the severity of Israeli warnings through his speech to the U.N. General Assembly in September 2012, where he dramatically displayed a cartoonish diagram of a nuclear bomb with a lit fuse with a literal "red line" to illustrate that Israel would not accept further nuclear advances by Iran. My own engagement with Pentagon officials at the time indicated their genuine concern about an Israeli military attack that could lead to unwanted escalation and put the United States in direct conflict with Iran.

Historian John Ghazvinian observes that, while some Israeli defense officials took a less alarmist view of Iran's nuclear pursuits, the American public was only getting Prime Minister Netanyahu's version of Iran, and that it was not a coincidence that this Israeli pressure emerged in the run-up to the 2012 presidential election when the president would be particularly sensitive about appearing hostile toward Israel. Trita Parsi similarly points to Israel for sabotaging Obama's early engagement attempts, including AIPAC's active lobbying efforts for increased sanctions on Iran.[63]

While this reading correctly identifies American domestic politics and discourse as influencing Iran policy, it exaggerates Israel's impact. Yes, it was clear that Netanyahu opposed diplomacy and encouraged talk of Israeli military options to help keep American pressure on Iran. But the key question is how much impact Israeli actions had on final policy decisions. Even Parsi acknowledges that the 2009 Iranian elections complicated Obama's interest in diplomacy and hardened the administration's approach.[64] As noted earlier, Iranian repression of the Green movement after the June 2009 elections, combined with the discovery of a covert Iranian nuclear fuel enrichment plant at a facility near Qom in September 2009, were more likely significant factors tilting balance away from diplomacy and toward increased sanctions than predictable Israeli opposition to engagement.

In fact, Netanyahu's active lobbying on Iran was not well received in Washington. In his memoir, William Burns notes that Obama was "irritated by Netanyahu's heavy-handed attempts to manipulate him in the run-up to the 2012 presidential elections."[65] Burns argues that Netanyahu's "badgering" had the opposite impact of what the prime minister intended, by increasing Obama's commitment to stop Iran's nuclear pursuits without a war. A former administration official similarly believes that Israel's threats to take military action may have been a "motivating factor" for Obama to go for a nuclear deal.[66]

According to another former senior U.S. official, the administration was talking to the Israelis "all the time" because Netanyahu and Israeli defense minister Ehud Barak were "making a lot of noise" about a military strike, and the United States did not want a military conflict with Iran that would drag in the United States.[67] A U.S.–Israel consultation group started in 2009 and met every few months to reassure the Israelis in what a former U.S. official said a colleague described to him as a "hug and punch" strategy: hold the Israelis tight and reassure, but make it clear there can be no military strike on Iran's nuclear program without warning the United

States.[68] The joint American-Israeli Stuxnet cyberattack targeting centrifuges at Iran's nuclear enrichment facility in Natanz was also part of this strategy designed to prevent a preemptive Israeli military strike by delaying Iran's nuclear advances.[69]

Former U.S. officials observe how Washington journalists who talked to the Israelis "all the time" were influenced by Israeli threats to launch a military strike, prompting articles like Jeffrey Goldberg's *Atlantic* piece, but the officials' own assessments were more measured. They took Israeli threats seriously but also understood that the Israelis were using the threat as leverage against the administration to put more pressure on Iran, which the administration was leaning toward in any case.

That said, a former U.S. official does believe that without Israel's influence in Congress, Obama might have "run the table longer on diplomatic engagement."[70] But once Obama did not think Israel was going to launch a strike by 2012, he was more willing to press on the diplomacy track despite continued Israeli objections. This was particularly true in Obama's second term, when the president was more willing to take on domestic political risks as he considered his legacy and viewed Iran diplomacy as among "several long plays."[71]

Former Israeli officials also raise examples of the administration pushing back and making policy decisions counter to Israeli demands. Former Israeli national security advisor Yaacov Amidror argues that the Obama administration "cheated" Israel twice: by changing American policy from dismantling Iran's nuclear program to postponing and monitoring it; and by not telling Israel about secret talks in Oman with the Iranians, which set the stage for the eventual nuclear agreement.[72] According to Amidror, the Israelis did not believe the administration would take an action like negotiating with Iranians directly without informing them, illustrating more distance in American policymaking from Israeli preferences than some accounts suggest.

A former U.S. official confirmed that the administration decided not to consult with the Israelis on the Oman channel.[73] Amidror even believes that some American experts advised Obama to involve the Israelis, but the president sided with advisors counseling against it.[74] Amidror did not win the internal Israeli debate about using military force against Iran, which he favored. He believes Israel was close to making a decision to attack Iran, but Netanyahu ultimately did not believe he had the support of Israeli intelligence (Mossad) and the Israel Defense Forces (IDF). Most of the security professionals in Israel thought the Iran challenge could be solved another way, in part because they were taking American preferences into account, not vice versa.[75]

Perhaps the starkest example of the limits of Israeli lobbying and influence on American policy was the failure of Netanyahu's high-profile campaign to derail the final nuclear agreement that emerged in President Obama's second term.

Obama's Take Two

THE ROAD TO A DEAL

The small, Gulf Arab state of Oman has long been viewed as a neutral regional state and a useful conduit for discreet diplomacy among adversarial parties. Under the long rule of the late Sultan Qaboos, Oman maintained good ties with both Iran and the United States, and had a reputation for quiet diplomacy, making it well positioned to host the initial back-channel talks between the Americans and Iranians toward the end of Obama's first term. Oman's credibility as a trusted broker increased after it helped the United States secure the release of two American hikers from an Iranian prison in September 2011, following the release of another American hiker the year before. Ben Rhodes says the hiker release showed that the "Omanis could do these things" and opened the way for the back channel, though Rhodes notes that at this early stage, and before Rouhani's election, "nothing really happened," as the talks were more about showing that a meeting with the Iranians was possible than about substantive negotiations.[76]

Burns also remained skeptical of new initiatives, given "the checkered history of American-Iranian contacts," but he recognized that Sultan Qaboos had good rapport with Iran's Supreme Leader and that Oman could serve as a reliable channel.[77] The Oman back channel began over the summer of 2012, despite continued talk about an Israeli war with Iran.[78] Or, as noted earlier, the talk of war may have only galvanized the administration to more seriously explore diplomatic options.

The talks started with a lower level preparatory meeting between American and Iranian officials, hosted by the Omanis, in which Jake Sullivan and Puneet Talwar represented the American side. At the time Sullivan was heading policy planning at the State Department and was considered a "rising star" among Washington's foreign policy elite.[79] Talwar had previously served on the State Department's policy planning staff in the second Clinton administration and had worked for Senator Biden as a staff member on the SFRC. He had also written a *Foreign Affairs* article in 2001 arguing for a shift from a containment policy to "moderate engagement," which in his view might "encourage and strengthen positive forces within Iran."[80] Tulwar had joined Burns for previous multilateral talks and was a key player in the TRR initiative. In order to help keep the talks under the radar, Sullivan and Talwar stayed at an empty U.S. government house rather than at a hotel where they might be recognized.[81]

But it was only after the 2012 U.S. election that diplomacy became more serious, with Kerry replacing Clinton as Obama's secretary of state and making Iran negotiations a priority. Ben Rhodes characterizes Kerry as "100 percent in favor of engaging the Iranians" and as one who believed "you can do anything with diplomacy."[82] Kerry had also previously helped facilitate the Oman channel as chair of the SFRC, when Sultan Qaboos reached out to him with the offer to facilitate U.S.–Iran engagement, which Kerry followed up with several trips to Oman to assess whether the offer was viable.[83]

After the election, the Omanis proposed meeting at a higher level, with Burns representing an experienced American team of senior diplomats, including Sullivan (at that point Vice President Biden's chief of staff) as well as nonproliferation experts Robert Einhorn, Jim Timbie, and Richard Nephew. Norman Roule, a senior advisor on Iran from the intelligence community, also joined the talks. Burns was careful to keep a tight lid on the Oman channel, however, acknowledging that only a handful of State Department and NSC officials knew about the secret talks because Obama knew the dangers of being "played" by Iran.[84]

Burns himself viewed the talks as transactional, favoring a focus solely on the nuclear issue since that is what the international community backed and what the Iranians were willing to discuss. He did not expect to the talks to lead to more fundamental change in U.S.–Iran relations. As he explains, the administration did not harbor "grand illusions of overnight transformations in Iranian behavior or U.S.–Iranian relations. I was a short-term pessimist about the prospect for such changes, given the cold-blooded nature of that regime, its resilience and practical capacity to repress, and the opportunities before it to meddle in a troubled Arab world."[85] Burns also understood that the administration could not detour too far from the traditional American playbook of keeping up the pressure on Iran, acknowledging that the team would need to "embed any progress on the nuclear issue in a wider strategy to push back against threatening Iranian behavior in the region."[86]

The talks made it clear that a zero-enrichment stance—the longstanding U.S. position that opposed any domestic enrichment activity by Iran—was not feasible by 2013. According to Burns, the president gave a green light to the team to show flexibility on this issue to demonstrate that the administration was serious about the negotiations; at the same time, the United States maintained military options, including "bunker buster" bomb development, if diplomacy failed.[87] Burns began direct engagement with senior Iranian officials in Muscat in February 2013.

The election of Rouhani, a more pragmatic Iranian leader, as president in June 2013 and the appointment of Javad Zarif, who had previously worked closely with Americans on Afghanistan, as Rouhani's foreign minister further accelerated diplomacy. Indeed, former U.S. officials believe that Rouhani's ascent was pivotal in moving the nuclear talks forward.[88] The talks led to a consensus on a "sanctions relief for nuclear freeze" formula, with the Americans briefing the P5 + 1 states on the back channel by the fall of 2013, when negotiations moved to the international multilateral format.

At this stage, public U.S.–Iran engagement would also become more routine. President Obama even sought a meeting with President Rouhani on the margins of the U.N. General Assembly in New York in September 2013; had it occurred, this would have been the highest level engagement between the United States and Iran since the revolution. But, in a sign that nuclear diplomacy could only go so far in altering U.S.–Iran relations, the meeting never transpired. As Rhodes recalls, Obama was waiting for a response from the Iranians while sitting in the secretary general's office, but the Iranians were indecisive and backed out.[89] Rhodes was told to tell the press that Obama was ready to meet Rouhani, but that the Iranians refused, which is when the Iranians appeared to regret their decision and requested a phone call with the president instead. While falling short of an in-person meeting, the Obama-Rouhani phone call nonetheless broke new ground and began to normalize the idea of American and Iranian leaders speaking directly, including subsequent calls between Zarif and Kerry.

U.S. diplomat Wendy Sherman first met her Iranian counterparts at the September 2013 U.N. General Assembly, which she called a "stiff" meeting but where Iranian officials intimated that Rouhani's election offered a new start to negotiations and that the Iranians were "ready to deal."[90] The talks led to an interim nuclear deal in Geneva on November 24, 2013, called the Joint Plan of Action (JPOA),[91] with Kerry and Sherman leading the negotiations toward a final agreement. But, as Burns observes, a deal was not inevitable, with the biggest obstacle being the overall strained nature of U.S.–Iran relations stemming from their own domestic politics: "the politics in Tehran and Washington were corrosive, offering little room for maneuver or incentive for risk-taking."[92]

Kerry was particularly attuned to the Iranian political context, taking care to avoid a U.S. posture that would give the impression that Iran was capitulating, because, as he explained in his memoir, he "knew the Iranians well enough by that point to understand that if they felt humiliated or condescended to, they were more likely to dig in than capitulate . . . Every move we made—every word we said—mattered enormously."[93] Indeed, a senior Iranian official complained to Burns during the Oman talks that the Iranians objected to the common American use of terms like "carrots and sticks" when discussing policy options to curtail Iran's program, noting that the "Iranians are not donkeys!"[94] Kerry was sensitive about avoiding such pitfalls. Former U.S. diplomats argue that this kind of "sensitivity to and awareness of the impact of U.S. rhetoric and tactics on the nuclear debate within Iran among U.S. negotiators appears to have played an important role in helping the U.S. secure critical concessions from Iran as part of the JCPOA."[95]

The Americans were also aware of their own domestic pressures. Ben Rhodes explains that administration officials understood that pushing the Iran deal forward "wasn't the best career move" and that once they started with the interim deal, it would take considerable "political capital" to reach a final nuclear agreement.[96] As Rhodes observed, the pro-Israel lobby AIPAC, which consistently backed Iran sanctions legislation and opposed the nuclear negotiations, "puts the effort in DC that no one else does."[97] If a member of Congress counters AIPAC talking points, "it's a decision to break from orthodoxy," Rhodes asserts, and not many do.[98]

Administration officials were willing to face political risks because, in Rhodes's view, they genuinely believed that without a diplomatic resolution they were heading toward war.[99] Lead negotiator Wendy Sherman was a strong supporter of diplomacy, arguing that military strikes would have only delayed Iran's nuclear program and incentivized Iranian leaders to accelerate it, while years of sanctions had failed to stop the program:

"By the time multilateral talks were back in full swing, in 2013, harsh sanctions had been in place for years . . . Yet, Iran now had 19,000 operating centrifuges."[100]

The interim agreement outlined the contours of the final bargain of nuclear rollbacks for sanctions relief, with Iran agreeing to some uranium enrichment cuts and increased international inspection of nuclear sites in exchange for some limited rollback of sanctions and access to frozen funds. This set the stage for the final, comprehensive nuclear agreement, announced on July 14, 2015, which imposed far more stringent limitations on Iran's nuclear enrichment and enhanced monitoring and verification, but offered Iran more significant sanctions relief.[101] Sherman characterizes the JCPOA as the "state of the art of professional multilateral diplomacy,"[102] and indeed the agreement was viewed by many in the administration, and in European capitals, as a key foreign policy achievement.

THE OBAMACARE OF FOREIGN POLICY

Despite the multilateral nature of the Iran deal and wide international backing, the agreement was not enthusiastically embraced in the region, or in Washington. Gulf Arab states resigned themselves to the reality of the deal, but remained concerned about its sole focus on Iran's nuclear capabilities without addressing its nonnuclear activities in the region—particularly its support for nonstate militant groups—that were a higher priority for them.[103] Israel was most strongly opposed, with Prime Minister Netanyahu leading the campaign to derail the agreement. Netanyahu was long associated with a strident public battle against Iran and its nuclear pursuits, often comparing Iran to the Nazi regime.[104] Netanyahu disparaged the final deal, calling it a "stunning historic mistake."[105]

Many other Israeli leaders shared Netanyahu's objections to the JCPOA and concerns about Iran's other regional activities threatening Israel. Foreign Minister Avigdor Lieberman likened the deal to the Munich agreement with Nazi Germany, while then defense minister Moshe Yaalon said the agreement was built on "lies and deceit" that granted Iran legitimacy.[106] Issac Herzog, then the opposition leader from Israel's Labor Party and later the president of Israel, joined Netanyahu's opposition, arguing that the deal would "unleash a lion from the cage" that would threaten Israel because Iran is an "empire of evil and hate that spreads terror across the region."[107]

Specific concerns about the deal's terms, including sunset clauses and verification measures, added to Israel's angst about the agreement, despite the belief among a large number of nonproliferation experts that the deal included robust monitoring and verification safeguards. Indeed, not all of Israel's own national security establishment viewed the JCPOA through the same lens as Netanyahu, and worried that Netanyahu's confrontational approach toward Washington might damage future US–Israeli relations.[108]

Some Israeli experts and former defense officials even supported the final agreement as the best alternative to contain Iran's program, given the shortcomings and failures of other options. Israeli politician and former IDF chief of staff Benjamin Gantz argued that while a better deal might have been reached, "I also see the half-full part of the glass here . . . And I see the achievement of keeping away the Iranians for ten, fifteen years into the future—and postponing their capabilities of having a nuclear capability—and with the right price."[109] Former Mossad head Efraim Halevy also argued that the agreement blocks the "road to Iranian nuclear military capabilities for at least a decade."[110] Other Israeli security analysts and former officials saw the value in an agreement that would delay the possibility of Iran acquiring a nuclear weapon by a decade or more.

Nonetheless, Netanyahu's strong opposition impacted the political debate in Washington, and his position was enthusiastically embraced by congressional Republicans who found this issue an easy target on which to challenge President Obama. While a number of congressional Democrats also expressed reservations about the deal, and ultimately voted against it, the JCPOA evolved into a partisan issue. Because sixty Senate votes are needed for ratification of a treaty in Congress, which would not be possible with Republican opposition, the administration did not advance the JCPOA as a treaty but rather as an executive action. While executive actions had by then become a common policy tool across Republican and Democratic administrations, the lack of bipartisan consensus only added to the intense politicization of the agreement.

Sherman observed that the deal's progress "seemed to energize the Republicans—and the Israelis, who began to act in concert with the GOP to foil our progress."[111] In March 2015 Netanyahu spoke to a joint session of Congress to denounce the deal, an unprecedented step that was viewed as partisan, given that Republican House speaker John Boehner invited Netanyahu without the knowledge or support of the White House. Sherman characterized the speech as akin to "throwing a grenade into the negotiations."[112]

Further complicating the agreement, Sen. Tom Cotton also published an open letter, signed by fellow Republican senators, warning the Iranians that any deal that was not approved by Congress could be revoked by a future administration. Interestingly, Sherman recalls how the U.S. negotiating team was able to make the most out of this opposition by using the Netanyahu speech and the Cotton letter to remind the Iranians that the administration could not concede more on the terms of the deal because of domestic pressure at home.[113]

Given the history of U.S.–Iran relations and the domestic framing of Iran in Congress over the years, such domestic resistance was not particularly surprising. But the opposition to the agreement was so forceful that in many ways the Iran deal became the "Obamacare of foreign policy," as one former Democratic member of Congress put it to me, referring to the partisan nature of the opposition that emerged over President Obama's healthcare initiative.

Indeed, the nuclear deal became a political football to an extent that had not been seen to that point, even when measured against the always contentious nature of debates about Iran in Washington. In 2013 and 2014, as the JCPOA began to come together, the Republican-led House Foreign Affairs Committee held nearly twenty hearings on Iran, largely airing hostile positions toward diplomacy and focusing on the shortcomings of the nuclear negotiations. House Republicans did everything they could to keep Iran front and center in the American mind, while Democrats in the Senate preferred to mute the issue, understanding that engagement with Iran was not a popular policy move in American politics.

Within the hearings themselves, the bipartisan antagonism toward Iran still reigned. Indeed, the rhetoric during the JCPOA hearings was fierce. For instance, Eliot Engel, a Democrat, warned that "ending the Iranian nuclear weapons program is the greatest national security challenge facing our Nation," asserting that "since the Iranian leadership has threatened to destroy the State of Israel, the dangers from this nuclear scheme are of the highest order."[114] Engel was deeply skeptical of trusting the Iranians. He warned that "the Iranian regime will only respond to pressure" and could not be trusted.[115] Across the aisle Ted Poe invoked similar phrasing, asserting, "The Iranians aren't acting in good faith. I don't see any evidence over the last few years they have ever acted in good faith."[116] Engel accused the Iranians of duplicity, saying, "While the regime feigns sincerity on negotiations for the international press, they continue to move full speed ahead with their nuclear weapons program."[117]

Chairwoman Ileana Ros-Lehtinen voiced similar concerns, both about the scale of the threat posed by Iran and about the difficulties of trusting Iran. Like Engel, she warned that "Iran continues to pose one of the greatest threats not only to U.S. national security, but also to global peace and security."[118] Ros-Lehtinen invoked the difficult post-1979 history in claiming that "diplomatic overtures have not [worked] and will not ever work with Iran." Brad Sherman, a Democrat, made perhaps the most inflammatory statement of the hearing when he accused the Iranian government of being a terrorist organization. Edward Royce reminded his colleagues of Iran's abysmal human rights record when he asserted that "a regime that is stoning women with one hand shouldn't be allowed with the other hand to get its grip on a nuclear weapon."[119] This statement is especially notable because it reprises the trope of construing Iran as a medieval regime and suggests that Iran's religious fundamentalism disqualifies it from normal diplomatic engagement. In other words, congressional debates on the Iran deal reinforced long-held narratives of Iran as an untrustworthy and irrational state.

Nonetheless, despite Israeli opposition, an active lobbying effort by AIPAC against the deal in Congress, increased politicization, and bipartisan expressions of dismay that Washington could strike a deal with a country like Iran, the administration was able to ultimately push the deal forward. Congress was not able to overturn the agreement, and the JCPOA went into force on "adoption day," October 18, 2015. In the following months, the International Atomic Energy Agency (IAEA) certified that Iran had met its obligations to restrict key elements of its nuclear program as required by the agreement, and the implementation of the JCPOA began on January 16, 2016, including the lifting of nuclear-related sanctions.

A TRANSACTIONAL, NOT TRANSFORMATIVE AGREEMENT

For all the vitriol directed against the JCPOA, and the energetic cheerleading supporting it from within and outside the administration, the reality of the agreement was much more modest. In the short time the deal was in place—through the end of Obama's final term and the first two years of the first Trump administration—the JCPOA neither brought total catastrophe to the region, as many opponents warned, nor did it prove to be a transformative stabilizing force for the wider region, as some of its supporters had hoped.

The JCPOA was at its core an arms control agreement, a diplomatic approach to contain Iran's nuclear program. Just as the United States and the Soviets had reached arms limitation agreements without resolving their adversarial political relationship, few should have expected an arms control agreement with Iran to lead the way toward a wider diplomatic breakthrough that would end the decades-long pattern of hostility. Expecting a more transformative impact from the agreement was unrealistic, particularly given the deep-rooted mindset in Washington (and among Iran's clerical rulers) resistant to accommodation.

Even policymakers who supported the deal viewed the agreement as a largely tactical, transactional arrangement to buy time; few were expecting the American policies on Iran to fundamentally change. In his remarks discussing the final nuclear deal, President Obama explained that, while the agreement "permanently prohibits Iran from obtaining a nuclear weapon . . . As was true in previous treaties, it does not resolve all problems; it certainly doesn't resolve all our problems with Iran. It does not ensure a warming between our two countries."[120]

The president made a forceful case for why he believed the agreement was the best one achievable to effectively prevent a nuclear-armed Iran, but he did not make the case that the agreement would inevitably, or even likely, lead to the end of animosity between the United States and Iran. Ben Rhodes says Obama even told his staff to avoid talking about how the deal would "moderate" the Iranians, understanding that any change that might occur within Iran would be a "ten-year bet" and would not happen on Obama's watch, and thus could not be sold as a reason to support the deal.[121] For Obama, the deal was all about the nuclear issue. The JCPOA was a major foreign policy achievement for the president, but the nuclear agreement was ultimately not a major detour in longstanding U.S. policies of confrontation toward the Islamic Republic.

In fact, even prominent foreign policy experts and former officials who supported the JCPOA argued that the need to bolster containment policies toward Iran would only increase in the wake of the agreement. Nicholas Burns, an experienced American diplomat who had worked on

Iran nuclear issues in President George W. Bush's second term, argued for accepting the nuclear deal, but moving quickly after its passing to a "parallel track" to contain Iran's regional ambitions.[122] Burns worried that the deal's economic relief would allow Iran to "make more trouble in the region" and thus required the United States to prepare a robust response to expected troublemaking, including putting the Iranians "on notice that we're not going to tolerate any diminution of American influence in the Persian Gulf."[123]

Such views were prevalent among the American foreign policy community, and certainly on Capitol Hill where few expected or desired transformational change in the U.S. approach to Iran. Indeed, if anything, the politically contentious domestic battle over the nuclear agreement only made the Iran file more polarizing in U.S. policy discourse. Those who supported the agreement were especially wary of not looking like "regime apologists," a popular slander by antiregime activists toward analysts or civil society actors who favored diplomacy.

Far from breaking the narrative on Iran, the nuclear deal further entrenched prevailing stances. Obama's unclenched fist ultimately yielded a limited, albeit important, arms control agreement. This was not the transformational moment Obama might have contemplated early in his presidency, but in the context of U.S. political domestic discourse on Iran, it was nonetheless an achievement.

Lingering Animosity

In his memoir, Obama reflected that he was seventeen years old at the time of the Iranian revolution and did not know anything about Iran, and yet "it's hard to overstate just how much, thirty years later, the fallout from these events still shaped the geopolitical landscape of my presidency."[124] Obama recognized the constraints he would face, globally but most critically domestically, because of the legacy he inherited and despite his desire to pursue a different path.

Given the track record of failed diplomatic efforts with Iran by the end of the Bush presidency, and Iran's considerably expanded nuclear program, it was foreseeable that the incoming Obama administration, like most previous administrations, would be tempted to consider new approaches to Iran, and in the end succeeded to a much greater extent than its predecessors. But even President Obama and the breakthrough on nuclear diplomacy during his second term did not ultimately change the deeply rooted framing and American posture toward Iran.

Those arguing against the deal tapped into longstanding frames of Iran as an untrustworthy pariah. Even those favoring the deal did not significantly depart from such framing, but nonetheless assessed that the arms control benefits would outweigh the risks of dealing with such an outlaw state. The lingering animosity toward and mistrust of Iran was in essence well established even with the success of the JCPOA, providing a natural starting point for the incoming Trump administration.

Still, few anticipated the extent of the disruption to emerge with the election of Donald Trump, who, unlike President Obama, entered the White House with little desire to improve relations with Tehran. In fact, in his first presidency he set out to do quite the opposite—to scuttle Obama's Iran policies and most specifically his signature foreign policy achievement, ensuring that whatever small opening the JCPOA might have offered for building better relations with Iran over time would be quickly squashed.

FIVE

The Worst Deal Ever

The contentious nature of U.S. Iran policy was on full display by the end of the Obama administration. I experienced firsthand the tense exchanges on the Iran nuclear deal during the many talks I gave on the subject over the course of 2015. But years later, one particular event brought home just how visceral and politically divisive the issue remained.

A group of mostly Iranian American women gathered one late summer afternoon in 2021 to mingle over tea at a garden salon featuring a prominent Iranian woman's rights activist. It was the type of small gathering in Los Angeles where you hear more Persian than English, not an uncommon experience in a city hosting one of the largest Iranian diaspora communities in the world.[1] The speaker shared a compelling story of overcoming hardships and discrimination as a woman in Iran, becoming an activist challenging the Islamic Republic rulers with a defiant campaign empowering women to shed their hijabs, or head coverings. As with many opponents of the Iranian government, her activism made her a target even while living abroad after brutal crackdowns on dissent made it too dangerous to return home. Her passionate plea for supporting human rights in Iran and holding its leaders accountable rallied wide support across the political spectrum, and her personal story showed great courage in standing up to repressive leaders. But then the discussion suddenly moved from inspiration to attack.

The speaker condemned mainstream human rights organizations, arguing that they selectively avoided criticism of Iran (although, in fact, major human rights organizations routinely issue reports critical of Iran's human rights record).[2] Skipping over Trump's handling of the Iran file over the previous four years, the activist resurfaced critiques of the Obama administration for its failure to support the Green movement, which even President Obama himself expressed regrets about, as noted in the previous chapter. Then the conversation took a more surprising turn. When the speaker began critiquing the Biden administration's handling of Iran policy in his early months in office, in her view wrongly prioritizing nuclear diplomacy over human rights, the event moderator interjected, "So they're [the Biden administration] regime apologists?" "Yes, absolutely," she responded. At the mention of President Biden's name, one woman in the audience yelled out, "He lost!"

I was shocked. Yes, I lived through the violence on January 6 and, like many Americans, worried about the health of American democracy. But to hear someone a few seats down from me contest the legitimacy of a U.S. presidential election was unsettling. The speakers ignored the disruption and went on with the panel. While the incident certainly did not represent the views of a diverse Iranian American community, it did reflect the especially divisive and political nature of Iran policy in America, particularly after the disruptive years of the Trump administration.

President Trump came into office promising to upend longstanding policies with his "America First" agenda, but when it came to Iran, he and his advisors were locked in the traditional framing of Iran as a fanatical, irrational, implacable enemy. Among his most consistent promises was his stated intention to scrap the Iran nuclear agreement, which he repeatedly called the "worst deal ever." He made good on that pledge in May 2018 when he unilaterally withdrew the United States from the global agreement, despite Iranian compliance at the time and against the advice of his own national security advisors. He promised to bring about a "better deal" and pursued a "maximum pressure" campaign—an onerous set of sanctions targeting Iran's banking and oil sectors in particular. The effort succeeded in devastating the Iranian economy, but it failed to bring about a new or stronger agreement. What it did instead was unleash more destructive Iranian activity across the region.

Unlike many previous incoming administrations, Trump officials did not seriously contemplate a new policy course with Iran in his first administration. On occasion President Trump mused about talking to the Iranians and striking a better deal; he showed interest in a meeting with

President Rouhani at the September 2017 U.N. General Assembly, only to be rebuffed by the Iranians, an outcome that pleased his more hawkish advisors.[3] But his convictions on Iran were in fact clearer from the outset of his presidency than his positions on many other policy issues. Trump viewed Iran as the source of the region's problems and accused the previous administration of being far too accommodating. Regional partners, particularly Saudi Arabia, the United Arab Emirates (UAE), and Israel, actively worked to shape Trump's Middle East outlook and reinforce his already hardline inclinations on Iran. All of his regional initiatives, from his first international trip to Riyadh to the Arab normalization agreements with Israel, were shaped by a desire to weaken and isolate Iran.

To the extent that debate emerged, it was in Trump's first year in office and focused on the narrow question of whether to stay in the JCPOA. Several of his top advisors argued in favor of remaining in the deal because they saw more damage to U.S. interests globally by withdrawing and preferred building on the agreement rather than abandoning it. European and Asian allies were making the same case, but Trump ultimately rejected these arguments and pursued the Iran policy he had promised on the campaign trail, which was in essence the quintessential hostile stance toward Iran built up over decades of American policymaking.

Domestic factors were again a strong driver of policy outcomes, aligned to a greater degree than in previous administrations with Israeli preferences. The veneer of strategic framing for Iran policies is often thin in American policymaking, but it was nearly undiscernible in the Trump era. Pro-Israel, anti-Iran policies fit with the Trump inner circle's worldviews. Despite Trump's otherwise erratic leadership style, his administration's policy direction on Iran was clear from the outset.

The Continuing Case for a Strategic Pivot

The Trump administration, like the Obama team, came into office determined to spend less time on the Middle East. Trump's "America first" brand reflected this preference, with Trump often arguing that the United States had wasted too much energy and money on foreign entanglements, neglecting priorities at home. Trump's December 2017 national security strategy forcefully promoted America First foreign policies.[4]

A Trump acquaintance told *New Yorker* writer Adam Entous, "He [Trump] quite honestly had very little interest in meddling in the Middle

East . . . all of this was an annoyance . . . 'The Sunnis, the Shias, the Jews, the Palestinians have been doing this for thousands of years, and I, Donald Trump, am not going to continue to add to the already outrageous investment of trillions of dollars in a region that breeds and funds terrorists against America while we starve our infrastructure investments at home!'"[5] Trump made no secret of his desire to avoid getting the United States involved in more Middle East wars. His postings on Twitter (later X), which became his signature conduit for revealing his administration's first-term policies, clearly reflected this preference. As he tweeted on October 7, 2019:

> I was elected on getting out of these ridiculous endless wars, where our great Military functions as a policing operation to the benefit of people who don't even like the USA. The two most unhappy countries at this move are Russia & China, because they love seeing us bogged . . . down, watching over a quagmire, & spending big dollars to do so. When I took over, our Military was totally depleted. Now it is stronger than ever before. The endless and ridiculous wars are ENDING! We will be focused on the big picture, knowing we can always go back & BLAST![6]

But Trump's fixation with undoing Obama's legacy in all arenas seeped into his obsession with overturning the Iran nuclear agreement, driving policies in directions counter to the strategic logic of investing less time in the Middle East and more time on global threats like China, as Trump's national defense strategy indicated.[7] Indeed, by the end of the Trump administration, following the U.S. killing of the IRGC head, General Qassem Soleimani, Iran launched its first direct attack on American forces since the Tanker War in the 1980s. While the strike did not result in American casualties—although it came closer than many realize and did lead to serious injuries among U.S. personnel stationed in Iraq—it underscored how Trump's policies fueling escalation with Iran worked at cross-purposes to the strategic rationale of extricating the United States from Middle East conflicts.

A Divided But Still Hawkish Team on Iran

Trump's closest advisors on the Middle East—including his son-in-law Jared Kushner, who became the administration's point person on the region— held views on Iran that aligned closely with those held by Israel, particularly with those of Prime Minister Benjamin Netanyahu. The Trump family had personal ties to Netanyahu, a longtime friend of Kushner's father. As several profiles of the Trumps have noted, Ivanka Trump and Jared Kushner maintained strong attachments to Israel, making large donations to Israeli charities, including to a yeshiva in a West Bank settlement; Netanyahu even stayed at the Kushner home in New Jersey on occasion.[8]

Kushner was also close with Israeli political operative Ron Dermer, whom Kushner calls Netanyahu's "right-hand man."[9] Kushner even acknowledges working with Dermer to oppose a U.N. Security Council resolution denouncing Israeli claims in the West Bank before Trump's inauguration, an unusual action during a presidential transition and one that violated protocol for an incoming administration. The resolution ultimately passed with a U.S. abstention in the final month of Obama's presidency, departing from the traditional U.S. practice of vetoing U.N. resolutions deemed critical of Israel. Kushner viewed the vote as an "unprecedented abandonment of Israel."[10]

Trump's pick for ambassador to Israel, David Friedman, also "held right-wing views of the Middle East and contributed money in support of the same West Bank settlement as Kushners."[11] Jason Greenblatt, an attorney who previously worked for the Trump Organization, served as the administration's lead envoy for the region. Greenblatt ran in similar circles as Friedman and Kushner, forming an ideologically aligned group of advisors solidly in the pro-Israel camp with little to no lobbying from Israel needed. Trump himself needed little coaxing, having long espoused pro-Israel sentiments. He filmed a campaign video in support of Netanyahu in 2013 in which he stated, "My name is Donald Trump and I'm a big fan of Israel . . . And you truly have a great Prime Minister in Benjamin Netanyahu. There's nobody like him."[12]

Trump and his closest advisors, who ultimately shaped his Middle East policies, also developed close relationships with other regional leaders who shared Netanyahu's perspectives on Iran at that time, particularly in Saudi Arabia and the UAE. UAE's ambassador to Washington, Yousef Al Otaiba, was among the most influential Arab diplomats across Washington's political spectrum, and he wasted no time in gaining "extraordinary access" to the Trump team, with Thomas Barrack, a Trump donor and friend of Otaiba's father, introducing the ambassador to Kushner during the campaign; Barrack was later indicted for failing to disclose his lobbying for foreign governments.[13]

The common denominator among Otaiba, Dermer, and Kushner was a shared concern about Iran. As Barrack wrote to Otaiba in 2016, when he was trying to cultivate his relationship with the administration: "You'll love him [Kushner] and he agrees with our Agenda!"[14] After Trump won the presidential election in 2016, Kushner met with UAE crown prince Mohammed bin Zayed (MBZ) in New York through Rick Gerson, a hedge fund manager and another friend of Trump. MBZ then proceeded to connect Kushner to the then Saudi deputy crown prince Mohammed bin Salman (MBS), who subsequently became the crown prince and de facto leader of Saudi Arabia. Kushner and MBS developed a close personal relationship through phone calls and texts.[15] Trump also maintained warm ties with MBS, even after the killing of *Washington Post* journalist Jamal Khashoggi in the Saudi Embassy in Istanbul, which U.S. intelligence later determined was approved by the Saudi government. Trump accepted Saudi denials about having had a role in the killing, even personally dictating a statement supporting MBS without consulting his advisors.[16]

Still, Trump's first foreign policy team was not a monolithic group. Some of his early advisors—National Security Advisor H. R. McMaster, Secretary of Defense James Mattis, and Secretary of State Rex Tillerson—did not share the same stance on the Iran deal as Trump's inner circle. Kushner expressed disdain for Tillerson in his memoir, calling him "risk-averse" and prone to managing problems rather than disrupting policies as Trump preferred, noting Tillerson's opposition to the U.S. Embassy move to Jerusalem.[17] As Kushner bluntly put it, "He hated me, and I hated him." (Ivanka Trump recommended the far more hawkish Mike Pompeo as his replacement after Trump fired Tillerson by tweet in early March 2018.)[18]

Former Obama advisors labeled this group the "axis of adults" within the administration because they believed these advisors would constrain Trump from dangerous decisions.[19] John Bolton, who would later replace McMaster as Trump's national security advisor, also used the term "axis of adults" frequently in his own memoir, but with a reading that was far less favorable—in his view, Trump's early advisors were holding him back from following through on the policies he wanted to pursue, including withdrawing from the Iran nuclear deal.[20]

That said, even this early group of more measured national security advisors shared Trump's critical views of Obama's handling of Iran. McMaster accused the Obama administration of taking "conciliation with Iran to a new level"[21] and acknowledged he was "sympathetic" to Trump's insistence that the JCPOA was the "worst deal ever."[22] Echoing longstanding American policymakers' framing of Iran as untrustworthy and incapable of change, given its revolutionary ideology, McMaster argued that the Obama administration was deluded in thinking the Iranian regime could change if the United States adjusted its policies. In his view, the enmity of the Islamic Republic to the United States is foundational to the regime, making conciliation with Iran impossible.[23]

Derek Harvey, a former Army colonel who served as the director on the Middle East at the NSC under Trump, similarly believed that the U.S. position had "deteriorated" during the Obama years and viewed what he saw as Obama's appeasement of Iran as neglecting close U.S. partners like Israel and Saudi Arabia. Harvey would come to work closely with Kushner, who served as his patron within the administration.[24]

Other advisors who later worked closely with Kushner on the Abraham Accords, the effort to integrate Israel into the broader Middle East, also maintained unusually close contacts with Gulf Arab and Israeli officials. General Miguel Correa, who joined the NSC in 2020, was a former defense attaché in the UAE, where he raised red flags by cultivating close personal ties with Emirati officials as a result of his role in rescuing an Emirati military helicopter in a 2017 Special Operations mission in Yemen. The uncle and father-in-law of one of the soldiers he rescued happened to be UAE leader MBZ. Correa was reported to leverage such access to conduct meetings with high-ranking Emirati leaders outside of official channels, leading the chargé d'affaires of the U.S. Embassy to remove Correa from his post, a measure backed by senior State and Defense Department officials.[25]

Mattis, the former head of CENTCOM from 2010 to 2013, also held an Iran-focused view of the region. He told journalist Dexter Filkins that his regional priorities were "Iran, Iran, Iran," and, according to journalists Peter Baker and Susan Glasser, emerged from his assignments in Iraq with an "abiding hatred of Iran."[26] As a former Marine, the devastating Marine barracks bombing in Beirut in 1983 also shaped Mattis's negative views of Iran.[27] One former aide said Mattis believed Iran "remained the greatest threat to the United States interests in the Middle East."[28] Even so, while Mattis opposed the Iran deal, he did not favor withdrawing from it once it existed as he thought the United States needed to honor its terms.[29] He gave congressional testimony in April 2018 that noted the deal's "pretty robust" verification measures.[30] Tillerson similarly tried to counter Trump's desire to leave the deal.

But it did not take long for the more hardline Iran hawks within the administration to oust this group and consolidate a uniformly anti-Iran stance among the top echelon of advisors, with one of the most hawkish voices on Iran in Washington, John Bolton, replacing McMaster in April 2018, just a month before Trump's withdrawal from the JCPOA. Mike Pompeo, who as CIA director "twice recommended in the Situation Room that Trump renounce the agreement" despite the norm against intelligence interference in policy decisions, became one of the most forceful voices in the administration favoring tougher Iran policies as he replaced Tillerson as secretary of state. As Baker and Glasser put it in their analysis of the first Trump administration, Pompeo and Bolton shared a "hardline approach to the use of American power in the Middle East and a focus on, even obsession with, Iran."[31] Vice President Mike Pence was also staunchly in the anti-Iran camp. When the chairman of the Joint Chiefs of Staff, Mark Milley, asked Pence in early 2020 why he was advocating for a military strike on Iran, Pence reportedly replied, "Because they are evil."[32]

Brian Hook, the administration's special representative on Iran, working the file daily, maneuvered among these warring camps throughout the administration, but was ultimately a loyal implementer of Pompeo's preferred maximum pressure policies before leaving the administration in August 2020. Hook was also Kushner's key interlocutor at the State Department[33] and maintained a tough stance against Iran even after leaving government.[34] The even more hawkish Elliott Abrams replaced Hook. Abrams believes that framing adversaries like Iran as evil—just as Reagan had done with the Soviet Union—is the right way to pursue foreign policy because it helps the United States look tougher, which in his view is good for negotiating positions.[35] But he also sees every deal with Iran as a "betrayal of the Iranian people," reflecting widespread views in Washington wary of engagement with adversaries.[36]

Swords and Orbs: A Message to Iran

Jared Kushner was the driving force behind Trump's decision to make his first foreign trip as president a trip to Saudi Arabia in an "epic snub" to America's democratic neighbors—every U.S. president's first trip abroad since Ronald Reagan had been to Canada or Mexico.[37] Derek Harvey, the NSC advisor for the region and a former intelligence officer at the Pentagon, backed Kushner's idea for the Saudi trip, believing it would also benefit Israel since both countries were hostile to Iran and were already establishing back-channel relations.[38]

However, McMaster did not like the plan, and especially Kushner's "out of channel" approach to organizing it.[39] At a March 2017 principals' meeting to discuss the trip, Tillerson similarly expressed reservations, arguing that the Saudis "always talk a big game" but that he was skeptical that they would deliver, based on his prior experience as an Exxon executive.[40] Mattis also thought the trip was a "bridge too far" and recommended waiting until the following year.[41] Kushner acknowledges that initially even Trump himself did not want to go, but when presented with the Saudi package—a high-profile summit of Arab and Muslim leaders, $300 billion in business deals, a new center to combat terrorism—and a promise to "roll out the red carpet for Trump," Trump agreed.[42]

Kushner also worked with deputy national security advisor Dina Powell to plan the trip, helping him overcome the "stiff internal resistance."[43] Most significantly, Kushner coordinated the trip with MBS, building on the personal ties they had developed during the campaign and transition period. After one situation room meeting in which Trump's senior advisors were debating the trip, Kushner called MBS and told him that everyone thought he was a fool for trusting MBS, warning the Saudi leader, "If I get to Saudi Arabia, and it's just a bunch of sand and camels, I'm a dead man."[44] The Saudis did not disappoint. Trump was greeted with an extravagant welcome during the late May 2017 visit—in contrast, Kushner points out, to the lackluster reception Obama had received on his visit to the kingdom the year before, when the Saudis refused to meet the president on the tarmac.[45]

In addition to performances of sword dancing and images of Trump and regional authoritarian leaders surreally staring at a glowing orb during their summit, the president's trip was ultimately intended to send a message to Iran. The visit would showcase that the Arab and Islamic world was united in the fight against extremist ideology, including a determination to confront Iran. Notably, no major Shia figure attended the gathering; Iraq was represented by its Kurdish Sunni president, Lebanon by its Sunni prime minister. The framing of extremism in sectarian terms and conflation of Iran-backed groups with Sunni-based terrorism was another shot against the Islamic Republic. Derek Harvey believed the summit sent a "strategic message" to Iran that Gulf Arab states and Israel were united against it.[46]

While the Trump administration put a stronger emphasis on Iran's links to terrorism, concerns about Iran's influence among nonstate militia groups across the region were not particularly new and had escalated significantly following the 2003 Iraq War and overthrow of Saddam Hussein, the ruthless Sunni dictator ruling over a Shia majority population. Regional fears grew that Iran would capitalize on the downfall of its primary Arab rival to gain control of four Arab capitals (Baghdad, Damascus, Beirut, and Sanaa), facilitating the perception of an expanding "Shia crescent" from Iran to the Mediterranean.[47] Syrian president Bashar al-Assad's ability to remain in power with Iranian and Russian support following the Arab uprisings reinforced these fears (Assad's regime only fell years later in a surprise assault by Syrian opposition forces in December 2024).

Israeli analysts, and some American think tanks, regularly referred to concerns about an Iranian land bridge extending from Tehran to Lebanon, where Iran's growing presence in Iraq and Syria allowed for the transfer of Iranian personnel and weaponry to Hizballah and other nonstate allies threatening Israel.[48] The Saudis were also concerned about Iranian missile transfers to Houthi forces in Yemen, creating a new cross-border threat in the context of the wider Saudi-Iranian political competition for regional influence. In reality, Iran's ability to expand its soft and hard power throughout the region faced serious limits, and a variety of actors actively pushed back against Iranian power projection over the years.[49] Iran's own vulnerabilities at home further diminished its power projection. Nonetheless, the perception of unfettered Iranian influence and hegemonic aspirations was widely held by many in the region and in Washington at that time, as was the belief that concerns about Iran would unite Arab states and Israel in common cause.

The Trump administration enthusiastically embraced this narrative to frame its regional posture and rhetoric. From the earliest days in the Trump administration, top advisors, such as the short-lived national security advisor Michael Flynn, spoke about "putting Iran on notice."[50] Other senior officials, such as the U.S. ambassador to the United Nations, Nikki Haley, repeatedly called out Iran's links to terrorist groups across the region. At one press conference, with Iranian missile fragments behind her to underscore Iran's support for Houthi rebels in Yemen, Haley called Iran the "arsonist" that is "fanning the flames of conflict in the region," arguing that it is hard to find a terrorist group in the Middle East "that doesn't have Iran's fingerprints all over it."[51] The Trump administration also began highlighting claims connecting Iran with Al Qaeda during the period when the president began challenging the Iran nuclear deal.[52] President Trump even used language in tweets following the 2017–2018 winter protests in Iran that were read as calls for regime change.[53]

The Riyadh summit demonstrated the administration's view of Saudi Arabia as a key pillar in confronting Iranian influence. Major arms sales and support for the Saudi campaign in Yemen accelerated following the president's trip. Multibillion-dollar U.S. arms sales to Saudi Arabia and other regional partners flowed with fewer constraints tied to human rights considerations.[54] The Trump administration considered an agreement for Saudi Arabia's nuclear energy development that would exceed the standards set for other regional states, despite proliferation risks (a proposal that resurfaced during the Biden administration).[55] The shift in leadership in Saudi Arabia to Crown Prince Mohammed bin Salman, who at the time expressed staunchly anti-Iranian views, further cemented the synergy between Washington and Riyadh on the Iran file.[56] As Baker and Glasser argue, MBS would end up "having far more influence over American foreign policy in the Trump years than the chancellor of Germany."[57]

Undoing the Nuclear Deal

The starkest example of a more confrontational approach was the Trump administration's position on the Iran nuclear deal, the JCPOA. Trump made no secret of his disdain for the nuclear deal during the presidential campaign. Nonetheless, many analysts thought the president would put his hostile rhetoric aside once in office and accept the agreement as long as Iran continued to comply with its terms. A career official who had worked on the nuclear deal and continued to serve in the Trump administration wrote a strategy paper for the incoming administration that made the case for the United States staying in the agreement as a way to keep pressure on Iran concerning regional issues, particularly Iran's support for militant groups through arms shipments and other covert activities. But the points made in the transition strategy paper "didn't stick and were watered down" in administration documents that emerged on Iran.[58]

Senior advisors in the administration who favored staying in the agreement argued that if Iran was complying with its terms, an American withdrawal could risk U.S. isolation and the loss of leverage in the future. The withdrawal discussion arose every ninety days because of a congressional requirement to recertify Iranian compliance, a "measure that infuriated

Trump" because it forced him to endorse a deal he despised.[59] Trump certified Iranian compliance twice after assuming office. After signing one of
these certifications, Trump reportedly told his advisors, "This is the last
time . . . It's a shitty deal,"[60] and "I'm never signing one of these certifications again . . . I can't believe I'm signing this one."[61] Even after the certifications were signed, McMaster designed a strategy on Iran that maintained
a confrontational approach, including "engagement, which was really a
subversion campaign to influence Iran's population" and "confrontation for
their malign actions."[62]

Meanwhile, deal opponents in Washington were actively encouraging
Trump to reverse course. Given the deeply rooted views in Washington of
Iran as an unchanging outlaw state and Trump's already hostile disposi-
tion toward Iran, this was not a difficult task. When Trump had to decide
whether to certify Iranian compliance with the JCPOA for a second time,
in July 2017, John Bolton—who was then a senior fellow at the conservative
think tank American Enterprise Institute—wrote an op-ed arguing that
"withdrawing from the JCPOA as soon as possible should be the highest
priority."[63]

Bolton claims his op-ed set off a battle in the White House with Mattis,
Tillerson, and McMaster succeeding in convincing Trump to certify the
agreement: "Trump ultimately succumbed, but not happily, and only after yet
again asking for alternatives, of which his advisors said there were none."[64]
Bolton says Trump called him a few days later to complain about advisors who
did not give him options; Bolton then told Trump's advisor, Steve Bannon,
that he would write a strategy for how Trump could withdraw from the deal,
which he published in the *National Review* in August 2017.[65] Kushner expressed his support for this step when he texted Bolton, "Steve [Bannon] and
I disagreed on many things, but we were in sync on Iran."[66]

By the third compliance decision, in October 2017, McMaster offered
Trump a third choice that tried to split the difference—the president could
decertify the agreement but not formally withdraw.[67] Some believed the decertification decision was only symbolic, offering a compromise that allowed
the president to register his disapproval of the agreement without ending
it, because only the reimposition of nuclear-related sanctions would violate
the deal. But in reality, the decision set in motion a chain of events that
raised questions about its future viability. The October decertification decision forced a sixty-day review period in Congress that could have reimposed
nuclear-related sanctions that would have killed the deal. After strong lob-

bying from Europe seeking to preserve the agreement, Congress did nothing during the sixty days, moving the fate of the deal back to the White House.

The next major decision point came in mid-January 2018, when the administration had to decide whether to continue waiving the nuclear-related sanctions necessary for the deal's survival. The president waived the sanctions,[68] but gave Europe one last chance to "fix" the agreement within 120 days or the United States would withdraw. The president outlined his major areas of concern with the JCPOA, primarily related to Iran's missile development, inspections of military sites, and sunset clauses.[69] The State Department engaged European partners to work on addressing these areas in an attempt to find a compromise that might save the agreement.[70] But some observers believe these efforts were largely a show. According to Baker and Glasser, former senator Bob Corker believed the talks were "strictly politics that made him [Trump] look like he was working on an Iran deal . . . he didn't really want it to be successful."[71]

Indeed, the core bargain of the JCPOA was Iran's nuclear rollback in exchange for economic relief through the lifting of sanctions. The uncertainty sparked by the Trump administration's threats created a chilling effect on international trade and investment in Iran even without the formal collapse of the JCPOA.[72] European firms were not willing to risk losing the U.S. market because of American secondary sanctions on Iran, and European government efforts to keep economic channels open to Iran ultimately failed to salvage the agreement.

The deal's fate was sealed by May 2018. Bolton had joined the administration as Trump's third national security advisor the month before and immediately focused on Iran. He told top European officials there was no way to fix the deal.[73] When French president Emmanuel Macron visited Washington in late April 2018, Trump told him he was leaving the deal, despite Macron's effort to persuade him otherwise.[74] Trump told Treasury Secretary Steven Mnuchin to prepare "the heaviest possible sanctions."[75] Bolton's summary of the demise of the JCPOA foreshadows the administration's more ambitious policies to challenge the regime itself: "It had taken one month to shred the Iran nuclear deal, showing how easy it was to do once somebody took events in hand . . . A lot remained to be done to bring Iran to its knees, or to overthrow the regime, Trump's stated policy to the contrary notwithstanding, but we were off to a great start."[76]

The Iran hawks in the administration had the advantage of pressing for a policy with which the president already agreed—Bolton reportedly hung in his office a framed copy of Trump's order to leave the JCPOA.[77] Despite the grave strategic consequences of this decision, its proponents celebrated locking in the already well-established pattern of hostility in American-Iranian relations, bringing it to new heights.

The Pressure Campaign Eclipses Talk of Talks

As the Trump administration exited the Iran deal, Trump repeatedly talked about how he could strike a better deal. Some speculated that if Trump's name could appear on a new deal, he just might agree to diplomacy over confrontation. But in the end, "maximum pressure" policies overshadowed talk of diplomacy and were backed by advisors who drove the administration's confrontational approach. Trump had little incentive to steer them in a different direction, given that being tough on Iran and unconditionally pro-Israel was popular with his political base.

By August 2018 Trump's second Secretary of State, Mike Pompeo, created a new team at the State Department called the Iran Action Group, led by Brian Hook, which was responsible for implementing increased economic and political pressure on Iran. The team's goal was to "ramp up pressure" and encourage other countries to reduce oil imports from Iran to zero.[78] As one account of the group explains, the team was staffed with experts under Hook who could add "muscle" to the administration's tough rhetoric on Iran.[79] The group worked on the assumption that "the U.S. economy and dollar are so central to the global economic system that American sanctions alone will isolate Iran's economy."[80] As *Bloomberg* journalists observed:

> Trump is going further than any previous president in using American financial power as a weapon—in direct confrontation with his allies, daring them to keep doing business with Iran, even if that brings the threat of U.S. economic punishment and denial to the American market, which is 60 times the size of the Iranian economy. As far as Hook is concerned . . . "Very few companies are going to choose Iran over the United States."[81]

Despite this tough posture, advisors like Bolton were pushing for even harsher sanctions enforcement and the end to any waivers of U.S. sanctions against countries still receiving Iranian oil exports. Bolton even called Pompeo "wobbly" on sanctions enforcement because of concerns that ending all waivers would spike oil prices if Arab oil-producing states did not make up for the loss of Iranian oil on the market.[82] Nonetheless, by April 2019 the White House announced an end of waivers, gaining wide Republican congressional support.[83] The administration also designated the IRGC as a foreign terrorist organization, subjecting Iran and members of this military arm of the government to further sanctions. Despite Iran's response—striking oil tankers in the Gulf and production facilities in Saudi Arabia over the summer of 2019—the administration maintained its pressure policies.

The administration also continued to exert pressure on allies to ensure the JCPOA could not be revived before the 2020 presidential election. In June 2020 the administration attempted to extend the U.N. arms embargo on Iran and trigger the "snapback" provision in the JCPOA that would reimpose all U.N. sanctions on Iran, but faced pushback from other JCPOA members (France, the United Kingdom, the European Union, Russia, and China), given that the United States was no longer a party to the agreement.[84]

Even in the midst of the maximum pressure campaign, Trump still believed he could find a way to talk to Iran and strike a deal. But his musings about diplomacy never went far. According to former advisors, Trump believed world leaders, including the Iranians, wanted to speak with him, but people were stopping them from getting through; Iranian foreign minister Zarif was even giving interviews claiming Trump wanted to talk, but advisors like Bolton and foreign leaders like Netanyahu and MBS were preventing it.[85] Bolton argues, however, that Rouhani had not made any effort to contact the administration, and that Zarif was just playing to Trump's vanity in media interviews.[86]

Trump was also convinced—even obsessed, by some accounts—that Obama's former secretary of state John Kerry was encouraging the Iranians to stay in the nuclear deal and wait Trump out, which in Trump's view was why the Iranians were not coming to him to talk. At one NSC principals' meeting on how to respond to Iranian escalation, Bolton quotes Trump as saying, "The Iranians aren't talking only because of John Kerry."[87] Trump even wanted to prosecute Kerry under the Logan Act, which prohibits U.S. citizens from negotiating with foreign governments.[88] According to Bolton, Trump asked Japanese prime minister Shinzo Abe to relay a message to the Iranians during a visit to Tehran that they should not listen to

Kerry, believing he "could do the negotiations in one day, not stretched out over nine to twelve months."[89] At the same time, Bolton says, "Of course, Trump was also totally prepared to go to war if he had to."[90]

It is thus not surprising that Bolton succeeded in talking Trump out of an idea proposed by French president Macron to meet with Zarif.[91] Macron was not the only politician trying to encourage Trump toward diplomacy with Iran. In a *New Yorker* article journalist Robin Wright wrote about an initiative by U.S. senator Rand Paul, which Trump apparently approved, to invite Zarif to visit the White House, an idea that Paul had raised with Zarif in a meeting in New York in mid-July 2019 amid escalating Iranian attacks on oil tankers and the shootdown of a U.S. drone in late June.[92] Indeed, Wright reports that during the first two years of his presidency, Trump reached out to Iran—through allies like the French— about possible meetings eight times, including twice when both Trump and Rouhani were in New York for the U.N. General Assembly.[93] Accounts from former Trump officials, however, assert that once the Trump meeting with Rouhani failed to materialize at the 2017 General Assembly, there were no subsequent discussions of such meetings again.[94]

In the case of the 2017 attempt, Wright notes that an offer to meet came just as Trump gave a speech calling Iran a "rogue state" whose "chief exports are violence, bloodshed, and chaos."[95] Rouhani unsurprisingly did not agree to meet. As Wright explains, the Iranians were concerned that any meeting with Trump would just be a photo opportunity, and they did not want the North Korea model as exemplified by the Singapore summit— theatrical optics but little substance, resulting in a two-page document that led nowhere.[96] In the end, no meeting ever took place between Trump and Iranian leaders; in fact, Trump sanctioned Zarif directly by late July 2019. Rand Paul responded to this news in a tweet: "If you sanction diplomats you'll have less diplomacy."[97]

Israel and Trump: Pushing on an Open Door

Given Trump's pro-Israel positions and advisors, the conventional view is that Israel was a driving factor in the administration's decision to withdraw from the nuclear deal and establish maximum pressure policies. Kushner himself argues that Netanyahu's press conference on April 18, 2018, on Israel's warehouse raid of the Iranian nuclear archives, where in Kushner's view Netanyahu provided "concrete evidence" that Iran had violated the deal, gave Trump the basis to make the withdrawal announcement on May 8, 2018. In fact, the nuclear archives pointed to past Iranian nuclear transgressions and did not produce evidence of Iranian violations of the JCPOA.[98]

But the reality was that the Israeli officials who favored the United States leaving the deal—and not all did—were pushing on an open door. Netanyahu may have helped make Trump's case that the Iranians could not be trusted. But it was not difficult to convince an administration dominated by policymakers already inclined to share Netanyahu's views on Iran. As Elliott Abrams put it to me, "every Republican already opposed the JCPOA because it was a bad deal . . . we didn't need the Israelis to make that case."[99] In fact, some Israeli security and defense experts were opposed to a U.S. withdrawal.[100] But such views did not end up swaying the administration.

Netanyahu and others in the antideal camp of course welcomed Trump's decision, but former senior Israeli officials believe that Trump would have left the deal even without Israel's encouragement.[101] In one Israeli official's view, Israel benefited from the Trump years but did not shape his agenda—Trump and Kushner wanted to do "good things" for Israel without any prodding.[102] On the JCPOA, Trump had campaigned on leaving the agreement, and the issue had become a key aspect of the domestic political debate, tied as much to critique of President Obama as to Israeli preferences.

Another former Israeli official believes that "Israel is credited more than deserved" on Iran policy, particularly given that Trump's positions on Iran were already well established.[103] He does acknowledge, however, that Israel often served as the "brain" for pressure policies, helping Trump's team with ideas for additional sanctions since "Trump wanted everything," even asking the Israelis why they weren't bombing Lebanon to pressure Iran.[104] The dynamic in which the U.S. administration was at times pushing for more measures against Iran than Israel itself created a "very weird" situation during the Trump years, according to a former Israeli official.[105] The chaotic nature of the Trump presidency, particularly the lack of a working bureaucracy, was welcomed by Israeli officials (and no doubt other foreign powers), because it "makes it easier" to share ideas that can be acted on quickly.[106]

But there were also instances in which the Israelis had no input into Trump administration initiatives, such as when Treasury Secretary

Mnuchin tried to coordinate a call between Trump and Rouhani, outreach that Israelis at the highest levels tried to prevent.[107] In this former Israeli official's assessment, if Trump had been able to strike a deal with Iran, Israel would not have been able to stop it.[108] That a deal never evolved had more to do with internal dynamics in Washington than it did with Israel.

Tapping into the Iranian Diaspora

While Israel and the pro-Israel lobby in Washington garner significant attention in discussions on U.S. policies in the Middle East, the role of the Iranian diaspora in the United States attracts far less notice despite its considerable size and prominence. Although the official count of Iranian Americans according to U.S. census data total just under half a million, some estimates suggest the community is between one and a half to two million people.[109] Surveys by nonpartisan Iranian American groups like the Public Affairs Alliance of Iranian Americans (PAAIA) suggest that this population maintains high levels of connection and communication with friends and family in Iran, with their highest priority being the promotion of democracy and human rights in the country.[110]

But the community is not monolithic, with diverse constituencies that are not always appreciated by U.S. politicians or the general public. While previous high-level U.S. officials, such as Secretary of State Albright, viewed the Iranian American community as somewhat of a constraint on engagement with Iranian leaders, a significant constituency of Iranian Americans has been more open to diplomacy. This was particularly the case at the height of U.S.–Iran engagement during the JCPOA negotiations. According to a PAAIA survey in 2020, 60 percent of Iranian Americans believed the Trump administration should have maintained the Iran nuclear deal.[111] The survey also indicated a strong preference for Biden over Trump in the 2020 election by a margin of 56 percent to 31 percent, and strong opposition (83 percent) to Trump policies like the travel ban executive order.[112] Such views contrasted with positive views of President Obama's handling of U.S.–Iran relations, with 71 percent approval.[113]

Nonetheless, the Trump administration actively sought to tap into the segment of the Iranian American community that held hawkish stances toward Iran. Senior officials like Pompeo delivered high-profile speeches promoting maximum pressure policies with titles like "Supporting Iranian Voices" to audiences that included a large representation of Iranian

Americans.[114] Surveys have shown that Iranian Americans who identify as Republicans are more likely to prioritize regime change and sanctions policies over diplomacy.[115] Groups within the community that embraced Trump's Iran policies, some of whom align themselves with the former Shah of Iran and his son Reza Pahlavi, view anyone talking to the government of Iran as a traitor.[116] While Pahlavi's rhetoric supports democracy and human rights principles, analysts of the Iranian diaspora observe that many of his supporters "cut a very different figure, brandishing aggressive, chauvinistic, exclusionary and ultra-nationalist politics that could be classified as far-right."[117]

Pro-diplomacy Iranian American groups on the left, such as the National Iranian American Council (NIAC), became a particularly popular target of right-leaning Iranian American groups during the JCPOA negotiations and beyond. While NIAC is a small nonprofit institution based in Washington whose influence likely peaked during the Obama and Rouhani JCPOA years, its former founder and head, Trita Parsi, became a lightning rod for those who opposed diplomacy with Iran. In the years following the nuclear deal, NIAC was often accused of being a lobby for the Iranian government, and its members were labeled as "regime apologists." On Twitter (X), for example, regime critics often referred to analysts whom they believed were too accommodating to the Iranian government as "NIACis." In a tragic twist, Iranian Americans who supported diplomacy and investment in Iran during the Obama years (and who had previous associations with NIAC) were also targeted by the Iranian government; for example, businessman Mohamed Bagher Namazi and his son Siamak Namazi were imprisoned for years in Iran.

Trump administration officials capitalized on divisions within the community, engaging Iranian American groups advocating against the Iranian regime to reinforce policies they were already pursuing, benefiting from the perception that Republicans are "tough" on Iran while Democrats are "weak."[118] Trump administration officials like Brian Hook amplified antiregime voices, actively seeking Iranian Americans who shared the administration's stance on Iran and whom they might invite to events.[119]

The State Department under Trump also funded controversial initiatives like the Iran Disinformation Project, which was in theory designed as a tool for criticizing the Iranian government through online platforms, but in practice was utilized to attack think tank analysts, human rights activists, and journalists—including U.S. citizens—deemed too supportive of diplomacy or insufficiently critical of the Iranian government. The project took to Twitter (X) to target individuals and groups that had supported the JCPOA, using hashtags like #NIACLobbies4Mullahs.[120] Even critics of Iran's harsh human rights practices and former prisoners in Iranian jails, such as *Washington Post* reporter Jason Rezaian, were targeted through this initiative, overreach that finally led the State Department to cut funding for the project by 2019.[121]

Senior U.S. officials have also embraced a controversial Iranian opposition organization based outside the country that actively seeks the overthrow of the Iranian government, the Mujahedin-e Khalq (MEK). The MEK attracts very little support among Iranian Americans and has an extremist track record, including aligning with Saddam Hussein in Iraq and killing U.S. citizens in Iran, that put the group on the U.S. terrorism list in 1997. Iranian American leaders who are stridently opposed to the Islamic Republic liken MEK to a cult and observe that despite the fractious nature of the Iranian American diaspora, the "evilness of the MEK" is one stance that all members of the community can agree on.[122]

Despite its unpopularity among Iranian Americans, MEK was delisted as a Foreign Terrorist Organization (FTO) in 2012 after a well-funded lobbying campaign in Congress and among former Republican and Democratic national security officials, demonstrating MEK's effectiveness in accessing current and former U.S. policymakers across the political spectrum.[123] Indeed, although MEK is popular in conservative American policymaking circles—Vice President Pence and other top officials in the Trump administration, including Pompeo and Bolton, have attended MEK conferences in the past[124]—the group's staunch opposition to the Islamic Republic has also resonated with prominent Democratic leaders. Former Senate Foreign Relations chair Bob Menendez and former chair of the Democratic National Committee Donna Brazile have spoken at MEK conferences, as have former senior Pentagon officials, such as Michele Flournoy.[125] It is well known that former U.S. officials are well paid for such appearances. That such a fringe group operating outside of the United States has managed to attract bipartisan support at the highest levels of the U.S. government—made easier by economic incentives but also because of the deeply rooted hostile framing of Iran—is a stark contrast to the still limited policy influence of the Iranian American community.

Indeed, as Iranian American experts pointed out to me, historically it is difficult to have influence on U.S. policy unless you are "completely adversarial to the regime," particularly when there are no relations between the two countries.[126] It is possible to see pockets of influence where Iranian American groups have been able to influence incremental policy measures, such as trade exemptions on telecommunication companies, that are important for Iranian civil society. But major policy decisions like the Iran nuclear deal would likely have emerged with or without groups like NIAC.[127] With growing repression inside Iran and the demise of the 2015 Iran nuclear deal, the number of Iranian Americans advocating for diplomacy dwindled by the time President Biden came into office.[128]

Divisions among the Iranian diaspora became particularly heated following the Mahsa Amini protests in the fall of 2022, during the Biden administration.[129] Despite the unifying cause of the "Woman, Life, Freedom" movement, the ferocity of attacks among diaspora groups reflects longstanding fissures within the community that have prevented a unified opposition from emerging.[130] While the Trump administration was especially capable of tapping into segments of this community that served its interests, the diaspora has long served more as a playing field for advancing political agendas in Washington than as a significant force in driving American policy on Iran. Many in the Iranian-American community remain dismayed by this fractured state of diaspora groups and their inability to translate their significant prominence and resources within American society into more cohesive and influential political platforms.

An Erratic Record on Military Force

Despite the Trump administration's confrontational postures on Iran, a conventional view emerged in Washington that Trump's overall foreign policy inclination was to avoid military conflict and above all another war in the Middle East. But multiple accounts by former advisors, historians, and journalists suggest that Trump was more open to force in his first administration than commonly understood, and his aversion to entangling the United States in another Middle East war did not prevent decisions that did indeed risk military conflict.

Such accounts paint a chaotic picture of how Trump handled decisions on the use of force, including when it came to military options against Iran. The president held no principled position; instead, decisions on military force were made on a whim, often based on who had last spoken with him or what he had last viewed on cable television news. At times such inputs worked in favor of using force, and at other times against it.

Early in his presidency, for example, Trump decided to launch a military strike in Syria to retaliate against a Syrian government nerve gas attack, despite his desire to withdraw U.S. forces from the country. According to Baker and Glasser, Trump made this "spur-of-the-moment decision" based on what he had seen on television.[131] But on other occasions, Trump decided against military responses. Starting in May 2019 Iran began its "maximum resistance" campaign in response to U.S. pressure policies with a series of attacks on oil tankers and facilities in neighboring Gulf Arab states. Bolton, believing that only regime change would solve the Iranian problem, argued that limited U.S. responses to such attacks in the past had only further emboldened Iran and thus stronger action against Iran was necessary, echoing longstanding views on how to deal with rogue states like Iran.[132]

In NSC discussions about the Iranian attacks, Bolton says that Trump demonstrated a willingness to use force to retaliate, expressing sentiments like "I have an unbelievable capacity for risk. Risk is good."[133] Nonetheless, Trump continued to return to the issue of how the United States was going to get its forces out of Syria and whether Gulf Arab states would pay for U.S. retaliatory strikes. To Bolton's frustration, Trump decided not to respond to the Iranian attacks against Gulf Arab partners of the United States, including a significant attack on Saudi oil facilities at Abqaiq.[134] A similar situation emerged when Bolton and Pompeo wanted to retaliate after a June 2019 Iranian shootdown of a U.S. drone in the Straits of Hormuz. Trump reportedly called off the attack at the last minute because of concerns about "too many body bags."[135] His decision was reflected, as was common in the Trump presidency, through a series of tweets:[136]

> President Obama made a desperate and terrible deal with Iran—Gave them 150 Billion Dollars plus 1.8 Billion Dollars in CASH! Iran was in big trouble and he bailed them out. Gave them a free path to Nuclear Weapons, and SOON. Instead of saying thank you, Iran yelled . . .
>
> . . . Death to America. I terminated the deal, which was not even ratified by Congress, and imposed strong sanctions. They are a much weakened nation today than at the beginning of my Presidency, when they were causing major problems throughout the Middle East. Now they are Bust! . . .

On Monday they shot down an unmanned drone flying in International Waters. We were cocked & loaded to retaliate last night on 3 different sights when I asked, how many will die. 150 people, sir, was the answer from a General. 10 minutes before the strike I stopped it, not . . .

. . . proportionate to shooting down an unmanned drone. I am in no hurry, our Military is rebuilt, new, and ready to go, by far the best in the world. Sanctions are biting & more added last night. Iran can NEVER have Nuclear Weapons, not against the USA, and not against the WORLD

Bolton argues that Trump initially agreed to what he calls the "breakfast package" in response to the drone shootdown—a consensus reached within the administration to strike functioning Iranian military targets inside the country, not just symbolic sites, despite an understanding that there would be a risk of casualties.[137] But according to Bolton, Department of Defense officials got the 150 body bags number into Trump's head, and the president backed down.[138] Baker and Glasser argue that the real motivation for Trump's restraint was political—he heard from advisors that the spiral of attacks coming from Iran was not good for the president heading into the 2020 election since Trump had promised to end "endless wars." Then Fox News host Tucker Carlson reportedly called Trump that week and told him "he could forget about re-election if he got into a war with Iran."[139]

But Trump did not always shy away from military force. Indeed, one of the most dramatic military actions of his presidency was his decision to kill IRGC commander Qassem Soleimani at the Baghdad airport in early January 2020. Tensions with Iran had escalated, including an Iranian attack that killed an American contractor in Iraq and threats by pro-Iranian militia groups in the county directed at the U.S. Embassy. According to Trump's secretary of defense, Mark Esper, Soleimani was planning attacks on the U.S. Embassy and other U.S. sites in and outside of Iraq.[140]

Trump's fourth national security advisor, Robert O'Brien, Vice President Pence, and Pompeo were pushing for a strike against Soleimani, but Joint Chiefs chairman General Mark Milley and Secretary Esper were more cautious, concerned that such a high-value strike could lead to further military escalation if not war with Iran. But in the end, Esper backed the operation, believing it was a necessary attack in which the risks of doing nothing would be higher than the risks of doing something, an assessment shared by CIA director Gina Haspel.[141] Trump agreed. Baker and Glasser argue that, again, political calculations were driving decisions, with Trump willing to risk war because of considerations related to impeachment hearings under way in Washington. According to their reporting, Trump called Tucker Carlson and put him on speakerphone where he claimed sixteen Republican senators demanded he do it (that is, kill Soleimani) "and they're running impeachment."[142]

The incident demonstrates less caution on Trump's part when it comes to the use of military force than is often appreciated. Even after the attack, which killed both Soleimani and a top Iraqi militia commander in a precision missile strike, Trump issued what his former advisors considered irresponsible statements to warn the Iranians against retaliating, even tweeting threats to strike cultural and historical sites in Iran, which Esper had to refute in media interviews as he gave assurances that the United States would follow the laws of war, which would prohibit these types of military actions.[143] According to Esper, Trump often drafted his Twitter (X) messages with whoever happened to be in the room, with no formal governmental coordination process,[144] demonstrating how dangerous Trump's actions could be—even on issues as consequential as the use of military force.

Trump demonstrated an interest in military options throughout his presidency. Bob Woodward and Robert Costa discuss one such instance when in a Situation Room meeting on Afghanistan, Trump diverted the discussion, as he often would, to ask about plans for military attacks on Iran. CENTCOM chief McKenzie diligently listed a range of options—air strikes, sabotage, cyberattacks, land invasion. They write that Trump responded, "Oh, wow," and asked how long it would take to do this.[145] Milley made sure McKenzie spelled out the risks of all the options, but it was clear that Trump's "curiosity" on force options had to "be managed."[146]

Trump considered further military action against Iran in the last months of his presidency. Shortly after the 2020 election and when the IAEA had announced that Iran had accelerated its uranium enrichment activities well beyond the restrictions of the JCPOA, General Milley was called to the White House to present military options on Iran. Trump reportedly asked about attacking ballistic missile sites inside Iran, and Milley responded with a warning that attacking Iran directly would amount to a war with Iran, recommending against a military option.[147] By some accounts, Milley believed Netanyahu was "pushing the president to hit Iran" before leaving office.[148]

Yet even Pompeo did not support military action at that point, arguing that the time for a strike had passed.[149] In the end Trump did not attack Iran, not even after Iran retaliated for Soleimani's killing by launching sixteen ballistic missiles at Al-Asad airbase in Iraq housing U.S. forces, which did not result in casualties but which senior military officials assessed was designed to "kill Americans" (and more than one hundred U.S. troops suffered traumatic brain injuries).[150] As Esper notes, "Nobody wanted another war in the Middle East, especially Trump."[151]

Iran Policy Starts and Ends with Hostility

Trump's antagonism toward Iran was a central driver of his Middle East policies, but this stance resonated because it built upon a longstanding foundation of framing Iran as an irrational, fanatical state that could not be trusted. And in Trump's case, a confrontational posture also served his political interest in disrupting the policies of his predecessor. His administration's decision to leave the nuclear deal met with some resistance domestically, but even many Democratic leaders did not contest his basic assumptions about Iran. Congressional debates about Trump's desire to withdraw from the agreement largely reinforced traditional framings of Iran, with even those opposing withdrawal making their arguments based on U.S. reputation concerns more than the reality of Iranian compliance.[152]

Even former Democratic officials involved in the negotiations leading to the nuclear deal, such as Jake Sullivan, stressed how the deal was not about preventing Iran's "malign" activities in the region, reminding members of Congress that the JCPOA was an arms control agreement, "not a treaty of goodwill."[153] In other words, Trump's specific decision to exit the deal was disruptive and led to long-term strategic consequences, but his overall animus toward Iran continued longstanding patterns in U.S. policy.

Because of Trump's deeply political decision-making calculus, one could argue that his foreign policy direction was unpredictable. Yet despite Trump's "impulsive and chaotic mind," his track record demonstrates longstanding convictions and a determination to pursue the goals he set.[154] This certainly was the case when it came to his Iran policies. Even though

his decisions on whether and when to use military force proved less predictable, he diligently and predictably followed through on his campaign
promise to withdraw from the Iran nuclear deal, a decision stemming from
domestic political concerns more than strategic logic.

The Trump administration considered Iran to be the core regional,
if not global, challenge. The other priorities—fighting extremism and
striking the "ultimate peace deal" between Israelis and Palestinians—
were framed in the context of confronting Iran. Trump's hostile rhetoric
toward Iran was on full display early in his administration, when he shared
the results of a "complete strategic review of our policy toward the rogue
regime in Iran" run by a "fanatical regime," and proceeded to document
the history of Iran's malign activities in the region and around the globe
since 1979.[155] Trump's strategy for Iran centered on increased sanctions in
what would later be characterized as his "maximum pressure" approach,
which endured through the end of his first term. While his administration
was dominated by advisors harboring well-known pro-Israel views, Israeli
preferences when it came to Iran policy were already deeply ingrained in
Trump's views of the region and domestic calculations about the benefits
of withdrawing from the nuclear agreement.

But his policies did not solve the Iran challenge, either on the nuclear
front or within the region. There would be no better deal—"talk of talks"
remained just that. By the end of the first Trump administration and
through the transition period after his election defeat, Iran continued to
advance its nuclear program, expanding enrichment activities to levels
well beyond the constraints of the JCPOA. Iran's regional activities only
became more belligerent as the so-called shadow war between Iran and
Israel escalated. The state of hostility not only continued but intensified by
the end of Trump's first term in office.

SIX

Death by Slow-Walking

As a candidate for president in 2020, Joe Biden did not hide his disdain for what he and most other Democrats saw as Trump's disruptive policies wreaking havoc around the globe and rupturing ties with America's closest allies. This included what he viewed as Trump's irresponsible withdrawal from the Iran nuclear deal. Biden published op-eds and gave speeches articulating a strategic critique of the Trump withdrawal and a desire to correct course, arguing for a revival of the deal as a foundation to build a "longer and stronger" framework that would also address nonnuclear issues of regional concern. Biden had made it clear that he believed Trump's withdrawal made Iran more dangerous and isolated the United States globally.[1]

Given the forcefulness of his critique, expectations were high that Biden, as president, would take early executive action to set the stage for a reversal of Trump's Iran decision, much as he did when he brought the United States back into the Paris climate agreement within his first month in office. But such expectations were never met. It turns out that Biden, as several former U.S. officials explained to me, was not fully committed to his own policy.

To be sure, returning to the nuclear deal was complicated. Iran had already made nuclear advances beyond the limits of the deal before Biden assumed the presidency in January 2021. By the end of the first Trump administration, Iran had resumed enriching uranium to 20 percent levels— well beyond the limit of 3.67 percent required by the agreement. The complex web of U.S. sanctions would also be difficult to untangle after additional measures imposed by the Trump administration. So-called "poison pill" sanctions targeting the IRGC and the Supreme Leader's office would be especially challenging for a future U.S. administration to lift.[2]

But in the early months of the Biden presidency, such obstacles appeared surmountable, assuming sufficient political will. It quickly became apparent, however, that the new Biden team would not be in a rush to make the effort. A chorus of top political appointees used similar cautionary language at confirmation hearings, parroting shared talking points to signal that a return to the nuclear deal would be a "long way" away. At regional track two meetings at the time, American experts with close connections to the incoming administration echoed the caution, with the ever popular leverage concept dominating the discourse—that is, that Biden should utilize the perceived leverage built up through Trump-era sanctions to press for a better deal rather than rush into a new agreement. Such a gambit was believed to be good strategy, not to mention good politics.

Never mind that the leverage might not have been as great as American analysts and policymakers assumed: the Iranians were not necessarily as desperate to return to the deal as they might have thought. After all, the U.S. withdrawal had politically exposed pro-deal diplomats and negotiators in Tehran, and sparked debate about whether Iran could trust any future U.S. commitments on sanctions relief. Iran's leaders also harbored misguided beliefs about their own leverage, believing that Iran's expanded nuclear activities would make the new administration eager for a deal to reverse course. Both sides miscalculated.

That the Iranians would play hardball could not have surprised observers in Washington; it fit perfectly into the framing of Iran as an untrustworthy state. But what surprised many, including some officials entering the new administration, was that Biden himself would be so hesitant. As one senior Biden administration official explained, it was clear to Biden that Congress did not like the agreement and that friends in the region "didn't want us to rush into it," so they took a view of "no rush . . . let them come to us." In this official's view, by the time "we got serious, they [Iran] weren't ready to do it."[3]

Such early calculations were particularly astounding given the widespread belief in Washington, Europe, and beyond that Biden's foreign policies would mark a sharp departure from the Trump years. Indeed, in contrast to Trump's conflation of personal with national interests,[4] Biden came into office with a professional foreign policy team, many of whom were alumni of the Obama years determined to undo what they saw as the damage done during the Trump administration. Reviving the Iran nuclear deal would have seemed to be high on their list. Biden himself had long been a proponent of arms control and nonproliferation initiatives, and viewed the JCPOA as an important step in containing the risk of nuclear proliferation. The administration's appointment of a pro-engagement Middle East expert and a member of the original JCPOA negotiation team, Robert Malley, as the special envoy on Iran heightened the sense that U.S. Iran policies were about to shift gears.

But the shifts, and a return to the nuclear deal, never materialized. Negotiations to restore the deal, which began in April 2021, came to a halt with the Iranian presidential election that June, which brought hardliner Ebrahim Raisi to power. It seemed unlikely that the Raisi administration would prioritize restoring the JCPOA as much as the previous Iranian team had. As expected, the Raisi team also took its time to return to negotiations. And when they did, the Iranians presented far less accommodating positions than had previously been anticipated, leading to tense rounds of talks and ultimately the failure to revive the agreement, despite negotiators coming close in the spring and summer of 2022. As a former U.S. official reflected, "we made big miscalculations," judging that the Iranians would accept a deal in August 2022.[5] The former official acknowledged that the American team were overconfident, believing they "could be masters of the timing," which clearly "didn't work out."[6]

The outbreak of the "Woman, Life, Freedom" protests in Iran in September 2022, combined with Iran's growing military alignment with Russia in support of its war against Ukraine, only served to put the nuclear file further on the back burner as U.S.–Iran tensions intensified. Military clashes increased as well. Iranian-backed militia groups launched sustained attacks on U.S. forces in Iraq and Syria until an informal U.S.–Iran de-escalation agreement in mid-2023 put an end to them. But the October 7 Hamas assault on Israel disrupted the lull, with attacks on U.S. forces not only resuming but intensifying before another pause in early February 2024, only to reignite by that summer.

The Biden administration also had to contend with unprecedented direct Israeli-Iranian conflict starting in the spring of 2024. In efforts to contain the escalation, the administration doubled down on longstanding policies of sanctions on Iran and increased military support to Israel to deter Iranian attacks. The election of a reformist Iranian president, Masoud Pezeshkian, following the unexpected death of Raisi in a May 2024 helicopter crash did little to ease rising tensions, despite Pezeshkian's stated interest in repairing ties with the West and eagerness to bring sanctions relief to Iran. Instead, Pezeshkian's rise coincided with a dramatic spike in the Israeli-Iranian conflict, including the killing of Hamas's and Hezbollah's top leadership, and a fundamentally altered regional landscape that significantly weakened Iran and its regional allies.

These events triggered yet another direct Israeli-Iranian clash in October, followed by the swift fall of Iran's ally, Bashar al-Assad, to a surprisingly effective Syrian rebel campaign in early December 2024. The Biden administration embraced Israel's military successes against Iran, and the election of Donald Trump in the U.S. 2024 presidential race signaled continued, if not strengthened, backing by Washington for offensive actions against Tehran. While Trump, as he did in his first term, sent signals during the campaign and after that he wanted a deal with Iran, Iran's growing vulnerabilities provided further fuel among Trump's more hawkish advisors who favored increased economic pressure and even military options.[7]

Iran's weakened state by the end of the Biden administration, combined with its nuclear advances, led to increased debate about the merits of a military strike and a growing chorus of voices in Washington viewing the altered strategic situation as an opportunity to attack Iran. Senior officials like National Security Advisor Jake Sullivan reportedly viewed Iran's options for retaliation and escalation as more limited, boosting the prospects for a successful strike.[8] Biden's former deputy special envoy for Iran, Richard Nephew, made the case for using military force against Iran if renewed attempts at diplomacy failed as Trump took office, arguing that an effective strike would require targeting not only Iran's nuclear facilities but also its regime assets, security forces, and even Iranian decision-makers.[9]

As a result, beyond limited de-escalation efforts to prevent a region-wide war, the Biden administration did little to reverse—and may have even accelerated—the enduring hostility between the United States and Iran. There is no doubt that Iran's own actions and the heightened regional tensions resulting from the Gaza war contributed to this outcome, but the domestic context within Washington played a major role in shaping the administration's approach, ultimately limiting the potential for setting the relationship on a different track.

A Desire to Do Less in the Middle East

For all the differences between them, Biden shared Trump's strong inclination to shift U.S. attention and resources toward confronting China. As a former senior U.S. official put it in the early months of the Biden presidency, "Now we have the third administration in a row trying to rebalance the United States from the Middle East to Asia and now a second administration wanting to center policy on great power competition."[10] This shifting global focus suggested a need to moderate perceptions of Iran as a strategic threat, though U.S. officials acknowledged that domestic politics would make changing postures on Iran difficult.[11]

Nonetheless, senior Biden advisors made no secret of their desire to reduce U.S. commitments in the Middle East. During the 2020 presidential campaign, Biden's future secretary of state, Antony Blinken, suggested, "Just as a matter of time allocation and budget priorities, I think we would be doing less not more in the Middle East."[12] Once in office, President Biden followed through on his determination to withdraw U.S. forces from Middle East–adjacent Afghanistan, even with the risks of bringing the Taliban back to power and abandoning close allies within the country. As a senior U.S. official explained, in the Obama years the Middle East still "loomed large" and prevented the desired pivot to Asia, but the Biden administration "was actually doing it."[13]

Administration officials sought to strengthen ties with the Saudis, despite Biden's campaign statements calling the country a pariah after the brutal killing of *Washington Post* columnist Jamal Khashoggi. They justified such outreach in part as empowering regional partners to take on more responsibility for regional security so the United States could turn its attention to Asia. The priority for the administration was to keep the region as quiet as possible so the United States could focus elsewhere. Just a week before the October 7, 2023 Hamas attack on Israel, Jake Sullivan argued that the shift was working, asserting, in one of the administration's worst-timed comments, that the "Middle East region is quieter today than it has been in two decades."[14] This strategy clearly did not work out as planned.

American strategic interests were arguably not served by further escalation and entanglements in the Middle East, given other pressing global priorities. And that was even before Russia's war against Ukraine, which only further incentivized the Biden administration to try to keep a lid on tensions with Iran, at least before Iran began supplying Russia with drones. But that logic only drove policy to a point, and ultimately it did not force a major reassessment.

Russia's growing alignment with Iran following the start of the Ukraine war reinforced the state of animosity between the United States and Iran. The war in Gaza—with Iran's backing of Hamas and nonstate militia groups attacking the United States and Israel—further diminished whatever political tolerance was left to engage Iran beyond narrow and largely indirect de-escalation efforts, particularly given the consolidation of hardliners within Iran's leadership and increased domestic repression.

The election of Pezeshkian during the summer of 2024 did not change U.S. views of Iran or the possibility for change. Iran's diminished regional position by the end of 2024 fueled arguments for more pressure to capitalize on Iranian vulnerability, arguments that found receptive audiences in Washington. Once again, an altered strategic landscape that arguably could have provided openings for reducing U.S.–Iran tensions were not the predominant factor shaping the relationship during Biden's presidency, particularly in the formative first year of his administration.

A Long Way Away: A Cautious Team on Iran

During the 2020 presidential campaign Biden signaled that his administration would make a clear break from Trump's policies. In an article for *Foreign Affairs* in the spring of 2020, Biden argued that he would use diplomacy as the "first instrument of American power" to bring the United States back to the "head of the table" to work with allies on common challenges, touting the JCPOA.[15] He noted that Trump "rashly cast the deal aside," which only led Iran to become more provocative, and warned that Trump's killing of IRGC leader Soleimani "raised the prospect of an ever-escalating cycle of violence in the region."[16] Biden also made it clear that if Iran returned to compliance with the nuclear deal, he would have the United States rejoin the agreement, and then work with allies to "strengthen and extend it, while more effectively pushing back against Iran's other destabilizing activities."[17] In a *CNN* op-ed less than two months before the election, Biden again argued that the United States had to urgently "change course" from the "dangerous failure" of Trump's Iran policy."[18]

But despite Biden's pro-diplomacy orientation, his rhetoric departed from Obama's early talk of reconciliation if Iran were to change its ways.

For Biden, it was less about trying to formulate a new way to deal with Iran and more about getting the deal back for the practical purposes of non-proliferation and alliance management. This stance fit with the traditional framing of Iran in Washington, even among pro-diplomacy proponents, which remained skeptical that wider openings with Iran were possible. Even when it came to the nuclear deal, Biden was less invested than many anticipated. As Obama's deputy national security advisor, Ben Rhodes, observed, Biden ultimately saw the JCPOA as an "Obama thing."[19]

Indeed, Rhodes's conversations with Biden's transition team indicated that going back to the JCPOA would not be a high priority, and they did not want "to do this out of the gate."[20] As another senior official characterized the early months of the Biden administration, "at first we were dragging our feet . . . frankly, the President wasn't into his own policy."[21] According to Rhodes and a number of other political observers, the primary reason for Biden's caution was domestic politics, specifically concerns about securing support from Iran hawks like Democratic senator Robert Menendez for Senate confirmation of Biden's political appointees. With an evenly divided Senate at the time, he needed full Democratic support to move his wider legislative agenda forward. According to Rhodes, the Biden team were hearing from the Hill that "doing the Iran deal" would put other policy priorities at risk.[22]

Biden's choice of top advisors reflected such caution. To be sure, many Biden appointees were veterans of the Obama administration, including officials who played significant roles in diplomacy with Iran. But former secretary of state John Kerry, one of the most active backers of diplomacy, joined the Biden administration as the climate envoy, limiting his influence over foreign policy issues like Iran. Biden's key foreign policy appointees—Antony Blinken as secretary of state and Jake Sullivan as his national security advisor—were considered more cautious and relatively hawkish when it came to Iran policy. As Rhodes observed, Blinken and Sullivan would not be the "first two draft picks" for getting the United States back into the nuclear deal.[23]

However, with Blinken bringing in his former colleague and childhood friend Robert Malley as the administration's special envoy on Iran, the outlook for renewed diplomacy improved. Malley had been a key member of Obama's team in JCPOA negotiations and had a reputation as a strong advocate for diplomacy as the former head of International Crisis Group, an international nongovernmental organization (NGO) promoting conflict prevention and resolution. Malley had long advocated engagement with adversaries without deploying the hostile rhetoric typical in Washington. His appointment bolstered the impression that the Biden team was serious about reversing Trump's policies and putting the Iran deal back on track.

Nonetheless, it became clear to administration allies that Malley would not have the upper hand. Administration officials—even Blinken—were slow to defend Malley when he faced attacks from Republicans in Congress and from pro-Israel groups who believed he would be too conciliatory toward Iran; according to Ben Rhodes, they "hung Rob out to dry for a bit" because "they didn't want a fight."[24] In a small but revealing example of the Biden team's risk-avoidance, Rhodes noted that the administration held off announcing Malley's appointment until after Blinken was confirmed; the Senate confirmed Blinken as secretary of state on January 26, 2021, and Malley's appointment was announced on January 28.[25] Such early decisions showed the administration was "already on the defense" when it came to Iran policy.[26]

Indeed, the "mood music" from the transition period through the early months of the administration indicated that Iran would not be a priority.[27] It was clear to former U.S. officials there would be slow-walking because the president did not want to look like he was "rushing" into a deal—both to avoid the appearance that the United States was desperate in negotiations and because such a stance "made political sense domestically."[28] It quickly became clear that Biden was more tepid on Iran diplomacy than President Obama had been. Senior officials were not putting the same "muscle" behind the efforts.[29]

Incoming officials conveyed more caution on Iran, despite previous involvement and support for the JCPOA. In interviews before Biden's inauguration, Jake Sullivan said the administration wanted to put Iran "back into the box" by forcing Iran to comply with the JCPOA's original terms.[30] In writings and interviews before the 2020 election, Sullivan expressed skepticism about a rapid return to the deal. While he argued that maximum pressure policies or regime change goals would not work, he believed the United States could put "more chips on the table" to get Iranians back to the negotiating table and argued that a U.S. return to the JCPOA would depend on "where we are" in terms of Iranian compliance.[31]

Sullivan's viewpoint only strengthened after Biden's election and was on public display during confirmation hearings for incoming senior officials. For example, director of national intelligence–designate Avril Haines told the Senate Intelligence Committee during her confirmation hearing in January 2021 that while the president-elect indicated that if Iran returned to compliance with the agreement, the United States would return as well, she believed that, "frankly, we're a long ways from that."[32] She added that the Biden administration would be looking into the issue of Iran's ballistic missiles and "other obviously destabilizing activities that Iran engages in."[33]

In his confirmation hearing Blinken used a similar formulation, stating that the United States would rejoin the deal if Iran returned to compliance, but that "we are a long way from there," adding that the United States would need to consult with allies and partners on "the take-off, not the landing."[34] Given that the Israelis were not hiding their opposition to a U.S. return to the deal, emphasizing the need to consult regional partners was well understood to mean that the administration would not likely be hurrying into a new agreement.

The mantra that the deal was a "long way away" became the defining message. According to former U.S. officials, the new administration did not want Iran to be the focus of attention in Biden's early months in office but rather wanted to keep attention on domestic challenges.[35] A senior official acknowledged that in the early months of the Biden administration, Iran "hasn't consumed a ton of energy."[36] These officials understood that the nuclear deal was not just a flashpoint with Republicans, given the bipartisan opposition to the original agreement by leading congressional Democrats. With expected congressional opposition to reviving the nuclear deal and messages from "friends in the region" who did not want the administration to "rush into it," senior officials took the "view of no rush" and "let them [Iranians] come to us."[37] The administration also did not follow through on campaign promises such as increasing humanitarian relief to Iranians because of domestic priorities and a reluctance to spend political capital on Iran early in the administration.[38]

Consequently, despite a circle of national security advisors that resembled an Obama 2.0 team, the "people in the administration who didn't want to pay the political price" with a swift return to the deal "got the upper hand."[39] Administration officials who favored a quick return to the JCPOA did not believe there would even be a debate on this issue and were surprised when they realized the "president wasn't in that place."[40] Congress appeared to be a major factor in Biden's calculations, with White

House advisors like Sullivan and Brett McGurk (Biden's key advisor on the Middle East) "going along to where Biden was," suggesting there were few voices in the administration fighting for a quick return.[41]

A proclivity toward caution also made administration officials reluctant to engage Iranian American groups as the Trump administration had done (albeit for different purposes). Some Iranian American leaders observed that Democrats are generally more cautious about engaging their community because they view Iran as a "hot potato" in American politics, helping explain the wariness of the Biden team in associating with Iranian American groups during the campaign and early in the administration.[42] While Republicans have found it useful to engage the community to reinforce the "Iran is evil" narrative, Democratic leaders tend to refrain from reaching out to Iranian Americans because they worry about political attacks by Republicans who would claim they are too "pro-regime."[43]

The Demise of the Nuclear Deal

As noted, Biden was clear about his desire to return to the Iran deal during the campaign. While influential columnists like Thomas Friedman were arguing that the administration should not resume the nuclear deal where it left off and instead should use the Trump-era "leverage" from oil sanctions to press Iran in other areas, such as missile exports across the region, Biden nonetheless told Friedman that he continued to believe that getting Iran's nuclear program "back under control and fully inspected" remained the overriding concern.[44] Biden worried about the regional proliferation risks in countries like Saudi Arabia, Turkey, and Egypt if Iran acquired nuclear weapons, and as Biden put it, "the last goddamn thing we need in that part of the world is a buildup of nuclear capability."[45] A return to the nuclear deal also tracked with Biden's general foreign policy preference for working multilaterally in support of international treaties and institutions.[46]

Nonproliferation analysts encouraged the new administration to make a "clean" return to the deal—where both the United States and Iran would take coordinated steps to return to the original terms of the agreement as opposed to attempts to negotiate a new deal. All sides arguably had incentives to return to the deal. Iran's president at the time, Hassan Rouhani, was associated with the original agreement and needed to respond to the dire economic situation in the country as a result of the increased economic pressures during the Trump years, making sanctions relief a high priority. Biden viewed the JCPOA as a critical multilateral nonproliferation agreement and as the best way to contain Iran's nuclear program while restoring America's credibility with key alliance partners in Europe and Asia that had strongly opposed Trump's withdrawal.

Technical hurdles, it was well understood, could impede a swift return, particularly when it came to the complex world of sanctions-lifting and determining which sanctions were "nuclear-related" and which would remain in place because they applied to other technologies, terrorism, or human rights.[47] Those hurdles could have likely been overcome through creative diplomacy. The problem was that, despite the strong strategic logic favoring a revived deal, concerns about domestic political costs were a complicating factor.

Even Democrats were arguing that technical and political aspects of the JCPOA at that time risked making the political costs of returning to the deal too high.[48] Concerns included the impending expiration of some restrictions on Iran outlined in sunset clauses in the original agreement—restrictions covering Iran's nuclear program, but also its missile production, arms exports, and conventional weapons.[49] American policymakers across the political spectrum were also wary of alienating regional allies, in addition to overall uneasiness about engagement with Iran. The Trump administration's attempt to keep the pressure on Iran through the transition period with a "flood" of new sanctions that went beyond the nuclear-related targets only increased the political costs of unraveling sanctions on Iran to bring them back into compliance with the agreement. Lifting sanctions on Iran was never a popular position in the American political system, certainly not when linked to sanctions on those associated with terrorism.

Israeli opposition to a U.S. return created additional difficulties. The assassination of top Iranian scientist Mohsen Fakhrizadeh in November 2020, shortly after Biden was elected, assumed to be the work of Israeli intelligence, was a clear signal to the incoming administration that Israel would take its own actions against Iran's nuclear progress. Netanyahu was not subtle in his speeches at conservative U.S. think tanks in expressing his continued opposition to the JCPOA and the possibility that the Biden administration might rejoin it.[50]

Iran also took actions during the presidential transition period that hindered diplomatic efforts. Most significantly, Iran accelerated uranium enrichment activities with the installation of advanced centrifuges at underground facilities, continuing to breach the terms of the agreement.[51] By the time Biden assumed the presidency, Iran was enriching uranium at twelve times the levels permitted in the deal.[52] Rather than making goodwill gestures to the incoming Biden administration to help restore trust after the turbulent Trump years,[53] Iranian leaders turned up the pressure on the Biden team, perhaps believing that further nuclear advancements would increase Tehran's leverage in future negotiations to restore the agreement. Some argued that since the U.S. withdrawal from the JCPOA, Tehran's calculations had changed, and its leadership was not as desperate for sanctions relief as Washington assumed, particularly as the country increasingly turned its strategic orientation toward China and Russia.[54]

But American policymakers and influential analysts in Washington saw things differently, believing Iran was on the back foot with the United States holding all the leverage. Many believed the United States maintained the upper hand in the aftermath of the devastating economic sanctions imposed on Iran's economy during the Trump years, assessing that Iran was in a particularly weak position as a result of the COVID-19 pandemic. Such reasoning led to arguments against the new administration rushing into a revived deal.

As one analyst explained in an assessment that reflected the thinking of many in Washington at the time: "Biden and his team will have time—and economic leverage—on their side. The incoming administration should take advantage of its strong position to diligently pursue its goal of strengthening and lengthening nuclear restrictions and should resist the pressure to act hastily."[55] According to this assessment, there was no urgency to strike a deal while the relatively pragmatic Iranian president was still in power and before Iran's June 2021 presidential elections because "the impending election will not fundamentally alter Tehran's strategic outlook or its openness to negotiations."[56] Iran experts who would later join Malley's team in the Biden administration made similar arguments before entering government.[57] Such arguments tracked with longstanding assumptions in Washington that it could expect little change from Tehran, regardless of leadership shifts, because of Iran's inherently hostile stance toward the United States.

These positions influenced the early policies of the administration, but events on the ground did not play out as such assessments anticipated. The election of Ebrahim Raisi in June 2021 did indeed halt nuclear diplomacy, with the new leadership indicating they were also in no rush to reach a deal. Malley acknowledged that the U.S. assessment of the Iranians' eagerness for a deal was a miscalculation.[58] But he noted that the Iranians were also miscalculating, believing the Biden administration wanted a deal more than was actually the case. As he put it, "each side overestimated how much the other side wanted a deal and underestimated the costs of not returning to it."[59]

Even before Raisi won, negotiators faced complications in the multiple rounds of negotiations that began in Vienna in April 2021, particularly on the thorny question of how to unravel the sanctions regime the Trump administration had built and provide assurances to the Iranians that the United States would not once again reverse course. But negotiations became more difficult after Raisi's election. European officials lamented the impact of American stalling, arguing that it would have been much easier before the Iranian elections.[60] These officials realized they had a "misguided hope" that Biden would quickly engage with nuclear diplomacy to restore the deal, and believed that Biden's caution cost several critical months to build expectations that might have led to a more successful outcome.[61] In their view, there was a "silence" about talking about Iran in the first months of the administration that was "off-putting" and a lost opportunity for preparing a strategy.[62]

A senior administration official acknowledged that the "people who didn't want to rush into a deal underestimated the ability of the Iranians to muddle through."[63] After considerable delay, Raisi sent a negotiating team back to Vienna, but Iranian positions were noticeably tougher. Iranian analysts argued that Raisi was anxious to demonstrate domestically that he could achieve a better agreement than the Rouhani and Zarif camp, reflecting typical political jockeying among factions within the Iranian system.[64]

The Vienna talks nonetheless continued, with the negotiating parties, under the coordination of the European Union, moving closer to a final text for reviving the deal by March 2022, only to reach a stalemate that continued until August 2022, when it once again appeared a deal was close. But the negotiators could not cross the finish line. A number of challenges stymied the talks, including Iranian demands for guarantees on sanctions relief and the end to IAEA investigations of past nuclear activity, as well as American and European demands that Iran end arms exports to Russia. European diplomats also believed that the U.S. "obsession" with the IRGC, particularly in the sensitive March–May 2022 period of the negotiations, slowed progress on the nuclear file.[65]

But Malley was skeptical that Raisi really wanted a deal, given Iran's response to the EU draft text in August 2022.[66] By the fall of 2022 Malley placed full blame for the demise of the nuclear negotiations on Iran.[67] His rhetoric also became more pointed toward nonnuclear issues, criticizing Iran's repression of the women-led protests and its military support for Ukraine. Malley was forced to take a leave from the State Department under murky circumstances in the spring of 2023, reportedly related to an investigation concerning his handling of classified documents.[68] Malley denied any wrongdoing, but the targeting of a pro-diplomacy senior U.S. official served as a cautionary tale about the career costs for those within the American system associated with Iran policy.

Midterm elections in the United States in the fall of 2022 added a further political dimension, making U.S. officials more sensitive about appearing to give concessions to Iran. Congressional letters in February and March 2022—signed by large numbers of Republicans in both the House and Senate—opposed a revived agreement without wide congressional approval, criticizing the administration's diplomacy with Iran.[69] The Iranian insistence that negotiations remain indirect since the United States was no longer a JCPOA member also made progress difficult, with EU negotiators forced to pass messages between the Iranians and Americans located in different Vienna hotels.

An International Crisis Group report summarized the situation as of September 2022: "With little sign of Iranian flexibility and growing reluctance among Democrats to engage in a polarizing Iran debate in Congress ahead of midterm elections, an imminent breakthrough appears unlikely."[70] That prediction proved accurate, with the JCPOA dead in all but name by the end of the Biden administration as Iran's nuclear advances consolidated. The IAEA condemned Iran's increase of enriched uranium to 60 percent levels and U.S. government and expert analysis assessed that Iran possessed sufficient uranium, if further enriched, to develop nuclear weapons should its government decide to do so, essentially moving Iran toward nuclear threshold status by the end of 2024.[71]

Israel's Influence, with Limits

As was the case with previous administrations, Israeli influence on Iran policy is most pronounced when its leaders are engaging U.S. officials already inclined to share similar assessments. In the Biden administration, early Israeli objections to a U.S. return to the JCPOA appeared to be less of a factor than domestic considerations in shaping the incoming administration's cautious stances. That said, there can be little doubt that pro-Israel sentiments in Congress affect the domestic political context for policymaking in the executive branch on Iran policy, particularly when Israel's security needs are already a predominant consideration for many U.S. officials.

When the new "change coalition" emerged in Israel's June 2021 elections under the leadership of Naftali Bennett and Yair Lapid, Israeli engagement with American policymakers appeared to support positions already held by key Biden advisors, particularly in the White House. Israeli officials maintained a strong relationship with National Security Advisor Jake Sullivan, who held nearly monthly meetings with Israeli officials in Washington.[72] According to former Israeli officials, Biden and his advisors appreciated Prime Minister Bennett's commitment to avoid arguing openly with the United States, in contrast to Netanyahu's stridently hostile public opposition to the Iran nuclear deal.

This approach appears to have paid off in Israel's view, with Biden telling Bennett in September 2021 that if Iran should ever have nuclear weapons, Israel would have a right to self-defense and the United States would not tie Israel's hands—the type of commitment Israeli officials say they never heard from President Obama.[73] In other words, it did not take a lot of Israeli coaxing when it came to Biden's positions. Israelis already saw him and his senior White House advisors as sympathetic to Israeli positions. The Israelis told Sullivan that they would not ultimately block a deal, but hoped the administration had a plan for how to "squeeze" Iran if a deal emerged.[74]

But the Israelis viewed Biden's State Department advisors more critically, particularly Iran envoy Malley. Some former Israeli officials believe that the negotiations to restore the JCPOA came extremely close to success in March and April 2022 and again in August 2022, an assessment that is also widely shared among former European negotiators. In the Israeli view, Malley's stance during the negotiations went further than the parameters conveyed to Israel by White House advisors, though there is little evidence that Malley's positions departed from White House positions.[75]

In the end, the Israelis believed they had effective influence because the Biden team went back to terms that were difficult for the Iranians to accept. However, it seems unlikely that the Israeli positions were the deciding factor, given that U.S. policymakers were themselves wary of looking vulnerable on Capitol Hill when it came to concessions on Iran, or of expending political capital on a deal with an increasingly hardline Iranian leadership. A former U.S. official argues that the United States did not take positions because they were what the Israelis wanted, but because they were based on the administration's own redlines, including refusing to close the IAEA file on past nuclear activities.[76] In this official's view, Israeli leaders had an interest in portraying their role as nudging the Americans toward tougher positions because of their own domestic politics; taking credit for stronger U.S. stances on Iran was a way to show that their government had influence in Washington.[77]

By the final round of negotiations in the late summer of 2022, it was in any case unclear whether the Iranians were still genuinely interested in reaching a deal as they toughened positions. As one former Israeli national security official put it, "Iran made it easy for Israel" by saying no in Vienna; if they had said yes, "Israel couldn't do anything" about it.[78]

And when it comes to Israeli preferences outside diplomacy, particularly on questions concerning the use of military force, former Israeli officials are consistently disappointed at what they perceive to be U.S. caution in employing force because of concerns about sparking a wider regional war. A dominant view among Israeli analysts and former officials is that force can quickly establish deterrence, while hesitancy will encourage Iran to continue its bad behavior.[79]

But such arguments have not always worked well in Washington, where successive administrations have been wary of getting the United States entangled in another Middle East war. For decades both Democratic and Republican administrations pushed back against Israeli leaders who advocated for direct U.S. military attacks against Iran and its nuclear program, even as U.S. officials, including President Biden, continued to defend Israel against Iranian attacks and to support Israeli attacks against Iran and Iranian-aligned groups across the region.

Protests, Ukraine, and Gaza: A Perfect Storm

The failure to revive the nuclear deal already signaled the continuing pattern of hostility between the United States and Iran; there would be no reverse-engineering of the JCPOA or, for that matter, of wider American-Iranian relations.[80] Ultimately, it was a constellation of developments within Iran, the region, and the global arena that reinforced and validated the hostile framing and dampened the appetite for more fundamental shifts in U.S. Iran policies. Particularly, starting in the fall of 2022, domestic developments in Iran, combined with wars in Ukraine and Gaza, all worked together to increase the toxicity of serious engagement with Iran, both in Washington but also increasingly within Europe.

The widespread "Woman, Life, Freedom" protests that erupted in Iran in September 2022 rapidly changed policymaker priorities. Administration officials faced increased scrutiny about dealing with Iran during a wave of domestic unrest and government repression. Iran's expanding relationship with Russia only further tarnished Iran's reputation in Washington and European capitals, particularly its decision to sell drones to Russia that were used in attacks on Ukrainian cities. Incentives to keep the pressure on Iran only increased; one senior U.S. official who was previously supportive of the JCPOA defended the administration's efforts to keep the pressure on Iran in a roundtable of foreign policy experts, saying, "We haven't lifted a single sanction Trump imposed—in fact we've added . . . sanctions designations."[81]

In the aftermath of the protests, even staunchly pro-diplomacy advocates like Malley suggested that, while the administration would not give up on diplomacy, the "inert" JCPOA negotiations were no longer their focus: "It's not on our agenda . . . There are protests in Iran. And there is this new decision by Iran to participate in a war in Europe by transferring drones to Russia. So that's what we're focused on because nothing's happening on the nuclear deal. We're not going to spend our time on it."[82] Senior administration officials Jake Sullivan and Antony Blinken began meeting publicly with Iranian civil society leaders to show their support for the protest movement, with Biden, Vice President Kamala Harris, and other senior officials voicing support for the protests and for additional measures to sanction Iran.[83]

American participants in track two meetings after the 2022 protests erupted were in agreement that sanctions relief for Iran was not politically feasible given such developments, not to mention the domestic U.S. political context of midterm elections in November 2022.[84] In this environment, the nuclear track moved into a "no deal" reality, or what Western policy circles referred to as the new "no deal, no crisis" status quo, where the goal became keeping "Iran off President Biden's desk by avoiding either a politically damaging political settlement or an escalation that risks conflict."[85]

Such a balance was difficult to strike, particularly with Iranian-backed attacks against U.S. forces in Iraq increasing in the spring of 2023. With the backdrop of the Ukraine war and Iran's support for Russia, the Biden administration supported Israel's mounting pressure to degrade Iranian capabilities, including assumed Israeli strikes on pro-Iranian groups in Damascus and even within Iran itself in a drone attack on a military site in Isfahan in early 2023. The United States held one of its largest joint exercises with Israel in the winter of 2023, which simulated offensive long-range strikes in what was widely viewed as a message to Iran.

Escalation also increased in the maritime arena. As the Biden administration sought to increase enforcement of sanctions on Iranian oil exports, including the seizing of Iranian oil tankers, Iran itself began seizing oil tankers in late April and early May 2023 in the Strait of Hormuz and the Gulf of Oman.[86] U.S. officials even began talking about placing Marines on commercial ships to deter Iranian attacks; the United States increased its rotation of ships and aircraft in the area in response to the uptick in Iranian assaults, claiming the Iranians had attacked nearly twenty internationally flagged commercial ships beginning in 2021.[87]

Even so, the United States and Iran managed to reach a set of limited, informal understandings brokered through the government of Oman to de-escalate tensions. The understandings reportedly included Iran ending its support for attacks on U.S. forces in Iraq, refraining from uranium enrichment beyond 60 percent levels, a mutual prisoner release, and the unfreezing of some Iranian assets.[88] The informal nature of agreement allowed the administration to bypass Congress, where opposition to engaging with Iran and even limited sanctions lifting remained politically contentious.

The Biden administration had already relaxed some sanctions enforcement even as it maintained Trump's economic pressure policies.[89] Specifically, the administration issued sanctions waivers to allow countries like China to import Iranian oil in efforts to keep global oil prices from rising, a growing concern after the onset of the war in Ukraine largely took Russian oil off the European market. The Biden administration also continued sanctions waivers started during the Trump administration to allow for Iranian energy exports to Iraq in a bid to maintain Iraqi stability even as officials emphasized their continued commitment "to reducing Iran's malign influence in the region."[90]

Such pragmatic easing of pressure on Iran to serve wider regional and global interests was a tactical departure from Trump's drive to eliminate Iran's ability to export oil, and Republicans were quick to criticize Biden for measures that, they argued, only helped fund Iran's support for terrorism. But at the strategic level, Biden's overall approach to Iran did not fundamentally differ: the containment and economic pressure on Iran remained largely in place, as did military deterrence.

Nonetheless, Ayatollah Khamenei reportedly green-lighted direct talks with U.S. officials in September 2023 and indicated that Ali Bagheri Kani, Iran's top nuclear negotiator and political deputy at the Foreign Ministry, was prepared to meet with Biden's Middle East advisor, Brett McGurk, after months of back-channel talks in Oman.[91] (Bagheri later became acting foreign minister after the death of Foreign Minister Hossein Amirabdollahian in the helicopter crash that killed President Raisi.) The understandings were largely transactional and short-term, but did create some months of calm—calm that was suddenly and violently upended with the October 7 Hamas assault on Israel.

Israeli–Iranian Confrontation, U.S. Elections, and a More Vulnerable Iran

The Gaza war quickly triggered conflict across the entire region by groups linked to Iran, including resumed attacks on U.S. forces in Iraq and damaging attacks on maritime shipping in the Red Sea by the Yemen-based Houthis. As the Gaza war continued through the end of 2024 (a ceasefire was only reached a day before Trump's inauguration in January 2025 though the war resumed two months later), U.S. tensions with Iran significantly increased with the intensification of Israeli-Iranian conflict. Israel and Iran moved beyond their "shadow war" of largely indirect and unattributed attacks into unprecedented direct military confrontation.

The confrontations began after an April 1, 2024, Israeli strike on an Iranian diplomatic facility in Damascus that killed several prominent IRGC generals. The Israelis did not believe the strike crossed Iranian redlines. Israel had for years targeted IRGC and Hezbollah operatives in Syria and had increased such attacks during the Gaza war without facing a significant response. Iran, in turn, had refrained from direct attacks against Israel to avoid a military response from the United States and had long relied on a forward defense strategy of backing nonstate militant forces to maintain military pressure on Israel while keeping conflict outside Iran's borders. The Israelis were consequently surprised when Iran decided to launch several hundred missiles and drones directly at Israel in retaliation for the Damascus strike.[92] While the United States coordinated an effective missile defense with Israel and other international partners that prevented significant damage (and Israel's retaliation remained limited to targeting Iran's air defenses at a single military base), the incident started a new escalatory pattern of direct Israeli-Iranian clashes that brought the United States into a military confrontation with Iran.

Tensions further escalated over the summer with a presumed Israeli targeted killing of Hamas leader Ismail Haniyeh in Tehran during his stay at a government guest house while visiting the capital for the inauguration of Pezeshkian. This was a particularly humiliating incident for the Iranians that only underscored Israel's intelligence penetration within Iran itself. Administration officials had already dismissed the significance of Pezeshkian's victory, adhering to longstanding views that saw Iran's enmity toward the United States as unwavering and foundational to the regime regardless of changes in leadership at the presidential level. When national security spokesman John Kirby was asked if the United States would consider new diplomacy with Iran or whether new openings were possible with the election of Pezeshkian, Kirby flatly answered no. When pushed to elaborate, he said, "It seems like a pretty easy question to answer," and then outlined the familiar list of U.S. concerns about Iran, reiterating that "we are not expecting any changes in Iranian behavior."[93]

The Haniyeh killing was followed by a relentless series of Israeli strikes on Hezbollah, starting with the explosion of pagers belonging to Hezbollah operatives and then the killing of Hezbollah leader Hassan Nasrallah, as well as a senior IRGC commander, in a massive Israeli airstrike in Beirut in late September. Israel also began a ground invasion into southern Lebanon. Iran responded by attacking Israel directly for a second time on October 1 with 180 ballistic missiles targeting military and intelligence sites, though damage was again limited given Israel's advanced missile defense capabilities and civil defense against missile attacks (and continued U.S. support).

The specter of Iranian attacks against Israel increased animosity toward Iran within Washington. Prominent Republican senators like Lindsey Graham pressed for a strong U.S. response, calling the Iranian regime "religious Nazis" and encouraging the Biden administration to hit Iran's oil refineries "hard."[94] Sen. Marco Rubio warned of the dangers of "appeasement" and asserted, "Only threatening the survival of the regime through maximum pressure and direct and disproportionate measures has a chance to influence and alter their criminal activities."[95] House Democratic leader Hakeem Jeffries issued a statement calling Iran a "sworn enemy of the United States," and promised that "America's commitment to the safety and security of Israel is ironclad and unbreakable."[96] President Biden reaffirmed support for Israel but cautioned against retaliation against nuclear sites or oil fields. Israel responded with a large-scale attack on multiple military sites across Iran in late October, showcasing its ability to penetrate Iranian air defenses.

With Iran continuing to face heavy losses from Israel's degradation of Hezbollah with its ground and air campaign in Lebanon, speculation increased that Iran might move toward weaponizing its nuclear program to compensate for its eroding conventional deterrence. After the IAEA board censured Iran in late November 2024 for failing to cooperate over its nuclear program, Foreign Minister Abbas Araghchi warned that Iranian leaders were debating whether the country should change its nuclear posture if international sanctions were reimposed.[97] The continuing nuclear standoff with Iran through the end of the Biden administration only added to the rising friction between the United States and Iran in the aftermath of the Gaza and Lebanon wars.

The U.S. presidential election of 2024 reflected the enduring hostility. When asked which foreign country she considered America's greatest adversary, Vice President Harris responded: "I think there's an obvious one in mind which is Iran. Iran has American blood on their hands."[98] As a presidential candidate, Harris held positions on the Middle East that were nearly indistinguishable from Biden's, including when it came to U.S. policies on Israel and Iran. Trump was typically hostile toward Iran throughout the campaign. A Justice Department indictment alleging an Iranian government-backed assassination plot against Trump and hacking efforts against his campaign almost certainly hardened Trump's views toward Tehran.[99]

Nonetheless, as in his first presidency, Trump periodically mused about making a deal. His multibillionaire campaign-supporter-turned-political-advisor, Elon Musk, even met with Iran's ambassador to the United Nations to reportedly defuse tensions just weeks after Trump's election win.[100] But Trump's messages on Iran were mixed. His early picks for national security positions harbored far more hawkish views on Iran and backed the continuation of his maximum pressure policies from his first administration.[101] With Iranian vulnerability increasing following the onslaught of Israeli military attacks and the fall of the Assad regime in early December, Trump's team was reported to discuss U.S. military options against Iran, including air strikes on Iran's nuclear facilities.[102] When asked about the chances of war with Iran, in an interview with *Time* magazine during the transition period, Trump replied, "Anything can happen."[103]

Unfulfilled Expectations

To sum up the Biden years, one might refer to them as unfulfilled expectations, a time when putting Iran's nuclear program "back in the box" had a moment's opportunity that quickly vanished as regional and domestic politics intervened. In fact, the administration intentionally chose not to seize the moment at the outset of Biden's presidency, finding the Iran issue too politically difficult and disruptive to other priorities. In this sense, it is particularly a story about the first year of the administration, when policy attitudes and positions were set in ways that limited future options. Dealing with Iran only got harder over the course of Biden's presidency.

Despite Biden's campaign promises that he would rapidly restart U.S. engagement and reverse the damage of the first Trump presidency, he and his team were more cautious in restoring diplomacy with Iran than many anticipated. Administration officials sent early signals that a restored deal was a long way away and believed time was on their side. They were not eager to expend political capital on such a politically divisive issue so early in Biden's presidency. Meanwhile, developments in Iran only worsened as the clock on reviving the nuclear agreement ran its course. Serious negotiations did eventually occur in Vienna, where the parties came close to a revived agreement. But stumbling blocks on all sides emerged in an environment of limited trust and high political costs, a common storyline in the history of U.S.–Iran relations.

Strong congressional opposition to reviving a nuclear deal that was never popular reinforced a domestic context already disinclined to take bold actions on Iran. Dealing with Iran was long viewed as politically risky—even before the intense politicization of the nuclear agreement—given the longstanding animosity built up over the years and the predominant view of Iran as a fanatical and unreliable state. The political costs for American policymakers engaging with Iran only increased with Iranian drone sales to Russia in the midst of the Ukraine war, on top of the Iranian government's crackdown on the "Woman, Life, Freedom" protests. The administration viewed its best option as trying to avoid a worse crisis and military escalation, leading to informal de-escalation arrangements in mid-2023. But there would be no return to the possibility of more extensive diplomacy as occurred during the Obama years.

The devastating October 7 Hamas attacks on Israel and ensuing war ensured that even limited de-escalation agreements would prove tenuous. Instead of Biden's aspirational "longer and stronger" deal, Iran essentially became a nuclear threshold state. Even with the unexpected death of a hardline Iranian president and the election of a reformist who expressed interest in renewed diplomacy with the West, few in Washington departed from the traditional framing, continuing to harbor low to zero expectations for significant change from Iran.

Nor were there expectations of significant shifts in Washington on Iran policy during an election year marked by war in the Middle East. Vice President Harris suggested little change in the U.S. approach to Iran during the presidential campaign and Trump's rhetoric also remained hostile, even as he dangled the possibility of being able to strike a new deal with Iran. But after winning the election, and with Iran's increased vulnerability following a series of Israeli attacks that significantly eroded Iran's regional alliance network, Trump and his advisors also began messaging the possibility of using military force against Iran's nuclear sites and once in office increased economic pressure.

Given Trump's unpredictable and highly personal leadership style, and competing views among his top advisors, his future policy direction on Iran remained unclear. Despite the opening of Oman-mediated U.S.–Iran talks in April 2025, the endgame for negotiations and the prospects for a new and sustainable nuclear deal were uncertain. The rapidly shifting regional landscape, and the continuing opposition to nuclear diplomacy with Iran among influential segments of Washington's foreign policy elite, provided plenty of ammunition to fuel the enduring hostility from the Biden years into the second Trump presidency.

CONCLUSION

Change Is Hard

For a wide range of reasons, there are likely few American policymakers—or for that matter, Americans—who do not harbor ill feelings toward the government of Iran. Fortunately, such animosity does not appear to extend to the people of both countries, suggesting that enmity between America and Iran need not be permanent. The rhetoric and actions of the Islamic Republic since its founding have made it difficult for many Americans to imagine anything other than an antagonistic relationship. Not only has this hostility endured, but both sides have had to endure it—and its associated costs—for nearly half a century. At this point, U.S.–Iran hostility has persisted longer than the Cold War.

Iran's hostility was on most dramatic and early display with the taking of American hostages at the U.S. Embassy in the early days of the revolution, leaving a scar on relations that has never fully healed. America's hostility toward Iran only hardened as Iran took other actions that harmed Americans in subsequent years, from the bombing of the Marine barracks in Beirut to militia attacks on American personnel in Iraq to the imprisonment of innocent Americans and other foreign nationals—a few examples in a long list of grievances. Alarm over how the Iranian government cracked down on protests at home as well as Iran's active support for Russia's war on Ukraine abroad intensified anti-Iranian sentiment in the United States, and increasingly in Europe. Iran's longstanding support for Hamas only further sullied its image following the October 7, 2023 attacks on Israel.

America's animus toward Iran is thus deep, understandable, and un-relenting, building over years and persisting across generations of poli-cymakers. A small personal vignette from a former government official reflects the longstanding representation of Iran as America's arch-enemy. This former official recalled his first image of Iran, from a grade school field trip to a local police station, where there was an image of Iranian leader Ayatollah Ruhollah Khomeini at the end of the firing range with the slogan, "put a holla in the ayatollah."[1] This official would later come to endorse diplomacy with Iran, demonstrating that overcoming animosity that has so deeply penetrated the American culture is not impossible.

In fact, multiple American policymakers across administrations from the 1980s to the present have attempted to engage Iranian leaders, believ-ing that doing so would be worth the effort in reducing the prospects of conflict. But such efforts have not been easy, and not only because of the troubling activities of the Iranians over time, who harbor their own long list of grievances against Washington. The efforts have been difficult be-cause, when so much animus has accumulated over time, and when the discourse on a topic becomes so divisive, the room for bold policy change becomes limited, and the political costs for doing so are perceived as too high.

The arc of U.S. Iran policy outlined across this book shows far less change in American policy outcomes than might be expected given the dramatic changes in the geostrategic environment and shifts in political leadership since the Iranian revolution. There were many moments when a change in the relationship would have made strategic sense, when the most senior policymakers even thought such change should be pursued, but ultimately it did not happen. This book has attempted to answer why this is so.

Strategic Drivers Do Not Always Win the Day

Starting with the Cold War, the overriding strategic concern among American policymakers was that oil-rich, strategically situated states like Iran could fall into the hands of the Soviets, leading some officials in the Reagan administration to contemplate a strategic opening to Iran to thwart Soviet influence. Senior administration officials secretly, if now fa-mously, visited Tehran in search of Iranian moderates. But such initiatives resulted in the Iran-Contra scandal rather than a strategic breakthrough.

It was in the early years of the Islamic Republic, following the trauma of the hostage crisis, when the framing of Iran as a fanatical state began to take root in U.S. policy discourse, playing a significant role in shaping and constraining U.S. positions during Cold War competition. The United States backed Iraq during the Iran-Iraq War, despite Iraq's own egregious and ruthless actions under Saddam Hussein's rule, to prevent the domination of the oil-rich region by revolutionary Iran. At the same time, the Reagan administration secretly sold arms to Iran in a bid to secure the release of American hostages held in Lebanon and reap what some Reagan advisors saw as the strategic benefit of minimizing Soviet influence. Even after the covert dealings were exposed, Reagan still forcefully defended his administration's contact with Iranians, arguing it was important to signal a new relationship was possible. But the episode only set the U.S.–Iran relationship further back as the two countries engaged in direct military confrontation during the Tanker War toward the end of the Reagan presidency. Iran-Contra also created a chill for future policymakers interested in engaging Iran because its legacy, in many officials' thinking, demonstrated the unacceptably high political cost of dealing with Iran and reinforced the belief that Iranian leaders could not be trusted.

With the end of the Cold War ushering in a new era of American primacy throughout the 1990s, brief periods emerged when American policymakers again considered new approaches to Iran. George H. W. Bush and Bill Clinton each pondered the possibility. Bush's inaugural speech even held out an olive branch, believing Iranian pragmatists might be able to help free American hostages in Lebanon, especially with the death of the virulently anti-American founder of the Islamic Republic, Ayatollah Khomeini, in 1989.

But despite the release of hostages, the Bush administration viewed the political costs of sanctions relief or more serious engagement with Iran as too high to be worth it; the domestic toxicity of Iran for policymakers who had experienced the hostage crisis and the subsequent Iran-Contra scandal was well understood. Iran's assassinations of dissidents in Europe only further undermined the case for a U.S. policy shift. Defense Secretary Robert Gates reflected a widespread sentiment in Washington when he characterized Iran as the third rail of American foreign policy.[2] Secretary of State James Baker similarly acknowledged that for American policymakers who had experienced the hostage crisis and the Iran-Contra episode, "we were all too well aware of the Ayatollah's destructive capacities in terms of domestic politics."[3]

The aftermath of the 1991 Gulf War may have provided yet another strategic opportunity to revisit relations, given that Iran welcomed the U.S. campaign to roll back Saddam Hussein's invasion of Kuwait. But a common enemy was not enough to move U.S.–Iran ties in new directions. Instead, the Bush administration focused on convening the Madrid peace conference to jump-start a new era of Arab-Israeli peacemaking. American policymakers viewed Iran not as a participant but as a sideshow and ultimately a spoiler.

When it took up the mantle of peacemaking, the Clinton administration did not contemplate an opening to Iran, as it viewed U.S. policy largely through the lens of the Arab-Israeli peace process. American policymakers placed Iran in the "rogue state" category of American adversaries as the administration developed a "dual containment" strategy toward both Iran and Iraq.[4] By the time the Clinton administration came around to considering openings to Tehran in its second term, the hostile framing of Iran was well entrenched within Washington, creating a difficult political environment for conciliatory gestures, made more difficult by the reluctance of Iranian leaders to engage the Americans as U.S. sanctions against Tehran strengthened.

With the war in Afghanistan following the 9/11 Al Qaeda attacks on the United States in 2001, another potential strategic opening emerged. Iran supported the U.S. attack on their common enemy, the Taliban. U.S. diplomats met with Iranian officials in the first significant direct talks since the arms for hostages dealings of the 1980s. U.S. officials also worked closely with Iranian counterparts in multilateral negotiations in Bonn to establish a post-Taliban government in Afghanistan.

Yet, in a repeat of past patterns, those favoring engagement met fierce resistance. Instead of testing new openings, George W. Bush identified Iran as a charter member of the "axis of evil." Bush's top political appointees perceived Iran as a dangerous and radical regime, making advocacy for engagement a losing battle. Neoconservative voices in the administration believed the Iranian government was on the brink of collapse and would follow Saddam Hussein's downfall. Such wishful thinking thwarted engagement policies, especially in Bush's first term, before Iraq deteriorated into another bloody battleground for U.S.–Iran conflict and while the nuclear issue was still relatively contained. Policymakers supporting engagement were conscious of not looking "weak" or pursuing policies that would be politicized as doing favors for Iran. Despite periodic attempts in Bush's second term to negotiate with Tehran through multilateral frameworks, the overriding policy results by the end of the Bush administration were a growing sanctions regime—alongside an expanding Iranian nuclear program.

This state of affairs continued through the first Obama administration, despite Obama's determination to reset relations with Iran and offer to extend his hand if Iran would "unclench its fist." President Obama saw the Middle East as weighing down the United States, distracting attention from his pivot to Asia to address a rising China in a new era of great power competition. The election of Hassan Rouhani as president of Iran in 2013, who was supported by reformist and more pragmatic factions within the Iranian system, built on the momentum of the pro-diplomacy personnel on Obama's team. The moment for a strategic breakthrough appeared possible with the success of the Iran nuclear agreement in 2015 in Obama's second term, when there were fewer domestic constraints and a new set of advisors with a different outlook on diplomacy.

Yet while some analysts hailed the nuclear agreement as a final chapter ending decades of American-Iranian confrontation, debates resurfaced about how far the United States could go in transforming its relationship beyond the nuclear deal. Even those within the administration who favored the agreement pushed back on using it for a wider opening, advocating continued pressure on Iran in other arenas. Indeed, the rhetoric of Iran as a malign and abnormal state shadowed every attempt of a president determined to do things differently, shaping what the administration thought was not only possible but politically palatable.

Donald Trump promised to disrupt longstanding policies with his "America First" agenda and a focus on competition with China globally, theoretically providing an incentive to lower the temperature on Middle East conflicts. But Trump's 2016 campaign promise to scrap the Iran nuclear agreement, which he repeatedly called the "worst deal ever," drove his policies once in office more than strategic logic did. He made good on his political promise by withdrawing the United States from the agreement in May 2018, despite continued Iranian compliance and against the advice of even his own advisors at the time. The Trump administration's "maximum pressure" policies succeeded in devastating the Iranian economy but failed to bring about Trump's promise of a "better deal." Instead, Tehran responded with "maximum resistance."

Unlike in most previous administrations, there was little debate about attempting a new course of policy toward Iran during Trump's first presidency. Reporting of Trump's erratic leadership style suggests he was personally interested in engaging the Iranian leadership, believing himself to be the ultimate dealmaker. But he surrounded himself with advisors who viewed Iran as the source of the region's problems and accused the previous administration of being far too accommodating—that is, those who were committed to the framing of Iran as an unchangeable, implacable, fanatical adversary.

Such deeply ingrained hostile views of the country among key advisors pushed policy in escalatory directions regardless of Trump's personal preferences. The veneer of strategic framing for Iran policies is often thin in American policymaking, but it was nearly indiscernible in Trump's first presidency. Anti-Iran policies fit with Trump's inner circle's worldviews and made for good tough-guy politics, but more than that, they were easy to explain and justify to a Washington audience that had marinated in anti-Iran rhetoric for nearly four decades. They also fit with Trump's strong political motivation to undo Obama's signature foreign policy achievement and were popular policies among segments of the pro-Israel community within the Republican party, including influential supporters like Sheldon and Miriam Adelson.[5]

Across many areas, President Biden sought to heal Trump-caused rifts with important allies in Europe and Asia. As a candidate he had promised to restore the Iran nuclear deal and build on it to forge a "longer and stronger" agreement, believing Trump's withdrawal was a strategic mistake that only made Iran more dangerous. But Biden administration policies did not prove to be as transformative as promised. Biden's new foreign policy team maintained a cautious stance, suggesting the administration was not in a rush to rejoin the deal, believing the United States had leverage to reach a better deal with Iran than ultimately proved to be the case. The administration was also sensitive about looking "weak" on Iran—in effect, to taking a position at odds with how members of Congress perceived Iran—when trying to gain confirmation for important political appointments. Yet, as many analysts at the time noted, time was not on the side of the nuclear deal's restoration, with Iran's nuclear program only advancing as Iranian leaders sought to increase their own leverage. With a new Iranian negotiating team after the June 2021 Iranian presidential election, Tehran would soon be presenting even less accommodating positions.

The political costs of dealing with Iran increased with Iran's military support of Russia in the Ukraine war and the Iranian government's repression of the "Woman, Life, Freedom" protests in 2022. The administration viewed its best option as trying to avoid a crisis and military escalation, leading to informal de-escalation arrangements by the summer and early fall of 2023. But the Gaza war abruptly challenged these arrangements, even leading Iran and the United States to a direct military exchange when Iran launched an unprecedented missile attack on Israel in April 2024 and again in October 2024.

Talk of military options against Iran intensified yet again as Iran's nuclear program advanced while its military and regional capabilities diminished in the aftermath of an onslaught of Israeli attacks and the unexpected fall of the Assad regime in Syria in late 2024. Despite the Biden administration's interest in lowering the temperature with Iran, the U.S. posture by the end of his presidency looked remarkably similar to the policies inherited from previous administrations. Military deterrence, economic pressure, and the continuing risk of military conflict continued to define U.S. policies on Iran while space for diplomacy remained limited.

It's Not Always—Or Only—Them

What this record illustrates is that geostrategic factors do not preordain policy outcomes. Foreign policies are choices, not strategic destiny. It also shows that the barriers to a more normal American relationship with Iran were not always about the bad things Iran has done over the years to Americans and, for that matter, to Iranians. Of course, a different American-Iranian relationship will depend on Iran going through its own transformation in how it sees the United States, how it acts in the region, and how it treats its own people. But American domestic politics and the orientation of the policymakers who have most influenced Iran policy are also a major and often neglected part of the story. These policymakers and the wider foreign policy community in Washington, as well as the public discourse, have largely internalized and framed Iran as an abnormal state. It is part of the DNA in American policy circles, within government but also among the think tank community and media ecosystem. Israel's animus toward Iran has contributed to these prevailing views, given Israel's influence across the political spectrum in Washington. But, even so, Israeli preferences on Iran did not always prevail. America's Iran policies, while subject to influence and reaction, are at their core homegrown.

Not all American policymakers have embraced the predominant framing of Iran as an abnormal state driven by leaders irrevocably committed to conflict with the United States. A number of American foreign policy experts see many Iranian actions as driven by national interests as much as by ideology, which can provide openings for accommodation because it allows for a better understanding of mutual threat perceptions. Indeed, debates about Iran policy have surfaced in every administration, with some policymakers advocating more aggressive policies and others backing more engagement, or at least the testing of diplomatic options.

At times such positions may have been influenced by where policymakers were situated—the "where you stand is where you sit" bureaucratic politics dynamic. For example, a former U.S. government official had a colleague who worked with General David Petraeus during the Iraq War and held a senior position at the Pentagon overseeing Middle East policy. He described his colleagues' view of Iran as "like 'fuck the Iranians, they're assholes, not misunderstood people.'"[6] This former official acknowledged that after spending a few years at the Pentagon, he too became more cynical about Iran and understood that being at the Pentagon impacted his views because "they're dovish on most things but not Iran," noting that the "military guys get shot at" while State Department officials deal with a different and less hostile part of the Iranian system.[7]

That being said, we see over time that regardless of bureaucratic differences—not all Pentagon officials opposed engagement, while many former State Department officials did—the engagement side of the debate nearly always loses when it comes to final strategic policy decisions on Iran. The success of the Iran nuclear agreement was a notable exception, but even then many backing the deal felt the need to compensate by keeping up the pressure on Iran in other arenas distinct from the nuclear file. The discourse and narratives that have shaped Iran policies for years did not fundamentally change. The onerous sanctions regime imposed on Iran—built up over decades—has not only endured but strengthened. U.S. military posture in the Middle East is still designed with an eye toward Iran. The increased politicization of American foreign policy has only further cemented the deeply rooted inclination to voice skepticism if not outright opposition toward diplomacy with Iran, particularly as the political costs of engagement have always been high.

Zalmay Khalilzad, a former U.S. ambassador and diplomat who engaged Iranian officials directly after the wars in Afghanistan and Iraq, discusses an interesting incident during the Reagan era in his memoir. Khalilzad recalls writing a memo addressing the debate about how to deal with Iraq following the Iran-Iraq ceasefire, including an option that considered easing economic sanctions on Iran. After the memo was leaked to *The New York Times*, Secretary of State George Shultz called a meeting with senior officials. He asked to see the memo, and while he was reading it, Khalilzad observed that "his face became redder and redder. Then he grabbed a marker and wrote a big "NO" across the first page. Cooling down a bit, he turned toward me [Khalilzad]. 'Zal, this makes great geopolitical sense but no political sense!'"[8] This political context, in which merely raising the possibility of easing pressure on Tehran is readily dismissed, has endured in the decades since, and in fact the space for robust debates about Iran policy has only narrowed over time as the list of objectionable Iranian actions has grown. No American policymaker wants to "look weak" on Iran or be accused of being an Iran "apologist."

But the constraints on changing U.S. Iran policy are not just about the political costs that have hamstrung American policymakers since the early days of Iran's revolution. The prevailing views of Iran also stem from genuine beliefs that the only way to deal with a country like Iran—a country widely believed in Washington to be driven by ideology and hegemonic ambitions—is continuous pressure. In this view, accommodating policies toward Iran will be futile because they will only embolden bad behavior. Abnormal states are destined to remain hostile and will not negotiate in good faith. Such readings of Iran remain widespread in Washington.

The writing of this book illuminated this dynamic. Early feedback on my project proposal from two anonymous former U.S. government officials was particularly revealing. These former policymakers could not fathom that any explanation other than Iran's bad faith and duplicitous policies was to blame for the sorry state of U.S.–Iran relations. If anything, they argued, American policies toward Iran have been accommodating, asserting, for example, that the United States could have invaded Iran after Iraq in 2003 but chose not to do so, or that the United States was restrained in deciding to assassinate Iranian IRGC general Qassem Soleimani in Iraq rather than in Iran. If the United States had wanted to, it could have confronted Iran militarily more often, argued one former official.[9]

Such arguments lauding American restraint given the U.S. track record in the Middle East might sound fantastical outside the Washington bubble, but they accurately reflect how many American policymakers see Iran and the American policy record on Iran. In the typical Washington assessment, any overture to Iran—Reagan's outreach in Iran-Contra, Clinton's overtures in his second term, Bush's engagement with Iran on Afghanistan, or Obama's negotiations over the nuclear deal—represents American magnanimity, only to be rejected by an obstinate and ideologically driven Iranian regime.

The common viewpoint in Washington is that the United States is the pragmatic party while Iran's anti-American ideology is the problem. The ideological barriers to accommodation come from Tehran, not Washington. It is no wonder that it is difficult for many American policymakers, or indeed others in the wider Washington foreign policy community, to look inward and consider fundamentally different approaches when they already believe American policy has tried and failed to accommodate Iran, and that in any case such efforts are fruitless.

"It's them, not us." The narrative is practically sacrosanct in Washington; arguing otherwise constitutes a foreign policy version of heresy. Even arguing *"it's both of us"*—as this book does—is a bridge too far for some. This is not a healthy state of affairs when it comes to dealing with critical foreign policy challenges like Iran, even if it's clear that Iran bears significant blame for a deeply adversarial relationship. Any chance of improving adversarial relationships requires honest and open debates, and reflection of policy choices and actions on all sides.

U.S. Foreign Policy Is Hard to Change

This deep dive into U.S. Iran policy illuminating some of the domestic dynamics shaping decisions could very well be at work on other critical national security challenges, potentially offering lessons for why American foreign policy has been difficult to change. First is the ever-present challenge of policy inertia. Once policies are firmly in place—a robust sanctions regime, for instance, or a view of an unchangeable enemy—it is difficult to shift course. As a former U.S. diplomat reflected: "Policymakers tend to live within existing constraints rather than challenging them."[10]

Changing postures toward adversaries is particularly difficult because of concerns about appearing weak and the common notion among American policymakers that talking to one's enemy is a concession, not necessarily a normal diplomatic practice.

Moreover, maintaining adversarial relationships may be not only politically safer but also good business. This is particularly true as the "revolving door" phenomenon—whereby former officials leverage their contacts forged during government service to establish consulting firms or join lobbying groups after leaving government—has only grown over time. Unlike many other Western democracies that rely on a cadre of civil servants for senior foreign policy positions and ambassadorships, the American system allows for an extensive political appointee system, as well as the common practice of appointing campaign donors to plum ambassadorial posts.

There can be advantages to tapping into a wider range of expertise across different sectors of the foreign policy elite who may bring in specialized knowledge and analytic insights that can help better inform complex global policies. But the downside of this system is that it allows for more vulnerability to foreign and special interest group access because former government officials often rely on such sources for funding projects upon leaving government when serving at consulting firms or policy think tanks and, at times, universities. This is not the case across the board, and many former government officials are extremely careful to avoid conflicts of interest. In many cases, political appointees may have paid a financial and personal cost for arduous government work because of a passion for public service.

The problem of the revolving door is nonetheless serious. Even if, as this book has argued, the particular attitude of American foreign policymakers toward Iran—and toward the possibility of productive strategic engagement with Iran—is homegrown, the attitude has found regular reinforcement through Washington's think tank and consulting culture over the years. For instance, foreign governments pay generously for access to former U.S. officials who, they believe, can connect them to current policymakers making decisions on issues of concern to them. Or they might see former officials as cooling their heels while waiting to return to new and possibly even more prominent positions of power. I witnessed such dynamics on various trips to the Middle East. On one occasion, when visiting an Emirati businessman to gauge his interest in joining a Middle East nonprofit advisory board, I was surprised, on entering the room for lunch, to find a recent former senior U.S. defense official sitting at the table engaged in what appeared to be a business pitch.

As a former U.S. official put it to me, the increased trend of Gulf Arab funding and links to Washington think tanks and consulting firms filled with former senior U.S. officials—Democrat and Republican—makes keeping up pressure on Iran "good business."[11] The former deputy national security advisor, Ben Rhodes, lifted the veil of such dynamics during the Obama years, explaining: "In addition to being the key producer of oil for the American-led global economy, the Saudis and Emiratis have poured money into the U.S. national security establishment—investing in think tanks, universities, corporate positions, lavish parties, and paid speaking opportunities for opinion journalists and people in the revolving door between the private sector and high-ranking government positions"— producing a "well-funded commentary advocating a harsh stance against Iran and, ultimately, the Obama foreign policy."[12]

Indeed, a number of Gulf Arab states have long been wary of Iran's regional influence and were unhappy with Obama's Middle East policies. When I visited Saudi Arabia just months after Trump's 2016 victory, the sense of excitement in Riyadh was palpable. I saw firsthand how senior Gulf officials enjoyed extraordinary access to top Trump administration officials, boasting about how their input was shaping decisions and President Trump's Middle East policies. They embraced Trump's hardline positions on Iran, though in subsequent years Emirati and Saudi leaders changed their tune and began mending ties with Tehran to avoid being in the crosshairs of U.S.–Iran conflict.

Former Trump advisors appeared particularly ready to cash in on their government service to strike lucrative business deals after leaving their public service positions. For example, General Miguel Correa, a former defense attaché at the U.S. Embassy in the UAE who worked with Jared Kushner on the Abraham Accords, became an advisor at Kushner's private equity firm, Affinity Partners, which attracted sizeable investments from Gulf Arab states.[13] Former senior Trump advisors like Kushner and former Treasury secretary Steven Mnuchin had already begun meeting with potential Gulf investors on official trips to the Middle East in the final weeks of the first Trump administration.[14] These type of access challenges are no doubt a factor in influencing other U.S. foreign policy areas, particularly when directed toward increasing pressure on adversaries already unpopular in Washington.

The Iran case may also help illuminate a broader career incentive system among a foreign policy elite that does not favor advocating for change. Pushing back on longstanding policies rarely helps advance one's career; better to stay the course and be a "team player." Why open yourself up to political scrutiny when trying to shift course on contentious issues like Iran? There is little to gain by standing out and making oneself vulnerable to accusations of naïveté or weakness. Such dynamics lend themselves to groupthink and an eagerness to show foreign policy "toughness," reinforcing common tropes about adversaries that become difficult to change.

Former U.S. policymakers acknowledge such factors at play when relaying stories about how, during internal discussions on Iran, senior officials would at times compete for who could look tougher on Iran or express more skepticism about Iranian motives. As Ben Rhodes put it to me, "all incentives for people in [the U.S.] government are to be hawks" on Iran.[15] Those who are "out of step" with conventional views understand there could be a cost on their foreign policy careers, such as jeopardizing the ability to secure a Senate confirmation for top government positions. Rhodes observes that because of such career concerns, even government officials "one layer down" who may have more nuanced views of foreign policy challenges like Iran may self-censor to conform to prevailing wisdom, at least in their public statements.[16]

Rob Malley calls this a sociological phenomenon, whereby the "social reproduction of a foreign policy" is fostered by creating "a system that rewards certain views despite a record of failure" and that lacks "accountability for the failures."[17] Even in internal deliberations officials feel the need to start discussions with critiques of policies they previously supported. Malley notes, for example, that during the transition period from Obama to Trump, some former Obama officials would say things like, "Let's agree the JCPOA wasn't perfect" or "the JCPOA needs to be strengthened" before making their point, thereby surrendering in advance to their opponents' view and waging the fight on their opponents' turf. They did this hoping to establish their credentials, when in reality it served to undermine their credibility. Malley observes that Democratic policymakers are particularly on the defensive when it comes to Iran policy, with constant "throat clearing" that ends up shaping policy in more hawkish directions, especially because there is no "ecosystem" for alternative foreign policy viewpoints.[18]

Such dynamics also pervade the think tank world. I have experienced sitting in briefings for former government officials where the experts in the room try to one-up each other on who can raise more examples of malign Iranian activities. There are of course exceptions, with many excellent analysts and former diplomats presenting complex and nuanced views of Iran and other foreign policy issues, often seeking to challenge conventional thinking while also appreciating the dangers Iran and other adversaries pose to American interests. I worked with a number of experts and former officials while at RAND who reflected such measured and thoughtful analysis. But pushing back on deeply accepted foreign policy narratives—such as Iran being the source of all problems in the Middle East—tends to be rare. Even presenting balanced assessments that take Iranian threat perceptions seriously may be considered too "dovish" in some Washington circles.

Career and reputational concerns may be at work in other areas of U.S. foreign policy, particularly when a hardline consensus against an adversary emerges that makes a departure from conventional views more costly. One study on U.S. policy toward China, for example, found that, despite diverging perspectives, many foreign policy professionals perceived "social and professional pressure to voice a more confrontational position towards China."[19] The study identifies strategies that foreign policy elites employ to cope with such pressures, including "mirroring hawkish rhetoric in their advice, modifying or self-censoring their views in public settings, and even exiting the field entirely"—demonstrating "how professional pressures and social dynamics among Washington's think tank community may constrain debate by shaping the content and expression of foreign policy advice."[20]

Such findings resonate with Iran policy dynamics. The experts who emerge as the most prominent voices in Washington or in the leading outlets of mainstream media on a subject like Iran are more likely to echo conventional framings than to challenge them.[21] How many times have we seen, for example, top experts on Iran or influential opinion columnists resort to "bazaar merchant" metaphors to explain why you can't trust the Iranians—likening dealing with Iran to shopping for a Persian carpet.[22] Such arguments are promoted to warn U.S. officials that if they show too much eagerness to strike a deal, adversaries like Iran will take full advantage. The reasoning is that Iran's revolutionary ideology and identity are fixed, so there is little the United States can do to change the equation.[23] Iran is the problem; Washington is off the hook. Such narratives shape the way members of the foreign policy elite view and discuss issues, and the boundaries they are reluctant to cross.

These types of factors combine in ways that make changing the direction of American foreign policy difficult, especially when it comes to how the United States deals with adversaries. Mindsets and incentive structures can impact policy choices, and it is always easier to continue status quo adversarial relationships than to risk political exposure by talking to the enemy, especially if the expectation is that the enemy is bent on an unrelentingly hostile and unchanging stance toward the United States. Without a game-changing external event to shake up policies on autopilot, the odds that policymakers will back new policies are low even if current postures are producing suboptimal results. It is extraordinary how long policies that seem unsustainable persist. The Iran case is a stark demonstration of this dilemma, but it no doubt reflects deeper structural and political challenges in the way U.S. foreign policy is formulated.

Can the Future Be Different?

The legacy of enduring hostility with Iran, and the political venom such hostility has engendered, has made major shifts in U.S. policy extremely difficult. There is little reason to believe a future change in direction is likely without a willingness to challenge longstanding beliefs, postures, and incentive systems—or, perhaps more realistically, a significant change in the nature or policies of the Iranian government that might help spark new debates and reassessments in Washington. Indeed, even for a rule-breaker like President Trump, who promotes himself as the ultimate dealmaker, charting a new course with Iran will prove difficult with the prevailing sentiments about Iran so deeply rooted in Washington, not to mention Trump's own previous track record of confrontation with Tehran.

But even without a change of government or adoption of radically different policies in Iran—which may eventually come in some form given its domestic and regional vulnerabilities—it is important to consider the costs of *not* changing policy directions. How well have America's Iran policies served American interests? Are there other ways forward that have not been tested? To consider such questions seriously, U.S. policymakers will need to recognize their own blind spots and engage in debates about the wisdom of current policies based largely on military, economic, and political pressure. It may be the case that, even if a future U.S. administration was willing to break new ground with Iran, Iranian leaders would not respond in kind and alter their own longstanding stance toward Washington. But as a number of former U.S. diplomats who have directly engaged Iran have argued, from a U.S. national security standpoint there is no rational reason to avoid trying.

This does not suggest an idealized view of what is possible to achieve with Iran's current government. Too often alternative policies toward Iran are dismissed as naïve because they are represented as unrealistic, transformative outcomes, such as a full normalization of ties between the United States and Iran. That is not likely a feasible goal given domestic considerations in both countries: the preceding chapters largely underscore the significant barriers within the American system, but barriers exist on Iran's side as well, as many other studies have demonstrated. On the other end of the spectrum, endless confrontation is also unsustainable and undesirable.

And yet, especially during times when Iran appears more vulnerable, there is a tendency in Washington to double down on confrontational policies, believing that hitting Iran hard while the country is on the ropes may lead to a regime collapse. Such policies have been tried and have failed. The Islamic Republic's system may one day collapse, but basing U.S. policies on that hope is not a strategy. Nor has the track record of regime change triggered by external actors been a positive one.

What might be possible and more productive to achieve over time—even with the continuation of diametrically opposed views of the global and regional order—is a version of détente.[24] The United States and Iran could come to an accommodation to reduce the possibility of military conflict, building on informal de-escalation arrangements that have already been established through third party mediators in the past to construct a more formal arrangement through direct talks. This would not be a peace treaty settling all differences between the United States and Iran or an acceptance of Iran's repression at home. Rather, détente would mean that Iran could become a *normal adversary*, allowing for both continued competition and the possibility of cooperation in limited areas where interests may overlap. Most critically, it could help reduce the specter of military conflict between the two countries, and between Iran and its neighbors, including eventually with Israel (Iran and its Arab neighbors have already been normalizing ties on their own accord).

A wider accommodation would also improve the prospects for a more viable nuclear agreement, particularly if such arrangements address a range of nonnuclear Iranian activities of concern in the region as well as Iran's own threat perceptions.[25] Restoring regular and direct diplomacy with Iranian leaders is essential to achieving any of these goals, and it need not—and should not—come at the expense of American leaders continuing to showcase and defend human rights abuses within the country, just as American policymakers did regularly when it came to diplomacy with the Soviets during the Cold War. Détente with an adversary and advocating for the people living within the adversary's borders are not mutually exclusive. Whether the United States will prioritize human rights issues in Iran or beyond remains to be seen.

It is too easy to create a strawman of unrealistic expectations and dismiss any possibility of change with a country as vilified in the American system as Iran, particularly when Iran's current leaders continue to engage in objectionable activities at home and abroad. There is good reason for pessimism, for seeing each side as so unchanging that there is no way forward other than continuous confrontation. Or, as former secretary of defense Robert Gates once put it, to believe that with such a politically contentious challenge there is "nothing to be done."

But a middle ground may be possible. The United States and Iran may not be able to achieve a full peace, but they might be able to end their state of endless hostility. That is a realistic vision American policymakers might work toward. It will take considerable political will on the American side and sustained diplomatic investments. It will take the Iranians producing more accommodating and pragmatic leaders in the years ahead who prioritize their people's needs as much as their own survival. Ultimately, it will take a willingness for each to challenge longstanding and deeply entrenched views of the other. In short, something can be done. But the long history of enduring hostility will not make it easy.

NOTES

Introduction

1. Martin Indyk, interview with author, April 28, 2021.

2. See, for example, John Ghazvinian, *America and Iran: A History, 1720 to the Present* (Knopf, 2021).

3. Dennis Ross, interview with author, January 19, 2022.

4. Ryan Crocker, interview with author, August 22, 2023.

5. "Track two" dialogues are unofficial closed meetings where experts and government officials, current and former, discuss challenging policy issues in efforts to generate new ideas for advancing policy solutions and reducing the prospects for conflict. In the Middle East, many track two dialogues emerged on Arab-Israeli issues throughout the 1980s and particularly following the 1991 Madrid peace conference, but a number of discussions in subsequent years focused on the Gulf region and Iran. For further details on track two dialogues, see Dalia Dassa Kaye, *Talking to the Enemy: Track Two Diplomacy in the Middle East and South Asia* (RAND, 2007).

6. Ghazvinian, *America and Iran*, presents the most comprehensive and detailed historical account of American-Iranian relations from both before and after the Islamic Revolution.

7. See, for example, Stephen Kinzer, *All the Shah's Men: An American Coup and the Roots of Middle East Terror* (Wiley, 2003); Roham Alvandi, *Nixon, Kissinger and the Shah: The United States and Iran in the Cold War* (Oxford University Press, 2014); Gary Sick, *All Fall Down: America's Tragic Encounter with Iran* (Random House, 1985); Gary Sick, *October Surprise: America's Hostages in Iran and the Election of Ronald Reagan* (Crown, 1991); Ray Takeyh, *The Last Shah: America, Iran, And the Fall of the Pahlavi Dynasty* (Yale University Press, 2021); and Mohsen M. Milani, *The Making of Iran's Islamic Revolution: From Monarchy to Islamic Republic* (Westview Press, 1988).

8. Examples in this genre include John Limbert, *Negotiating with Iran: Wrestling the Ghosts of History* (U.S. Institute of Peace, 2009); Barbara Slavin, *Bitter Friends, Bosom Enemies: Iran, the U.S., and the Twisted Path to Confrontation* (St. Martin's Press, 2007); and James A. Bill, *The Eagle and the Lion: The Tragedy of American-Iranian Relations* (Yale University Press, 1988). The critical oral history book, James G. Blight et al., *Becoming Enemies: U.S.–Iran Relations and the Iran-Iraq War, 1979-1988* (Rowman and Littlefield, 2012), similarly reviews misconceptions in U.S.–Iran relations focused on the period of the Iran-Iraq War.

9. See Hussein Banai, Malcolm Byrne, and John Tirman, *Republics of Myth: National Narratives and the US–Iran Conflict* (Johns Hopkins University Press, 2022).

10. Banai, Byrne, and Tirman, *Republics of Myth*.

11. Robert S. Litwak draws on Iran as a case study in both *Rogue States and U.S. Foreign Policy: Containment after the Cold War* (Woodrow Wilson Center Press, 2000) and *Regime Change: U.S. Strategy through the Prism of 9/11* (Johns Hopkins University Press, 2007). Jeffrey Fields also examines a range of U.S. relationships with rogue states, including Iran, to illustrate the impact of ideology and perceptions of American predominance in shaping foreign policy after the Cold War. See Fields, "Engaging Adversaries: Myths and Realities in American Foreign Policy," *Diplomacy and Statecraft* 26, no. 2 (2015): 294–321.

12. Two notable examples include David Crist, *The Twilight War: The Secret History of America's Thirty-Year Conflict with Iran* (Penguin Books, 2012); and Kenneth M. Pollack, *The Persian Puzzle: The Conflict between Iran and America* (Random House, 2004).

13. A prominent book falling into this camp is Trita Parsi, *Losing an Enemy: Obama, Iran, and the Triumph of Diplomacy* (Yale University Press, 2017). This book builds on Parsi's earlier books, including *A Single Roll of the Dice: Obama's Diplomacy with Iran* (Yale University Press, 2012); and *Treacherous Alliance: The Secret Dealings of Israel, Iran, and the United States* (Yale University Press, 2008).

14. See Dana H. Allin and Steven Simon, *The Sixth Crisis: Iran, Israel, America, and the Rumors of War* (Oxford University Press, 2010).

15. George Lakoff has written and spoken extensively about the power of framing to shaping political debate. See, for example, Lakoff, *Moral Politics: How Liberals and Conservatives Think* (University of Chicago Press, 2016).

16. Some scholars argue that emotional and ideological factors underlying perceptions of American superiority and exceptionalism became more prevalent following the end of the Cold War because of the increased saliency of domestic politics and concerns about reputation. See, for example, Fields, "Engaging Adversaries." Fields notes that U.S. engagement with adversaries becomes more exceptional than was the case during the Cold War because American exceptionalism reinforces the norm against having relations with the "other," or "deviant" and "rogue" regimes. However, in the case of Iran, such dispositions among American policymakers predated the end of the Cold War. But the popularity of the term "rogue" after the end of the Cold War certainly reinforced these preexisting frames of Iran.

17. See, for example, Defense Department, report to Congress, "Unclassified Report on Military Power of Iran," UNCLASSIFIED, April 2010, in Malcolm Byrne and Kian Byrne, *Worlds Apart: A Documentary History of US–Iranian Relations, 1978–2018* (Cambridge University Press, 2022), 250–256.

18. National Intelligence Council, National Intelligence Estimate, "Iran: Nuclear Intentions and Capabilities," November 2007, https://www.dni.gov/files/documents/Newsroom/Reports%20and%20Pubs/20071203_release.pdf.

19. Fields, "Engaging Adversaries."

20. Brian Hook, prepared testimony before Senate Foreign Relations Committee hearing, "Tehran's Shadow Army: Addressing Iran's Proxy Network in the Middle East," February 28, 2024, https://www.foreign.senate.gov/imo/media/doc/0217a85a-ae50-89b2-e9d2-a20d47ffabbc/022824_Hook_Testimony.pdf.

21. CIA Intelligence Memorandum, SECRET, "Middle East Terrorism: The Threat and Possible U.S. Responses," U.S. Central Intelligence Agency Directorate of Intelligence Office of Near Eastern and South Asian Analysis, February 25, 1985, https://search.proquest.com/government-official-publications/middle-east-terrorism-threat-possible-u-s/docview/2321518989/se-2?accountid=25333.

22. CIA Intelligence Memorandum, SECRET, "Middle East Terrorism: The Threat and Possible U.S. Responses."

23. Quoted in Ghazvinian, *America and Iran*, 284.

24. See, for example, Ray Takeyh, "The Coup against Democracy That Wasn't," *Commentary*, December 2021, https://www.commentary.org/articles/ray-takeyh/iran-1953-coup-america/.

25. American Embassy, Tehran, telegram, L. Bruce Laingen for the Secretary of State, "Shah's Desire to Reside in the U.S.," SECRET, July 28, 1979, in Byrne and Byrne, *Worlds Apart*, 33.

26. Cited in Ghazvinian, *America and Iran*, 319.

27. Quoted in Ghazvinian, *America and Iran*, 323.

28. Madeleine K. Albright, oral history transcript, Miller Center, University of Virginia, August 30, 2006, https://millercenter.org/the-presidency/presidential-oral-histories/madeleine-k-albright-oral-history.

29. Gary Sick, interview with author, May 3, 2021.

30. Gary Sick, interview with author, May 3, 2021.

31. Gary Sick, interview with author, May 3, 2021.

32. White House, memorandum, Zbigniew Brzezinski for President Carter, "Black Room Report," TOP SECRET, November 20, 1979, in Byrne and Byrne, *Worlds Apart*, 42.

33. White House, memorandum, Zbigniew Brzezinski for President Carter, "Black Room Report," TOP SECRET, November 20, 1979, in Byrne and Byrne, *Worlds Apart*, 42.

34. See letter from assistant secretary of state Julia Frifield to Edward R. Royce, chairman, House Foreign Affairs Committee, March 17, 2016, https://foreignaffairs.house.gov/wp-content/uploads/2016/08/03.17.16-DOS-Response-Concerns-re-1.7-Billion-Payout-to-Iran.pdf.

35 "The Situation in Iran," hearing before Committee on Foreign Relations,

U.S. Senate, 96th Congress, 2nd sess., May 8, 1980, https://heinonline.org/HOL /LandingPage?handle=hein.cbhear/sitiranoo01&div=2&id=&page=.

36. "The Situation in Iran," hearing before Committee on Foreign Relations, U.S. Senate, 96th Congress, 2nd sess., May 8, 1980 (italics added).

37. "The Iran Agreements," hearings before Committee on Foreign Relations, U.S. Senate, 97th Congress, 1st sess., February 17, 18, and March 4, 1981, https:// heinonline.org/HOL/LandingPage?handle=hein.cbhear/cbhearings1429&div= 2&id=&page=.

38. "The Iran Agreements," hearings before Committee on Foreign Relations, U.S. Senate, 97th Congress, 1st sess., February 17, 18, and March 4, 1981.

Chapter One

1. Dennis Ross, interview with author, January 19, 2022.

2. Malcolm Byrne, *Iran-Contra: Reagan's Scandal and the Unchecked Abuse of Presidential Power* (University Press of Kansas, 2014).

3. President Ronald Reagan, speech about Iran-Contra affair, March 4, 1987, https://web.archive.org/web/20080302164911/http://www.pbs.org/wgbh/amex/ reagan/filmmore/reference/primary/irancontra.html.

4. "Address to the Nation on the Iran Arms and Contra Aid Controversy," November 13, 1986, Ronald Reagan Presidential Library and Museum, https:// www.reaganlibrary.gov/archives/speech/address-nation-iran-arms-and-contra -aid-controversy-november-13-1986.

5. "Address to the Nation on the Iran Arms and Contra Aid Controversy," November 13, 1986, Ronald Reagan Presidential Library and Museum.

6. "Address to the Nation on the Iran Arms and Contra Aid Controversy," November 13, 1986, Ronald Reagan Presidential Library and Museum (italics added).

7. Bruce Riedel, interview with author, April 22, 2021.

8. Bruce Riedel, interview with author, April 22, 2021.

9. Bruce Riedel, interview with author, April 22, 2021.

10. Bernard Gwertzman, "McFarlane Took Cake and Bible to Tehran, Ex-- C.I.A. Man says," *The New York Times,* January 11, 1987.

11. Dennis Ross, interview with author, January 19, 2022.

12. Dennis Ross, interview with author, January 19, 2022.

13. See, for example, Dennis Ross, "America Should Get Behind Saudi Ara- bia's Revolutionary Crown Prince," *The Washington Post*, February 12, 2018.

14. Dennis Ross, interview with author, January 19, 2022.

15. See Riedel quoted in James G. Blight et al., *Becoming Enemies: US–Iran Relations and the Iran-Iraq War, 1979–1988* (Rowman and Littlefield, 2014), 147.

16. U.S. National Security Council, Top Secret NSC Action Memorandum, "U.S. Policy toward Iran and Strategic Recommendations; Includes Attach- ments," April 18, 1985, https://search.proquest.com/government-official-publica tions/iran-u-s-policy-toward-strategic-recommendations/docview/2321518652/se -2?accountid=25333.

17. U.S. National Security Council, Top Secret NSC Action Memorandum,

"U.S. Policy toward Iran and Strategic Recommendations; Includes Attachments," April 18, 1985.

18. U.S. National Security Council, Top Secret NSC Action Memorandum, "U.S. Policy toward Iran and Strategic Recommendations; Includes Attachments," April 18, 1985.

19. U.S. National Security Council, Top Secret NSC Action Memorandum, "U.S. Policy toward Iran and Strategic Recommendations; Includes Attachments," April 18, 1985.

20. U.S.National Security Council, Top Secret National Security Decision Directive (NSDD), "U.S. Policy toward Iran," June 17, 1985, https://search. proquest.com/government-official-publications/u-s-policy-toward-iran-attached -cover-memorandum/docview/2321518878/se-2?accountid=25333.

21. U.S.National Security Council, Top Secret National Security Decision Directive (NSDD), "U.S. Policy toward Iran," June 17, 1985.

22. U.S.National Security Council, Top Secret National Security Decision Directive (NSDD), "U.S. Policy toward Iran," June 17, 1985.

23. David Crist, *The Twilight War: The Secret History of America's Thirty-Year Conflict with Iran* (Penguin, 2013), 176.

24. Crist, *The Twilight War*, 176.

25. Colin Powell, *My American Journey* (Ballantine, 2003), 305.

26. Powell, *My American Journey*, 305.

27. Powell, *My American Journey*, 305.

28. Powell, *My American Journey*, 305.

29. Powell argues that, despite opposition from senior administration officials, the plan moved forward because Reagan was attracted to the promise of releasing American hostages. Powell, *My American Journey*, 343.

30. Crist, *The Twilight War*, 67.

31. Crist, *The Twilight War*, 67.

32. U.S. National Security Council, Top Secret National Security Decision Directive (NSDD), "U.S. Policy toward Iran," June 17, 1985.

33. U.S. National Security Council, Top Secret National Security Decision Directive (NSDD), "U.S. Policy toward Iran," June 17, 1985.

34. U.S. National Security Council, Top Secret National Security Decision Directive (NSDD), "U.S. Policy toward Iran," June 17, 1985.

35. U.S. National Security Council, Top Secret National Security Decision Directive (NSDD), "U.S. Policy toward Iran," June 17, 1985.

36. "Address to the Nation on the Iran Arms and Contra Aid Controversy," November 13, 1986, Ronald Reagan Presidential Library and Museum.

37. "Address to the Nation on the Iran Arms and Contra Aid Controversy," November 13, 1986, Ronald Reagan Presidential Library and Museum (italics added).

38. U.S. Department of State, Bureau of Near Eastern and South Asian Affairs, Assistant Secretary, and U.S. Department of State, Bureau of Political-Military Affairs, Assistant Secretary, Secret Information Memorandum, "U.S. Policy on Third-Country Transfers of U.S. Arms to Iraq," February 4, 1987, https:

//search.proquest.com/government-official-publications/u-s-policy-on-third
-country-transfers-arms-iraq/docview/2321521269/se-2?accountid=25333.

39. U.S. Department of State, Bureau of Near Eastern and South Asian Af-
fairs, Assistant Secretary, and U.S. Department of State, Bureau of Political-
Military Affairs, Assistant Secretary, Secret Information Memorandum, "U.S.
Policy on Third-Country Transfers of U.S. Arms to Iraq," February 4, 1987.

40. Blight et al., *Becoming Enemies.*

41. Blight et al., *Becoming Enemies.*

42. Blight et al., *Becoming Enemies*, 102. This quote is sourced to former U.S.
ambassador to Iraq David Newton.

43. Blight et al., *Becoming Enemies*, 103.

44. Crist, *The Twilight War.*

45. Quoted in Blight et al., *Becoming Enemies*, 107–108.

46. Blight et al., *Becoming Enemies*, 107.

47. U.S. Joint Chiefs of Staff, Joint Staff, Secret Memorandum, "U.S. Arms
Transfer Policy toward Iran," September 3, 1981, https://search.proquest.com/
government-official-publications/u-s-arms-transfer-policy-toward-iran/docview/
2321518962/se-2?accountid=25333.

48. U.S. Joint Chiefs of Staff, Joint Staff, Secret Memorandum, "U.S. Arms
Transfer Policy toward Iran," September 3, 1981.

49. Crist, *The Twilight War*, 56.

50. Crist, *The Twilight War.*

51. Blight et al., *Becoming Enemies.*

52. See, for example, "Won't Let 'Barbaric' Iran Close Oil Routes—Reagan:
Doesn't Say What U.S. Will Do," *Los Angeles Times*, May 27, 1987.

53. Crist, *The Twilight War*, 163.

54. These two hearings focused in particular on the Tanker War: "U.S. Policy
in the Persian Gulf," hearings before Committee on Foreign Relations, U.S.
Senate, 100th Congress, 1st session, May 29, June 16, October 23 and 28, 1987,
https://heinonline.org/HOL/LandingPage?handle=hein.cbhear/usppgooo1&div
=2&id=&page=. Also "Antiterrorism Policy and Arms Export Controls," hearing
and markup before Committee on Foreign Affairs and its subcommittees on
Arms Control, International Security, and Science on International Economic
Policy and Trade, and on International Operations, House of Representatives,
100th Congress, 2nd session on H.R. 3651, March 17 and April 19, 1988, https://
heinonline.org/HOL/LandingPage?handle=hein.cbhear/cbhearings4156&div=
2&id=&page=.

55. Statement of Richard Murphy, Assistant Secretary of State for Near Eastern and South Asian Affairs, "U.S. Policy in the Persian Gulf," hearings before
Committee on Foreign Relations, U.S. Senate, 100th Congress, 1st session, May
29, June 16, October 23 and 28, 1987, https://heinonline.org/HOL/LandingPage?
handle=hein.cbhear/usppgooo1&div=2&id=&page=.

56. Statement of Caspar Weinberger, Secretary of Defense, "U.S. policy in the
Persian Gulf," Hearings before the Committee on Foreign Relations, United
States Senate, 100th Congress, 1st session, May 29, June 16, October 23 and 28,

1987, https://heinonline.org/HOL/LandingPage?handle=hein.cbhear/usppgooo1
&div=2&id=&page=.

57. Statement of Richard Murphy, "U.S. Policy in the Persian Gulf."

58. Statement of Sen. Larry Pressler, "U.S. Policy in the Persian Gulf," hearings before Committee on Foreign Relations, U.S. Senate, 100th Congress, 1st session, May 29, June 16, October 23 and 28, 1987, https://heinonline.org/HOL/LandingPage?handle=hein.cbhear/usppgooo1&div=2&id=&page=.

59. Statement of Richard Murphy, "U.S. Policy in the Persian Gulf."

60. Hearings before Committee on Foreign Relations, "U.S. Policy in the Persian Gulf."

61. Hearings before Committee on Foreign Relations, "U.S. Policy in the Persian Gulf."

62. Statement of Sen. Claiborne Pell, "U.S. Policy in the Persian Gulf," hearings before Committee on Foreign Relations, U.S. Senate, 100th Congress, 1st session, May 29, June 16, October 23 and 28, 1987, https://heinonline.org/HOL/LandingPage?handle=hein.cbhear/usppgooo1&div=2&id=&page=.

Chapter Two

1. Richard Haass, interview with author, April 13, 2023.

2. Richard Haass, interview with author, April 13, 2023.

3. President George H. W. Bush, "Inaugural Address," January 20, 1989 (emphasis added); full text and audio available from the Miller Center, University of Virginia, https://millercenter.org/the-presidency/presidential-speeches/january-20-1989-inaugural-address.

4. Richard Haass, interview with author, April 13, 2023.

5. Transcript of interview with Robert M. Gates, July 23–24, 2000, College Station, Texas, George H. W. Bush Oral History Project, University of Virginia, https://millercenter.org/the-presidency/presidential-oral-histories/robert-m-gates-deputy-director-central (italics added).

6. James A. Baker III, *The Politics of Diplomacy: Revolution, War & Peace, 1989-1992* (Putnam, 1995), 262.

7. Robert S. Litwak, *Rogue States and U.S. Foreign Policy: Containment after the Cold War* (Woodrow Wilson Center Press, 2000).

8. White House, National Security Review 10, "U.S. Policy Toward the Persian Gulf," February 22, 1989, https://irp.fas.org/offdocs/nsr/nsr10.pdf.

9. CIA Secret Memorandum, U.S. Central Intelligence Agency, National Intelligence Officer for the Near East and South Asia, "Response to National Security Review-10: U.S. Policy toward the Persian Gulf," March 3, 1989, https://search.proquest.com/government-official-publications/response-national-security-review-10-u-s-policy/docview/2321518886/se-2?accountid=25333.

10. White House, National Security Directive 26, "U.S. Policy toward the Persian Gulf," October 2, 1989, https://irp.fas.org/offdocs/nsd/nsd26.pdf.

11. White House, NSD 26, "U.S. Policy toward the Persian Gulf," October 2, 1989.

12. Hussein Banai, Malcolm Byrne, and John Tirman, *Republics of Myth: Na-*

tional Narratives and the U.S.–Iran Conflict (Johns Hopkins University Press, 2022).

13. George H. W. Bush and Brent Scowcroft, *A World Transformed* (Vintage, 1999), 566.

14. White House, Memorandum of Telephone Conversation, "Telcon with Chancellor Kohl of Germany," SECRET, February 18, 1991, George H. W. Bush Presidential Library, Memcoms and Telcons, printed in full in Malcolm Byrne and Kian Byrne, *Worlds Apart: A Documentary History of US–Iranian Relations, 1978–2018* (Cambridge University Press, 2022), 146–149.

15. Transcript of interview with Robert M. Gates, July 23–24, 2000, College Station, Texas, George H. W. Bush Oral History Project, University of Virginia.

16. Bush and Scowcroft, *A World Transformed*, 433.

17. See David Crist, *The Twilight War: The Secret History of America's Thirty-Year Conflict with Iran* (Penguin, 2013).

18. Dennis Ross, interview with author, January 19, 2022.

19. Dennis Ross, interview with author, January 19, 2022.

20. Dennis Ross, interview with author, January 19, 2022.

21. See Dalia Dassa Kaye, *Beyond the Handshake: Multilateral Cooperation in the Arab-Israeli Peace Process* (Columbia University Press, 2001).

22. Dennis Ross, interview with author, January 19, 2022.

23. See the *New York Times* report: https://www.nytimes.com/1989/08/01/world/group-beirut-says-it-hanged-us-colonel-2d-threat-issued-bush-convenes-security.html.

24. White House, Memorandum of Conversation, "Telephone Conversation with Sultan Qaboos of Oman," CONFIDENTIAL, August 3, 1989; original source, George H. W. Bush Presidential Library, Memcons and Telcons, printed in Byrne and Byrne, *Worlds Apart*, 142–145.

25. White House, Memorandum of Conversation, "Telephone Conversation with Sultan Qaboos of Oman," CONFIDENTIAL, August 3, 1989, in Byrne and Byrne, *Worlds Apart*, 142–145.

26. White House, Memorandum of Conversation, "Telephone Conversation with Sultan Qaboos of Oman," CONFIDENTIAL, August 3, 1989, in Byrne and Byrne, *Worlds Apart*, 142–145.

27. Banai, Byrne, and Tirman, *Republics of Myth*, 116.

28. Banai, Byrne, and Tirman, *Republics of Myth*, 116.

29. Bruce Riedel, interview with author, April 22, 2021.

30. Bruce Riedel, interview with author, April 22, 2021.

31. Banai, Byrne, and Tirman, *Republics of Myth*, 117, quoting from the memoir, Giandomenico Picco, *Man without a Gun: One Diplomat's Secret Struggle to Free the Hostages, Fight Terrorism, and End a War* (Crown, 1999), 3–4.

32. Henry Rome, "United States Iran Policy and the Role of Israel, 1990–1993," *Diplomacy and Statecraft* 30, no. 4 (2019): 729–754.

33. For an account of these interactions from a former U.N. diplomat, see Picco, *Man without a Gun*.

34. Kenneth M. Pollack, *The Persian Puzzle: The Conflict between Iran and America* (Random House, 2004).

35. John Ghazvinian, *America and Iran: A History, 1720 to the Present* (Knopf, 2021).

36. Elaine Sciolino, "After a Fresh Look, U.S. Decides to Still Steer Clear of Iran," *The New York Times*, June 7, 1992.

37. Richard Haass, interview with author, April 13, 2023. Also see Miller Center, George H. W. Bush Oral History Project, transcript, Interview with Richard Haass, May 27, 2004, https://millercenter.org/the-presidency/presidential -oral-histories/richard-haass-oral-history.

38. Ghazvinian, *America and Iran*, 390. Ghazvinian argues that Israel had major impact on U.S. thinking during this period and that Israel has a unique ability "to influence public narratives in the United States" (396).

39. Rome, "United States Iran Policy and the Role of Israel, 1990–1993."

40. Rome, "United States Iran Policy and the Role of Israel, 1990–1993."

41. Rome, "United States Iran Policy and the Role of Israel, 1990–1993."

42. Bruce Riedel, interview with author, April 22, 2021. Riedel reiterated that Clinton's containment policies toward Iran were essentially a continuation of where Bush had left U.S. policy.

43. Martin Indyk, *Innocent Abroad: An Intimate Account of American Peace Diplomacy in the Middle East* (Simon and Schuster, 2014), 31.

44. Madeleine Albright, interview with author, July 27, 2021.

45. Madeleine K. Albright, oral history transcript, August 30, 2006, Miller Center, University of Virginia, https://millercenter.org/the-presidency/presiden tial-oral-histories/madeleine-k-albright-oral-history.

46. Indyk, *Innocent Abroad*, 6.

47. Martin Indyk, interview with author, April 28, 2021. Indyk shared that his main exposure to Iran before entering the U.S. government was during the revolutionary period, when he worked for the Australian government. As an analyst, he wrote an assessment suggesting that the fall of the Shah's regime was likely but was not able to convince his superiors, who were influenced by American intelligence officials who thought the "sun will never set" on the Shah.

48. Martin Indyk, interview with author, April 28, 2021.

49. Martin Indyk, interview with author, April 28, 2021.

50. Martin Indyk, interview with author, April 28, 2021.

51. See Indyk, *Innocent Abroad*.

52. Martin Indyk, interview with author, April 28, 2021.

53. See Martin Indyk, "The Clinton Administration's Approach to the Middle East," keynote address to the Soref Symposium, Washington Institute for Near East Policy, May 18, 1993, https://www.washingtoninstitute.org/policy-analysis/ clinton-administrations-approach-middle-east.

54. Martin Indyk, interview with author, April 28, 2021.

55. Martin Indyk, interview with author, April 28, 2021.

56. Martin Indyk, interview with author, April 28, 2021.

57. I was not able to verify the fatwa order with other U.S. officials serving during that time. Indyk died before the publication of this book.

58. Martin Indyk, interview with author, April 28, 2021.

59. Dennis Ross, interview with author, January 19, 2022.

60. Dennis Ross, interview with author, January 19, 2022.

61. Indyk, *Innocent Abroad*.

62. Todd S. Purdum, "Clinton to Order a Trade Embargo against Tehran," *The New York Times*, May 1, 1995.

63. Purdum, "Clinton to Order a Trade Embargo against Tehran."

64. Purdum, "Clinton to Order a Trade Embargo against Tehran."

65. Indyk, *Innocent Abroad*, 168.

66. Martin Indyk, interview with author, April 28, 2021.

67. Martin Indyk, interview with author, April 28, 2021.

68. Howard Berman, interview with author, September 29, 2021.

69. Howard Berman, interview with author, September 29, 2021.

70. Howard Berman, interview with author, September 29, 2021.

71. Howard Berman, interview with author, September 29, 2021.

72. "U.S. Sanctions on Iran: Next Steps," hearing before House Subcommittee on International Economic Policy and Trade of Committee on International Relations, 104th Congress, May 2, 1995, https://heinonline.org/HOL/Page?public=true&handle=hein.cbhear/cblhacteoo01&div=2&start_page=1&collection=congrec&set_as_cursor=1&men_tab=srchresults.

73. "U.S. Sanctions on Iran: Next Steps," hearing before House Subcommittee on International Economic Policy and Trade of Committee on International Relations, 104th Congress, May 2, 1995.

74. "U.S. Sanctions on Iran: Next Steps," Hearing before House Subcommittee on International Economic Policy and Trade of Committee on International Relations, 104th Congress, May 2, 1995.

75. "U.S. Sanctions on Iran: Next Steps," Hearing before House Subcommittee on International Economic Policy and Trade of Committee on International Relations, 104th Congress, May 2, 1995.

76. "U.S. Sanctions on Iran: Next Steps," Hearing before House Subcommittee on International Economic Policy and Trade of Committee on International Relations, 104th Congress, May 2, 1995.

77. Martin Indyk, interview with author, April 28, 2021.

78. Indyk, *Innocent Abroad*, 216.

79. Madeleine Albright, interview with author, July 27, 2021.

80. Madeleine Albright, *Madam Secretary: A Memoir* (Miramax, 2001), 320.

81. Albright, *Madam Secretary*.

82. Martin Indyk, interview with author, April 28, 2021.

83. Albright, *Madam Secretary*, 323.

84. Byrne and Byrne, *Worlds Apart*, 164. The full text of the letter is reproduced on pages 164–165 as document 35, White House, Letter, President Clinton for President Khatami, "Message to President Khatami from President Clinton," Classification Unknown, June 1999.

85. Secretary of State Madeleine K. Albright, remarks before American-Iranian Council, March 17, 2000, Washington, D.C., https://1997-2001.state.gov /statements/2000/000317.html.

86. Secretary of State Madeleine K. Albright, remarks before American-Iranian Council, March 17, 2000, Washington, D.C.

87. Madeleine Albright, interview with author, July 27, 2021.

88. Madeleine Albright, interview with author, July 27, 2021. It is important to note that views among the Iranian American community are diverse and have evolved since Albright's time, as I address in later chapters.

89. Former senior State Department official, interview with author, November 1, 2024.

90. Madeleine Albright, interview with author, July 27, 2021.

91. Bruce Riedel, interview with author, April 22, 2021.

92. Bruce Riedel, interview with author, April 22, 2021.

93. Bruce Riedel, interview with author, April 22, 2021.

94. Bruce Riedel, interview with author, April 22, 2021.

95. Martin Indyk, interview with author, April 28, 2021.

96. Martin Indyk, interview with author, April 28, 2021.

97. Litwak, *Rogue States and U.S. Foreign Policy*.

Chapter Three

1. White House, President George W. Bush, "President Delivers State of the Union Address," The President's State of the Union Address, The United States Capitol, Washington, DC, January 29, 2002, https://georgewbush-whitehouse. archives.gov/news/releases/2002/01/20020129-11.html.

2. Stephen Hadley, interview with author, May 25, 2023.

3. See George W. Bush, *Decision Points* (Crown, 2010), 233.

4. Condoleezza Rice, *No Higher Honor: A Memoir of My Years in Washington* (Crown, 2011), 150.

5. Rice, *No Higher Honor*, 150.

6. Ryan Crocker, interview with author, August 22, 2023.

7. Ryan Crocker, interview with author, August 22, 2023.

8. Ryan Crocker, interview with author, August 22, 2023.

9. Ryan Crocker, interview with author, August 22, 2023.

10. See Stephen J. Hadley, "The George W. Bush Administration," *The Iran Primer*, U.S. Institute of Peace, October 5, 2010, https://iranprimer.usip.org/ resource/george-w-bush-administration, 2.

11. See Michael Singh, "Postscript," in Stephen J. Hadley, ed., *Hand-Off: The Foreign Policy George W. Bush Passed to Barack Obama* (Brookings Institution Press, 2023), 295.

12. Crist argues that the Pentagon's Joint Staff recommended building on Clinton's outreach. See David Crist, *The Twilight War: The Secret History of America's Thirty-Year Conflict with Iran* (Penguin, 2013).

13. Crist, *The Twilight War*.

14. Ryan Crocker represented the U.S. side in these talks. In his interview with

me, Crocker acknowledged that his Iranian counterparts included representatives of the IRGC as well as Foreign Ministry diplomats. Ryan Crocker, interview with author, August 22, 2023.

15. Ryan Crocker, interview with author, August 22, 2023.

16. Zalmay Khalilzad, *The Envoy: From Kabul to the White House, My Journey through a Turbulent World* (St. Martin's Press, 2016), 119.

17. Khalilzad, *The Envoy*, 120.

18. Rice, *No Higher Honor*, 163

19. Rice, *No Higher Honor*, 164.

20. William J. Burns, *The Back Channel: A Memoir of American Diplomacy and the Case for Its Renewal* (Random House, 2019), 179.

21. Elliott Abrams, interview with author, November 20, 2024.

22. Burns, *The Back Channel*, 196.

23. Richard Haass, interview with author, April 13, 2023.

24. Ryan Crocker, interview with author, August 22, 2023.

25. Ryan Crocker, interview with author, August 22, 2023.

26. Ryan Crocker, interview with author, August 22, 2023.

27. Ryan Crocker, interview with author, August 22, 2023.

28. Ryan Crocker, interview with author, August 22, 2023.

29. Ryan Crocker, interview with author, August 22, 2023.

30. Ryan Crocker, interview with author, August 22, 2023.

31. Ryan Crocker, interview with author, August 22, 2023.

32. Ryan Crocker, interview with author, August 22, 2023.

33. Ryan Crocker, interview with author, August 22, 2023.

34. Ryan Crocker, interview with author, August 22, 2023.

35. James Dobbins, interview with author, October 1, 2021.

36. James Dobbins, "Negotiating with Iran: Reflections from Personal Experience," *The Washington Quarterly* 33, no. 1 (2010): 152.

37. James Dobbins, interview with author, October 1, 2021.

38. James Dobbins, *Foreign Service: Five Decades on the Frontlines of American Diplomacy* (Brookings Institution Press, 2017), 235.

39. Dobbins, *Foreign Service*, 235.

40. Dobbins, *Foreign Service*.

41. James Dobbins, interview with author, October 1, 2021.

42. Dobbins, *Foreign Service*.

43. Khalilzad notes that he and Dobbins had coffee with Zarif and Taherian every morning during the talks. See Khalilzad, *The Envoy*, 120.

44. Dobbins, *Foreign Service*, 239.

45. George Tenet, *At the Center of the Storm: My Years at the CIA* (Harper Collins, 2007), 311.

46. Tenet, *At the Center of the Storm*, 311–312.

47. Tenet, *At the Center of the Storm*, 312.

48. Tenet, *At the Center of the Storm*, 314.

49. Tenet, *At the Center of the Storm*, 314.

50. Elliott Abrams, interview with author, November 20, 2024.

51. Dobbins, *Foreign Service.*

52. Hadley, "The George W. Bush Administration."

53. Dobbins, *Foreign Service*, 258.

54. Dobbins, *Foreign Service.*

55. James Dobbins, interview with author, October 1, 2021.

56. Quoted in Barbara Slavin, "The Global War on Terror Wrecked Relations with Iran," Atlantic Council, September 7, 2021, https://www.atlanticcouncil.org /commentary/article/the-global-war-on-terrorism-wrecked-relations-with-iran/.

57. Richard Haass, interview with author, April 13, 2023.

58. Richard Haass, interview with author, April 13, 2023.

59. Richard Haass, interview with author, April 13, 2023.

60. Burns, *The Back Channel*, 340.

61. Burns, *The Back Channel*, 340.

62. Burns, *The Back Channel*, 340.

63. Khalilzad, *The Envoy*, 164.

64. Khalilzad, *The Envoy*, 165.

65. Khalilzad, *The Envoy*, 165.

66. Khalilzad, *The Envoy*, 165.

67. Ryan Crocker, interview with author, August 22, 2023.

68. Ryan Crocker, interview with author, August 22, 2023.

69. Bush, *Decision Points*, 415.

70. Bush, *Decision Points*, 416.

71. Bush, *Decision Points*, 417.

72. Bush, *Decision Points*, 420.

73. "What's Next in the War on Terrorism?" Hearing before Committee on Foreign Relations, U.S. Senate, 107th Congress, 2nd session, February 7, 2002, https://heinonline.org/HOL/LandingPage?handle=hein.cbhear/ cbhearings71328&div=2&id=&page=.

74. "Hearings to Examine Threats, Responses, and Regional Considerations Surrounding Iraq," Hearings before Committee on Foreign Relations, U.S. Senate, 107th Congress, 2nd session, July 31 and August 1, 2002, https://heinonline .org/HOL/LandingPage?handle=hein.cbhear/cbhearings71538&div=2&id= &page=.

75. Hadley, "The George W. Bush Administration."

76. Crist, *The Twilight War.*

77. Elliott Abrams, interview with author, November 20, 2024.

78. Edward P. Djerejian (with William Martin), *Danger and Opportunity: An American Ambassador's Journey through the Middle East* (Threshold Editions, 2008), 203.

79. State Department official, interview with author, September 8, 2022.

80. For details about the evolution of the Iran Watcher initiative and State Department diplomatic efforts to cover Iran, see Jillian Burns, "The Iran Watcher Program: A Different Kind of Teleworking," *The Foreign Service Journal*, March 2015, https://afsa.org/iran-watcher-program-different-kind-teleworking.

81. State Department official, interview with author, September 8, 2022.

82. Jillian Burns, "The Iran Watcher Program."

83. William Burns, *The Back Channel*, 341.

84. Rice discusses this initiative in *No Higher Honor*, 626.

85. Rice, *No Higher Honor*, 626.

86. Rice, *No Higher Honor*, 626.

87. Elliott Abrams, interview with author, November 20, 2024.

88. Elliott Abrams, interview with author, November 20, 2024.

89. Rice, *No Higher Honor*, 627.

90. Rice, *No Higher Honor*, 628.

91. Former senior State Department official, interview with author, November 1, 2024.

92. Elliott Abrams, interview with author, November 20, 2024.

93. Gary Sick made this argument in interview with author, May 3, 2021.

94. Jonah Goldberg, "Baghdad Delenda Est, Part Two: Get On with It," *National Review*, April 23, 2002.

95. Dobbins, *Foreign Service*, 245.

96. David Johnston, "Pentagon Analyst Gets 12 Years for Disclosing Data," *The New York Times*, January 20, 2006.

97. Nathan Guttman, "Once Labeled an AIPAC Spy, Larry Franklin Tells His Story," *The Forward*, July 1, 2009.

98. Richard Haass, interview with author, April 13, 2023.

99. Frederic Wehrey et al., *The Iraq Effect: The Middle East after the Iraq War* (RAND, 2010).

100. Richard Haass, interview with author, April 13, 2023.

101. Richard Haass, interview with author, April 13, 2023.

102. The most prominent advocates of the argument that the pro-Israel lobby influences U.S. foreign policy are John J. Mearsheimer and Stephen M. Walt, *The Israel Lobby and U.S. Foreign Policy* (Farrar, Straus and Giroux, 2007).

103. "Increasing Our Nonproliferation Efforts in the Former Soviet Union," Hearing before Committee on Foreign Relations, U.S. Senate, 107th Congress, 2nd session, April 23, 2002, https://www.govinfo.gov/content/pkg/CHRG-107shrg81833/html/CHRG-107shrg81833.htm.

104. Hadley, "The George W. Bush Administration."

105. National Security Council, Memorandum for the Record, January 16, 2009, in Hadley, ed., *Hand-Off*, 287.

106. Rice, *No Higher Honor*, 336.

107. Rice, *No Higher Honor*, 337.

108. Rice, *No Higher Honor*, 461.

109. Rice, *No Higher Honor*, 461.

110. Jack Straw, "The West Should Risk Doing a Deal with Iran," *The Telegraph*, September 24, 2014.

111. Rice, *No Higher Honor*, 461.

112. Rice, *No Higher Honor*, 463.

113. Rice, *No Higher Honor*, 463.

114. Rice, *No Higher Honor*, 464.

115. Rice, *No Higher Honor,* 537.

116. Rice, *No Higher Honor,* 537.

117. Rice, *No Higher Honor,* 465.

118. Bush, *Decision Points,* 419.

119. The five permanent members of the U.N. Security Council are the United States, Russia, China, France, and the United Kingdom. The P5 + 1 consists of these five permanent members plus Germany. The grouping is also referred to as the E3 + 3, incorporating the three primary European players (United Kingdom, France, and Germany) as well as global powers (United States, China, and Russia).

120. Hadley, ed., *Hand-Off.*

121. Hadley, ed., *Hand-Off.*

122. John Ghazvinian, *America and Iran: A History, 1720 to the Present* (Knopf, 2021), 476.

123. NSC transition memo, reprinted in Hadley, ed., *Hand-Off,* 292.

124. Dobbins, "Negotiating with Iran."

125. Stephen Hadley argues that such talks accomplished very little and deteriorated once Iran supported terrorist groups attacking U.S. forces. See Hadley, "The George W. Bush Administration."

126. NSC memo, reprinted in Hadley, ed., *Hand-Off,* 292.

127. NSC memo, reprinted in Hadley, ed., *Hand-Off,* 293.

128. Singh, "Postscript," 295.

Chapter Four

1. Howard Berman, interview with author, October 8, 2021.

2. Howard Berman, interview with author, October 8, 2021.

3. John Ghazvinian, for example, makes this argument in *America and Iran: A History, 1720 to the Present* (Knopf, 2021).

4. Ben Rhodes, interview with author, November 4, 2024.

5. Ben Rhodes, interview with author, November 4, 2024.

6. Ben Rhodes, interview with author, November 4, 2024.

7. For an explanation of the Green movement's origins and evolution, see Abbas Milani, "The Green Movement," *The Iran Primer,* U.S. Institute of Peace, October 6, 2010, https://iranprimer.usip.org/resource/green-movement.

8. Ben Rhodes, interview with author, November 4, 2024.

9. See David Crist, *The Twilight War: The Secret History of America's Thirty-Year Conflict with Iran* (Penguin, 2013).

10. Stephen Heintz, interview with author, November 8, 2024. Heintz, the president of the Rockefeller Brothers Fund (RBF), has supported and participated in track two dialogues with Iranian experts and former officials for more than twenty years and introduced Senator Kerry to influential Iranians, including former diplomats, through an initiative that started through the United Nations Association. For further details on RBF's Iran initiative, see "RBF Releases Report on U.S.–Iran Track II Dialogue," August 3, 2010, https://www.rbf.org/news/rbf-releases-report-us-iran-track-ii-dialogue.

11. Trita Parsi, for example, argued that the JCPOA was not just a nuclear deal but "the final chapter of a thirty-five year battle over the geopolitical order in the region" (Parsi, *Losing an Enemy* [Yale, 2017], 9).

12. Former senior U.S. official, interview with author, April 19, 2021.

13. "Full Text: Obama's Foreign Policy Speech," *The Guardian*, July 16, 2008.

14. "Full Text: Obama's Foreign Policy Speech," *The Guardian*, July 16, 2008.

15. "Remarks by the President at the University of Cairo," June 4, 2009, White House Archives, https://obamawhitehouse.archives.gov/the-press-office/remarks -president-cairo-university-6-04-09.

16. "Remarks by President Obama to the Australian Parliament," November 17, 2011, White House Archives, https://obamawhitehouse.archives.gov/the-press -office/2011/11/17/remarks-president-obama-australian-parliament.

17. "President Barack Obama's Inaugural Address," January 21, 2009, White House Archives, https://obamawhitehouse.archives.gov/blog/2009/01/21/ president-Barack-obamas-inaugural-address.

18. "Obama Tells Al Arabiya Peace Talks Should Resume," transcript of interview with Hisham Melham, *Al Arabiya*, January 27, 2009, https://english.alarabiya .net/articles/2009%2F01%2F27%2F65087.

19. Videotaped Remarks by the President in Celebration of Nowruz, The White House Archives, March 20, 2009, https://obamawhitehouse.archives.gov/ the-press-office/videotaped-remarks-president-celebration-nowruz.

20. William J. Burns, *The Back Channel: A Memoir of American Diplomacy and the Case for its Renewal* (Random House, 2019), 346.

21. Burns, *The Back Channel*, 346.

22. Burns, *The Back Channel*, 347.

23. Burns, *The Back Channel*, 348.

24. Burns, *The Back Channel*, 348.

25. Burns, *The Back Channel*, 348.

26. Ben Rhodes, interview with author, November 4, 2024.

27. Burns, *The Back Channel*, 348.

28. Quoted in Kenneth Katzman, "Iran: U.S. Concerns and Policy Responses," Congressional Research Service Report, March 11, 2010, https://www.everycrsre port.com/files/20100311_RL32048_c58c1381139a62322a4c7533ac6124deafc16c99 .pdf.

29. Katzman, "Iran: U.S. Concerns and Policy Responses."

30. Stephen Collinson, "A Rare Moment of Public Self-criticism by a Former President," CNN, October 18, 2022.

31. Former senior U.S. official, interview with author, April 19, 2021.

32. Steven Hurst, "The Iranian Nuclear Negotiations as a Two-Level Game: The Importance of Domestic Politics," *Diplomacy and Statecraft* 27, no. 3 (2016): 551.

33. Barack Obama, *A Promised Land* (Crown, 2020), 318.

34. Former senior U.S. official, interview with author, April 19, 2021.

35. Hurst, "The Iranian Nuclear Negotiations as a Two-Level Game."

36. Hurst, "The Iranian Nuclear Negotiations as a Two-Level Game."

37. Ghazvinian, *America and Iran,* 487.

38. Former U.S. official, interview with author, July 28, 2021.

39. Dennis Ross, interview with author, January 19, 2022.

40. Obama, *A Promised Land,* 454.

41. Obama, *A Promised Land,* 454.

42. Howard Berman, interview with author, October 8, 2021.

43. See, for example, "No Deal Is Better Than a Bad Deal," *Jewish Standard,* July 23, 2015.

44. Howard Berman, interview with author, October 8, 2021.

45. Howard Berman, interview with author, October 8, 2021.

46. Daniel Poneman and Sahar Nowrouzzadeh, "The Deal That Got Away: The 2009 Nuclear Fuel Swap with Iran," Belfer Center for Science and International Affairs Paper, Harvard University, January 2021, https://www.belfercenter.org/publication/deal-got-away-2009-nuclear-fuel-swap-iran. Both authors of this Belfer Center report were former U.S. government officials serving in the Obama administration. As deputy secretary of energy, Poneman led the U.S. delegation in the technical negotiations over the TRR fuel swap proposal in October 2009.

47. Poneman and Nowrouzzadeh, "The Deal That Got Away."

48. Poneman and Nowrouzzadeh, "The Deal That Got Away," 12.

49. Poneman and Nowrouzzadeh, "The Deal That Got Away," 17.

50. Poneman and Nowrouzzadeh, "The Deal That Got Away," 40.

51. Poneman and Nowrouzzadeh, "The Deal That Got Away," 41.

52. Burns, *The Back Channel,* 353.

53. Former U.S. official, interview with author, July 28, 2021.

54. Quoted in Poneman and Nowrouzzadeh, "The Deal That Got Away," 38–39.

55. Burns, *The Back Channel,* 353.

56. Quoted in Poneman and Nowrouzzadeh, "The Deal That Got Away," 30.

57. Burns, *The Back Channel,* 354.

58. Former U.S. official, interview with author, July 28, 2021.

59. Former U.S. official, interview with author, July 28, 2021.

60. For an account of the congressional pressure on President Obama and the influence of AIPAC, see Ghazvinian, *America and Iran,* 497.

61. Jeffrey Goldberg, "The Point of No Return," *The Atlantic,* September 2010.

62. Ronen Bergman, "Will Israel Attack Iran," *The New York Times Magazine,* January 25, 2012.

63. Trita Parsi, *A Single Roll of the Dice: Obama's Diplomacy with Iran* (Yale, 2012).

64. Parsi, *A Single Roll of the Dice,* 105.

65. Burns, *The Back Channel,* 355.

66. Former U.S. official, interview with author, July 28, 2021.

67. Former senior U.S. official, interview with author, April 19, 2021.

68. Former U.S. official, interview with author, July 28, 2021.

69. See Ellen Nakashima and Joby Warrick, "Stuxnet Was the Work of U.S. and Israeli Experts, Officials Say," *The Washington Post,* June 2, 2012.

70. Former senior U.S. official, interview with author, April 19, 2021.

71. Former senior U.S. official, interview with author, April 19, 2021.

72. Yaacov Amidror, interview with author, February 28, 2023.

73. Former U.S. official, interview with author, July 28, 2021.

74. Yaacov Amidror, interview with author, February 28, 2023.

75. Yaacov Amidror, interview with author, February 28, 2023.

76. Ben Rhodes, interview with author, November 4, 2024.

77. Burns, *The Back Channel*, 356.

78. Parsi, *Losing an Enemy*, 169.

79. Parsi, *Losing an Enemy*, 169.

80. Puneet Talwar, "Iran in the Balance," *Foreign Affairs*, July–August 2001.

81. Parsi, *Losing an Enemy*, 169.

82. Ben Rhodes, interview with author, November 4, 2024.

83. Wendy Sherman, "How We Got the Iran Deal: And Why We'll Miss it," *Foreign Affairs*, September–October 2018.

84. Burns, *The Back Channel*, 359.

85. Burns, *The Back Channel*, 361.

86. Burns, *The Back Channel*, 361.

87. Burns, *The Back Channel*, 362.

88. Ben Rhodes, interview with author, November 4, 2024.

89. Ben Rhodes, interview with author, November 4, 2024.

90. Sherman, "How We Got the Iran Deal."

91. For the text of the interim agreement, see U.S. Institute of Peace, "The Interim Nuclear Deal," *The Iran Primer*, June 11, 2015, https://iranprimer.usip.org/resource/interim-nuclear-deal.

92. Burns, *The Back Channel*, 383.

93. Cited in Poneman and Nowrouzzadeh, "The Deal That Got Away," 41.

94. Burns, *The Back Channel*, 365.

95. Poneman and Nowrouzzadeh, "The Deal That Got Away," 41.

96. Ben Rhodes, interview with author, November 4, 2024.

97. Ben Rhodes, interview with author, November 4, 2024.

98. Ben Rhodes, interview with author, November 4, 2024.

99. Ben Rhodes, interview with author, November 4, 2024.

100. Sherman, "How We Got the Iran Deal."

101. For the full text of the final agreement, see "Joint Comprehensive Plan of Action, Vienna, 14 July 2015," https://2009-2017.state.gov/documents/organization/245317.pdf.

102. Sherman, "How We Got the Iran Deal."

103. Dalia Dassa Kaye and Jeffrey Martini, *The Days after a Deal with Iran: Regional Responses to a Final Nuclear Agreement* (RAND Corporation, 2014).

104. See "Netanyahu Likens Iran to Nazis," *DW*, April 16, 2015 , https://www.dw.com/en/netanyahu-likens-iran-to-nazis-in-holocaust-remembrance-speech/a-18386607.

105. Dalia Dassa Kaye, *Israel's Iran Policies after the Nuclear Deal* (RAND Corporation, 2016).

106. Kaye, *Israel's Iran Policies after the Nuclear Deal.*

107. Kaye, *Israel's Iran Policies after the Nuclear Deal.*

108. Dalia Dassa Kaye, "A Different Israeli Take on Iran," *Los Angeles Times*, November 12, 2013.

109. Kaye, *Israel's Iran Policies after the Nuclear Deal.*

110. Kaye, *Israel's Iran Policies after the Nuclear Deal.*

111. Sherman, "How We Got the Iran Deal."

112. Sherman, "How We Got the Iran Deal."

113. Sherman, "How We Got the Iran Deal.".

114. "Preventing a Nuclear Iran," Hearing before Committee on Foreign Affairs, House of Representatives, 113th Congress, 1st Session, May 15, 2013, https://www.govinfo.gov/content/pkg/CHRG-113hhrg80940/html/CHRG-113hhrg80 940.htm.

115. "Preventing a Nuclear Iran," Hearing before Committee on Foreign Affairs, House of Representatives, 113th Congress, 1st Session, May 15, 2013.

116. "Implementation of the Iran Nuclear Deal," Joint Hearing before Subcommittee on Middle East and North Africa and Subcommittee on Terrorism, Nonproliferation, and Trade of Committee on Foreign Affairs, House of Representatives, 113th Congress, 2nd Session, January 28, 2014, https://docs.house.gov/meet ings/FA/FA13/20140128/101679/HHRG-113-FA13-Transcript-20140128.pdf.

117. "Preventing a Nuclear Iran," Hearing before Committee on Foreign Affairs, House of Representatives, 113th Congress, 1st Session, May 15, 2013.

118. "Preventing a Nuclear Iran," Hearing before Committee on Foreign Affairs, House of Representatives, 113th Congress, 1st Session, May 15, 2013.

119. "Implementation of the Iran Nuclear Deal," Joint Hearing before Subcommittee on Middle East and North Africa and Subcommittee on Terrorism, Nonproliferation, and Trade of Committee on Foreign Affairs, House of Representatives, 113th Congress, 2nd Session, January 28, 2014.

120. White House, "Remarks by the President on the Iran Nuclear Deal," American University, Washington, D.C., August 5, 2015, https://obamawhitehouse .archives.gov/the-press-office/2015/08/05/remarks-president-iran-nuclear-deal#:~ :text=We%20now%20have%20the%20opportunity,be%20proud%20of%20this% 20achievement.

121. Ben Rhodes, interview with author, November 4, 2024.

122. Gerald F. Seib, "An Expert View: Accept the Deal But Move to Contain Iran," *The Wall Street Journal*, July 20, 2015.

123. Seib, "An Expert View: Accept the Deal but Move to Contain Iran."

124. Obama, *A Promised Land*, 452.

Chapter Five

1. The United States hosts the largest numbers of the Iranian diaspora in the world, though many Iranian emigrants migrated to European countries. Germany, the United Kingdom, and Sweden host the largest numbers of Iranians in Europe. In the United States, California, particularly Los Angeles, has traditionally attracted the largest numbers of Iranian migrants, but migration patterns

among the Iranian diaspora, particularly younger Iranians, appear to be changing. See "Mapping the Iranian Diaspora in America," featuring the work of UCLA professor Kevan Harris, UCLA International Institute, February 16, 2023, https://international.ucla.edu/institute2/article/262699.

2. See, for example, the Iran pages of Human Rights Watch and Amnesty International, respectively: https://www.hrw.org/middle-east/north-africa/iran; https://www.amnesty.org/en/location/middle-east-and-north-africa/middle -east/iran/.

3. Elliott Abrams, who became Trump's special representative on Iran in 2020, asserts that this meeting was a "serious possibility" and he's "happy it didn't happen." Elliott Abrams, interview with author, November 20, 2024.

4. White House, "National Security Strategy of the United States of America," December 2017, https://trumpwhitehouse.archives.gov/wp-content/uploads/2017/ 12/NSS-Final-12-18-2017-0905.pdf.

5. Adam Entous, "Donald Trump's New World Order: How the President, Israel, and the Gulf States Plan to Fight Iran—and Leave the Obama Years Behind," *The New Yorker*, June 11, 2018.

6. Donald J. Trump, Twitter (X) account @realDonaldTrump, October 7, 2019.

7. Helene Cooper, "Military Shifts Focus to Threats by Russia and China, Not Terrorism," *The New York Times*, January 19, 2018.

8. Entous, "Donald Trump's New World Order"; Peter Baker and Susan Glasser, *The Divider: Trump in the White House, 2017–2021* (Anchor Books, 2022), 513.

9. Jared Kushner, *Breaking History: A White House Memoir* (Broadside Books, 2022), 61.

10. Kushner, *Breaking History*, 61.

11. Entous, "Donald Trump's New World Order."

12. Entous, "Donald Trump's New World Order."

13. Entous, "Donald Trump's New World Order."

14. Baker and Glasser, *The Divider*, 68.

15. Baker and Glasser, *The Divider*, 69.

16. Baker and Glasser, *The Divider*, 291.

17. Kushner, *Breaking History*, 79.

18. Kushner, *Breaking History*, 167.

19. Peter Baker and Susan Glasser attribute the phrase to former Obama (and Biden) senior Pentagon official Colin Kahl. See Baker and Glasser, *The Divider*, 66.

20. Bolton refers to the "axis of adults" unfavorably throughout his memoir. See John Bolton, *The Room Where It Happened: A White House Memoir* (Simon and Schuster, 2020), 1–2, 20–21, 213, 237.

21. H. R. McMaster, *Battlegrounds: The Fight to Defend the Free World* (Harper, 2020), 312.

22. McMaster, *Battlegrounds*, 293.

23. McMaster, *Battlegrounds*, 320.

24. Bob Woodward, *Fear: Trump in the White House* (Simon and Schuster, 2018), 110–112.

25. Daniel Lippman, "Inside an Explosive Whisper Campaign That Tried to Sink a Biden Ambassador Pick," *Politico*, December 27, 2021.

26. Baker and Glasser, *The Divider*, 106.

27. Woodward, *Fear*, 52.

28. Woodward, *Fear*, 52–53.

29. Baker and Glasser, *The Divider*, 183.

30. U.S. Institute of Peace, "Secretary Mattis on Iran Nuclear Deal," *The Iran Primer*, April 30, 2018, https://iranprimer.usip.org/blog/2018/apr/27/secretary-mat tis-iran-nuclear-deal.

31. Baker and Glasser, *The Divider*, 182.

32. Quoted in Baker and Glasser, *The Divider*, 591.

33. Kushner, *Breaking History*, 115.

34. See Brian Hook's testimony to SFRC, February 28, 2024, https://www.foreign.senate.gov/imo/media/doc/0217a85a-ae50-89b2-e9d2-a20d47ffabbc/022824_Hook_Testimony.pdf.

35. Elliott Abrams, interview with author, November 20, 2024.

36. Elliott Abrams, interview with author, November 20, 2024.

37. See Office of Historian, U.S. Department of State, "Travels Abroad of the President," https://history.state.gov/departmenthistory/travels/president.

38. Woodward, *Fear*, 111.

39. Woodward, *Fear*, 112.

40. Quoted in Woodward, *Fear*, 112.

41. Quoted in Woodward, *Fear*, 112.

42. Kushner, *Breaking History*, 87.

43. Kushner, *Breaking History*, 89.

44. Kushner, *Breaking History*, 89.

45. Kushner, *Breaking History*, 87.

46. Woodward, *Fear*, 114.

47. King Abdullah of Jordan coined the phrase "Shia Crescent" to capture Iran's growing regional reach in the aftermath of the 2003 Iraq War. For an assessment of the impact of the war on Iran's regional influence and its limits, see Javad Heiran-Nia, "Retrospective: U.S. Invasion of Iraq Was a Mixed Blessing for Iran," Commentary, Henry L. Stimson Center, March 17, 2023, https://www.stimson.org/2023/retrospective-us-invasion-of-iraq-was-a-mixed-blessing-for-iran/.

48. See, for example, David Adesnik and Behnam Ben Taleblu, with foreword by LTG (Ret.) H. R. McMaster, *Burning Bridge: The Iranian Land Corridor to the Mediterranean* (Foundation for Defense of Democracies Press, June 2019).

49. Michael Wahid Hanna and Dalia Dassa Kaye, "The Limits of Iranian Power," *Survival* 57, no. 5 (2015): 173–198.

50. Karen DeYoung, "Trump Administration Says It's Putting Iran 'On Notice' Following Missile Test," *The Washington Post*, February 1, 2017.

51. Nikki Haley, news conference on Iran nuclear agreement, December 14, 2017, https://www.youtube.com/watch?v=SXaoJKIAxRk.

52. Ned Price, "Why Mike Pompeo Released More bin Laden Files," *The Atlantic*, November 8, 2017.

53. One of the president's tweets stated: "Iran is failing at every level despite the terrible deal made with them by the Obama Administration. The great Iranian people have been repressed for many years. They are hungry for food & for freedom. Along with human rights, the wealth of Iran is being looted. TIME FOR CHANGE!" See Daniella Diaz and Dan Merica, "Trump on Iran: 'Time for change!'" CNN, January 1, 2018.

54. Jack Deutsch, "US Still Pouring Weapons into Yemen War," *Al Monitor*, March 8, 2018, https://www.al-monitor.com/pulse/originals/2018/03/yemen-us-wea pons-saudi-arabia-uae.html.

55. Michael R. Gordon, Timothy Puko, and Summer Said, "U.S. Pursues Saudi Nuclear Deal, Despite Proliferation Risk," *The Wall Street Journal*, February 20, 2018.

56. Sara Elizabeth Williams, "Iran Supreme Leader Is 'New Hitler' Says Saudi Crown Prince," *The Telegraph*, November 25, 2017.

57. Baker and Glasser, *The Divider*, 68.

58. U.S. official, interview with author, July 30, 2021.

59. Baker and Glasser, *The Divider*, 183.

60. Woodward, *Fear*, 130.

61. Woodward, *Fear*, 133.

62. Woodward, *Fear*, 133.

63. John Bolton, "Trump Must Withdraw from Iran Nuclear Deal—Now," *The Hill*, July 16, 2017.

64. Bolton, *The Room Where It Happened*, 23–24.

65. Bolton, *The Room Where It Happened*, 24. Also see Bolton, "How to Get Out of the Iran Nuclear Deal," *National Review*, August 28, 2017.

66. Bolton, *The Room Where It Happened*, 25.

67. See McMaster, *Battlegrounds*.

68. "Trump Extends Iran Nuclear Deal Again," *Politico*, January 12, 2018.

69. White House, "Statement by the President on the Iran Nuclear Deal," January 12, 2018, https://www.whitehouse.gov/briefings-statements/statement-presi dent-iran-nuclear-deal/.

70. "For Now, U.S. Wants Europeans Just to Commit to Improve Iran Deal," Reuters, February 18, 2018.

71. Baker and Glasser, *The Divider*, 184.

72. "Uncertainty over Iran Nuclear Agreement Could Heighten Economic Tensions with Europe," *USA Today*, October 11, 2017.

73. Bolton, *The Room Where It Happened*, 66.

74. Bolton, *The Room Where It Happened*, 69.

75. Bolton, *The Room Where It Happened*, 70.

76. Bolton, *The Room Where It Happened*, 74.

77. Baker and Glasser, *The Divider*, 326.

78. See, for example, Robbie Gramer and Colum Lynch, "Pompeo Creates New Team to Pressure Iran," *Foreign Policy*, August 16, 2018.

79. Team members included: "a former explosives ordnance expert, Jason Shell; David Tessler, a mild-mannered sanctions expert with two tweets to his name; Michelle Giuda, who was once Newt Gingrich's spokeswoman and was also a national gymnastics champion at the University of California at Los Angeles; and a former New York ad man, Len Khodorkovsky, whose family fled the Soviet Union when he was a child and who now coordinates Pompeo's anti-Iran messaging campaign." See Nick Wadhams and Javier Blas, "The Iran Action Group Puts Muscle behind Trump's Iran Bluster," *Bloomberg*, October 4, 2018.

80. Wadhams and Blas, "The Iran Action Group Puts Muscle behind Trump's Iran Bluster."

81. Wadhams and Blas, "The Iran Action Group Puts Muscle behind Trump's Iran Bluster."

82. Bolton, *The Room Where It Happened*, 369.

83. Bolton, *The Room Where It Happened*, 369.

84. Keith Johnson and Colum Lynch, "Trump Rushes to Kill Off Iran Nuclear Deal before Election," *Foreign Policy*, June 12, 2020.

85. Bolton, *The Room Where It Happened*, 371.

86. Bolton, *The Room Where It Happened*, 371.

87. Bolton, *The Room Where It Happened*, 383.

88. Bolton, *The Room Where It Happened*, 376.

89. Bolton, *The Room Where It Happened*, 386.

90. Bolton, *The Room Where It Happened*, 386.

91. Bolton, *The Room Where It Happened*, 422.

92. Robin Wright, "Iran's Foreign Minister Was Invited to Meet Trump in the Oval Office," *The New Yorker*, August 2, 2019.

93. Wright, "Iran's Foreign Minister Was Invited to Meet Trump in the Oval Office."

94. Elliott Abrams, interview with author, November 20, 2024.

95. Wright, "Iran's Foreign Minister Was Invited to Meet Trump in the Oval Office."

96. Wright, "Iran's Foreign Minister Was Invited to Meet Trump in the Oval Office."

97. Wright, "Iran's Foreign Minister Was Invited to Meet Trump in the Oval Office."

98. Kushner, *Breaking History*, 170.

99. Elliott Abrams, interview with author, November 20, 2024.

100. Dalia Dassa Kaye and Shira Efron, "Israel's Evolving Iran Policy," *Survival* 62, no. 4 (2020): 7–30.

101. Former senior Israeli official, interview with author, March 2, 2023.

102. Former senior Israeli official, interview with author, March 2, 2023.

103. Former Israeli national security official, interview with author, February 27, 2023.

104. Former Israeli national security official, interview with author, February 27, 2023.

105. Former Israeli national security official, interview with author, February 27, 2023.

106. Former Israeli national security official, interview with author, February 27, 2023.

107. Former Israeli national security official, interview with author, February 27, 2023.

108. Former Israeli national security official, interview with author, February 27, 2023.

109. Iranian American experts, interview with author, October 14, 2021.

110. PAAIA Executive Summary, 2020 survey, https://paaia.org/wp-content/uploads/2020/10/Executive-Summary.2020.pdf.

111. PAAIA Executive Summary, 2020 survey.

112. PAAIA Executive Summary, 2020 survey.

113. PAAIA Executive Summary, 2020 survey.

114. "Secretary Pompeo Delivers Remarks on 'Supporting Iranian Voices' at the Ronald Reagan Foundation and Library, Simi Valley, California," July 22, 2018, https://www.youtube.com/watch?v=XR7aGNhYrMs.

115. PAAIA Executive Summary, 2020 survey.

116. Iranian American expert, interview with author, October 11, 2021.

117. Arash Azizi, "The Fiasco of Iranian Diaspora Politics," *New Lines Magazine*, April 22, 2024.

118. Iranian American experts, interview with author, October 14, 2021.

119. Iranian American experts, interview with author, October 14, 2021.

120. Julian Borger, "US Cuts Funds for 'Anti-propaganda' Iran Group That Trolled Activists," *The Guardian*, May 31, 2019.

121. Jason Rezaian, "The State Department Has Been Funding Trolls. I'm One of Their Targets," *The Washington Post*, June 4, 2019.

122. Iranian American expert, interview with author, October 11, 2021.

123. Scott Shane, "For Obscure Iranian Exile Group, Broad Support in the U.S.," *The New York Times*, November 26, 2011.

124. Nadeen Ebrahim, "A Darling of US Conservatives, Iran's Top Opposition Group May Face an Uncertain Future," CNN, July 10, 2023.

125. Matthew Petti and Eli Clifton, "Biden-linked Expert Backs Regime Change at Event Sponsored by Iranian Militant Group," *Responsible Statecraft*, July 13, 2021, https://responsiblestatecraft.org/2021/07/12/biden-linked-expert-backs-regime-change-at-event-sponsored-by-iranian-militant-group/.

126. Iranian American experts, interview with author, October 14, 2021.

127. Iranian American experts, interview with author, October 14, 2021.

128. Iranian American experts, interview with author, October 14, 2021.

129. Daniel Block, "'I'll Burn You Alive,'" *Politico*, April 22, 2023.

130. Arash Azizi, *Opposition Politics of the Iranian Diaspora: Out of Many, One—But Not Just Yet*, Clingendael, October 27, 2023, https://www.clingendael.org/iran?p=4.

131. Baker and Glasser, *The Divider*, 72.

132. Bolton, *The Room Where It Happened*, 374.

133. Trump quoted in Bolton, *The Room Where It Happened*, 381.

134. Bolton, *The Room Where It Happened*, 397.

135. Baker and Glasser, *The Divider*, 328.

136. The full texts of the tweets are reproduced in Bolton, *The Room Where It Happened*, 407.

137. Bolton, *The Room Where It Happened*, 401.

138. Bolton, *The Room Where It Happened*, 401.

139. Quoted in Baker and Glasser, *The Divider*, 328.

140. Mark T. Esper, *A Sacred Oath: Memoirs of a Secretary of Defense during Extraordinary Times* (William Morrow, 2022), 146.

141. Esper, *A Sacred Oath*.

142. Baker and Glasser, *The Divider*, 389.

143. Esper, *A Sacred Oath*, 158.

144. Esper, *A Sacred Oath*, 158.

145. Bob Woodward and Robert Costa, *Peril* (Simon and Schuster, 2021), 104.

146. Woodward and Costa, *Peril*, 105.

147. Baker and Glasser, *The Divider*, 591. Also see Bob Woodward and Robert Costa, *Peril*, 159.

148. Baker and Glasser, *The Divider*, 592.

149. Woodward and Costa, *Peril*, 161.

150. Esper, *A Sacred Oath*, 175.

151. Esper, *A Sacred Oath*, 176.

152. See "Confronting the Full Range of Iranian Threats," Hearing before Committee on Foreign Affairs, House of Representatives, 115th Congress, 1st Session, October 11, 2017, https://www.govinfo.gov/content/pkg/CHRG-115hhrg27160/pdf/CHRG-115hhrg27160.pdf.

153. "Confronting the Full Range of Iranian Threats," Hearing before Committee on Foreign Affairs, House of Representatives, 115th Congress, 1st Session, October 11, 2017.

154. Reuben Steff, *US Foreign Policy in the Age of Trump* (Routledge, 2021), 2.

155. "Remarks by President Trump on Iran Strategy," October 13, 2017, https://trumpwhitehouse.archives.gov/briefings-statements/remarks-president-trump-iran-strategy/.

Chapter Six

1. Joe Biden, "There's a Smarter Way to Be Tough on Iran," CNN, September 13, 2020.

2. For these and other challenges facing the revival of the JCPOA when Biden took office, see Brian O'Toole, "Rejoining the Iran Nuclear Deal: Not So Easy," Issue Brief, Atlantic Council, January 2021, https://www.atlanticcouncil.org/in-depth-research-reports/issue-brief/rejoining-the-iran-nuclear-deal-not-so-easy/.

3. Former senior U.S. official, interview with author, October 5, 2021.

4. Peter Baker and Susan Glasser, *The Divider: Trump in the White House, 2017–2021* (Anchor Books, 2022), xiii.

5. Former U.S. official, interview with author, November 12, 2024.

6. Former U.S. official, interview with author, November 12, 2024.

7. Alexander Ward and Laurence Norman, "Trump Team Weighs Options, including Airstrikes, to Stop Iran's Nuclear Program," *The Wall Street Journal*, December 13, 2024.

8. Barak Ravid, "Scoop: Biden Discussed Plans to Strike Iran Nuclear Sites If Tehran Speeds toward Bomb,"*Axios*, January 2, 2025.

9. Richard Nephew, "A Last Chance for Iran: America Should Give Diplomacy a Final Shot—While Preparing to Use Military Force," *Foreign Affairs*, January 2, 2025.

10. Former senior U.S. official, interview with author, April 2021.

11. Former senior U.S. official, interview with author, April 2021.

12. Walter Russell Mead, "Transcript: Dialogues on American Foreign Policy and World Affairs: A Conversation with Former Deputy Secretary of State Antony Blinken," Hudson Institute, July 9, 2020, https://www.hudson.org/foreign-policy/transcript-dialogues-on-american-foreign-policy-and-world-affairs-a-conversation-with-former-deputy-secretary-of-state-antony-blinken.

13. Former senior U.S. official, interview with author, October 5, 2021.

14. Gal Beckerman, "'The Middle East Region Is Quieter Today Than It Has Been in Two Decades': A Week Ago, Joe Biden's National Security Advisor, Jake Sullivan, Sounded Optimistic about the Region," *The Atlantic*, October 7, 2023.

15. Joseph R. Biden Jr., "Why America Must Lead Again: Rescuing U.S. Foreign Policy after Trump," *Foreign Affairs*, March–April 2020.

16. Biden, "Why America Must Lead Again."

17. Biden, "Why America Must Lead Again."

18. Biden, "Joe Biden: There's a Smarter Way to Be Tough on Iran."

19. Ben Rhodes, interview with author, November 4, 2024.

20. Ben Rhodes, interview with author, November 4, 2024.

21. Former senior U.S. official, interview with author, October 5, 2021.

22. Ben Rhodes, interview with author, November 4, 2024.

23. Ben Rhodes, interview with author, November 4, 2024.

24. Ben Rhodes, interview with author, November 4, 2024.

25. These dates are included in the Department of State profiles of both officials. See U.S. Department of State, "Antony J. Blinken, Secretary of State," and U.S. Department of State, "Robert Malley, Special Envoy for Iran," respectively, https://www.state.gov/biographies/antony-j-blinken/; https://www.state.gov/biographies/robert-malley/.

26. Former U.S. official, interview with author, November 12, 2024.

27. Former U.S. official, interview with author, November 12, 2024.

28. Former U.S. official, interview with author, November 12, 2024.

29. Former U.S. official, interview with author, November 12, 2024.

30. Gordon Lubold and Joshua Jamerson, "Biden National Security Advisor Sees U.S. Rejoining Iran Nuclear Deal," *The Wall Street Journal*, December 7, 2020.

31. "Jake Sullivan: U.S. Grand Strategy in the Middle East," CSIS, June 22, 2020, https://www.csis.org/events/jake-sullivan-us-grand-strategy-middle-east.

32. U.S. Institute of Peace, "Avril Haines on Iran," *The Iran Primer*, January 21, 2021, https://iranprimer.usip.org/blog/2021/jan/21/avril-haines-iran.

33. U.S. Institute of Peace, "Avril Haines on Iran," *The Iran Primer*, January 21, 2021.

34. Arms Control Association, "Biden Officials Express Support for Rejoining Iran Nuclear Deal," https://www.armscontrol.org/blog/2021-01/p4-1-iran-nuclear-deal-alert.

35. Former U.S. official, interview with author, July 28, 2021.

36. Former senior U.S. official, interview with author, October 5, 2021.

37. Former senior U.S. official, interview with author, October 5, 2021.

38. Former U.S. official, interview with author, July 28, 2021.

39. Former senior U.S. official, interview with author, October 5, 2021.

40. Former senior U.S. official, interview with author, October 5, 2021.

41. Former senior U.S. official, interview with author, October 5, 2021.

42. Iranian American experts, interview with author, October 14, 2021.

43. Iranian American experts, interview with author, October 14, 2021.

44. Thomas L. Friedman, "'We Got to Figure Out How to Work Together,'" *The New York Times*, December 3, 2020, A23.

45. Friedman, "'We Got to Figure Out How to Work Together,'" A23.

46. Robin Wright, "The Seven Pillars of Biden's Foreign Policy," *The New Yorker*, November 11, 2020.

47. O'Toole, "Rejoining the Iran Nuclear Deal: Not So Easy."

48. Eric Brewer, "A Clean Return to the Iran Nuclear Deal Should Be Biden's First Option," *Bulletin of Atomic Scientists*, January 11, 2021.

49. For further details on the timing of the JCPOA's sunset clauses, see U.S. Institute of Peace, "Explainer: Timing of Key Sunsets in Nuclear Deal," *The Iran Primer*, October 18, 2023, https://iranprimer.usip.org/blog/2023/jan/11/explainer-timing-key-sunsets-nuclear-deal.

50. "Transcript: A Conversation with Israeli Prime Minister Benjamin Netanyahu," Hudson Institute, December 4, 2020, https://www.hudson.org/foreign-policy/transcript-a-conversation-with-israeli-prime-minister-benjamin-netanyahu.

51. François Murphy, "Iran Tells IAEA It Will Accelerate Underground Uranium Enrichment," Reuters, December 4, 2020.

52. For an assessment of the challenges and opportunities for the incoming Biden administration to return to the nuclear deal, see Dalia Dassa Kaye, "Reverse Engineering: Can Revival of the Nuclear Deal Spark a New Regional Security Dialogue?" *The Wilson Quarterly*, Winter 2021.

53. Robert S. Litwak and Haleh Esfandiari, "Iran Should Take the First Step," Wilson Center, November 24, 2020, https://www.wilsoncenter.org/article/iran-should-take-first-step.

54. Mohammad Ayatollahi Tabaar, "No Matter Who Is U.S. President, Iran Will Drive a Harder Bargain Than Before," *Foreign Affairs*, October 20, 2020.

55. Henry Rome, "Opinion: Iran Is Escalating Its Nuclear Program. Biden Should Not Rush to Respond," NPR, January 8, 2021.

56. Rome, "Opinion: Iran is Escalating Its Nuclear Program."

57. Ariane Tabatabai, who first joined the Biden administration as an advisor on Iran at the State Department, co-authored an article with Henry Rome before the 2020 election arguing against the next administration rushing to revive the nuclear agreement given increased U.S. leverage. See Ariane Tabatabai and Henry Rome, "For Iran, Negotiations Aren't Optional: With Its Economy in Trouble, Tehran Will Have to Talk to Washington. But the Next Administration Shouldn't Rush Things," *Foreign Policy*, September 15, 2020.

58. Robert Malley, interview with author, November 12, 2024.

59. Robert Malley, interview with author, November 12, 2024.

60. European officials, interview with author, October 25, 2023.

61. European officials, interview with author, October 25, 2023.

62. European officials, interview with author, October 25, 2023.

63. Former senior U.S. official, interview with author, October 5, 2021.

64. Such arguments were made during track two dialogues that the author attended over the course of 2021 and 2022.

65. European officials, interview with author, October 25, 2023.

66. Robert Malley, interview with author, November 12, 2024.

67. See, for example, an interview with Robert Malley by *Foreign Policy*, November 30, 2022, https://foreignpolicy.com/live/rob-malley-u-s-special-envoy-for-iran/.

68. Josh Rogin, "Inside the Saga of the State Department's Missing Iran Envoy," *The Washington Post,* September 6, 2023. Also see Nahal Toosi and Joe Gould, "FBI Probes Whether Iran Envoy Malley Committed Crimes in Handling of Classified Info," *Politico*, May 10, 2024.

69. See Zachary Basu, "Scoop: House GOP Moves to Tank Biden's Iran Diplomacy," *Axios*, February 16, 2022; and press release from SFRC, "49 Senate Republicans Tell President Biden: An Iran Agreement without Broad Congressional Support Will Not Survive," March 14, 2022, https://www.foreign.senate.gov/press/rep/release/49-senate-republicans-tell-president-biden-an-iran-agreement-without-broad-congressional-support-will-not-survive.

70. International Crisis Group, "Is Restoring the Iran Nuclear Deal Still Possible?" September 12, 2022, https://www.crisisgroup.org/b87-middle-east-north-africa/gulf-and-arabian-peninsula/iran/restoring-iran-nuclear-deal-still.

71. See Alexander Cornwell, François Murphy, and John Irish, "Exclusive: Iran Dramatically Accelerating Uranium Enrichment to Near Bomb Grade, IAEA Says," Reuters, December 6, 2024; and U.S. Institute of Peace, "U.S. Intelligence on Iran's Nuclear Advances," *The Iran Primer*, December 10, 2024, https://iranprimer.usip.org/blog/2024/dec/10/us-intelligence-iran%E2%80%99s-nuclear-advances.

72. Multiple former senior Israeli officials, interviews with author, late February and early March 2023.

73. Multiple former senior Israeli officials, interviews with author, late February and early March 2023.

74. Multiple former senior Israeli officials, interviews with author, late February and early March 2023.

75. Multiple former senior Israeli officials, interviews with author, late February and early March 2023.

76. Former U.S. official, interview with author, November 12, 2024.

77. Former U.S. official, interview with author, November 12, 2024.

78. Multiple former senior Israeli officials, interviews with author, late February and early March 2023.

79. Multiple former senior Israeli officials, interviews with author, late February and early March 2023.

80. Kaye, "Reverse Engineering."

81. Comments by a former senior U.S. official at an online foreign policy roundtable the author joined, September 28, 2022.

82. U.S. Institute of Peace, "Malley on U.S. Iran Policy," *The Iran Primer*, December 1, 2022, https://iranprimer.usip.org/blog/2022/nov/01/malley-us-iran-policy.

83. U.S. Institute of Peace, "U.S. Supports Iran Protests," *The Iran Primer*, November 14, 2022, https://iranprimer.usip.org/blog/2022/oct/03/us-supports-iran-protests.

84. Author participation in track two dialogue in Europe, October 2022.

85. Henry Rome and Louis Dugit-Gros, "'No Deal, No Crisis' Is No Plan for Iran," Washington Institute for Near East Policy, March 29, 2023, https://www.washingtoninstitute.org/policy-analysis/no-deal-no-crisis-no-plan-iran.

86. Soufan Center, "IntelBrief: Iranian Tanker Seizures Dampen Hopes for Regional De-escalation," May 9, 2023, https://thesoufancenter.org/intelbrief-2023-may-9/.

87. U.S. Naval Forces Central Command Public Affairs, "U.S. Prevents Iran from Seizing Two Merchant Tankers in the Gulf of Oman," July 5, 2023, https://www.cusnc.navy.mil/Media/News/Display/Article/3448159/us-prevents-iran-from-seizing-two-merchant-tankers-in-gulf-of-oman/.

88. Michael Crowley, Ronen Bergman, and Farnaz Fassihi, "Prisoner Deal Could Smooth Effort to Contain Iran's Nuclear Program," *The New York Times*, August 10, 2023.

89. For an assessment of Iran's oil exports and U.S. sanctions, see Henry Rome, "Iran's Oil Exports Are Vulnerable to Sanctions," PolicyWatch 3669, Washington Institute for Near East Policy, November 9, 2022, https://www.washingtoninstitute.org/policy-analysis/irans-oil-exports-are-vulnerable-sanctions.

90. U.S. Department of State, Department Press Briefing, December 3, 2024, Vedant Patel, Principal Deputy Spokesperson, https://www.state.gov/briefings/department-press-briefing-december-3-2024/.

91. Amwaj Media, "Scoop: Khamenei 'Grants Permission' for Direct Iran–US Nuclear Talks," September 25, 2023, https://amwaj.media/article/scoop-khamenei-grants-permission-for-direct-iran-us-nuclear-talks.

92. Author discussions with a number of Israeli analysts and defense officials

during a June 2024 visit to Tel Aviv made it clear that Israeli planners had miscalculated, as they did not expect a direct Iranian response to the April 1 strike in Damascus.

93. "White House Press Secretary Karine Jean-Pierre and NSC's John Kirby Hold a Briefing—7/8/24," CNBC Television.

94. Lindsey Graham, X post, October 1, 2024, https://x.com/LindseyGrahamSC/status/1841163062834815144.

95. Marco Rubio, X post, October 1, 2024, https://x.com/marcorubio/status/1841178807702581581.

96. See "Leader Jeffries Statement on the Iranian Attack against Israel," October 1, 2024, https://jeffries.house.gov/2024/10/01/leader-jeffries-statement-on-the-iranian-attack-against-israel/.

97. Patrick Wintour, "Iran Says It Could End Ban on Possessing Nuclear Weapons If Sanctions Reimposed," *The Guardian*, November 28, 2024.

98. Brit McCandless Farmer, "Kamala Harris and Tim Walz: More from Their *60 Minutes* Interviews," *CBS News*, October 7, 2024. A shorter clip of the Iran answer in the interview appears on the *Washington Post* website.

99. Glenn Thrush and David E. Sanger, "U.S. Charges Iranians with Hacking Trump Campaign," *The New York Times*, September 27, 2024.

100. Farnaz Fassihi, "Elon Musk Met with Iran's U.N. Ambassador, Iranian Officials Say," *The New York Times*, November 14, 2024. Subsequent reports during the presidential transition alleged that Musk intervened with Iranian officials to help secure the release of an Italian journalist in exchange for the release of an Iranian engineer detained in Italy at the request of the U.S. Justice Department; the Iranian faced accusations of supporting a militia group that killed three American military personnel at a U.S. base in Jordan. See Farnaz Fassihi, Emma Bubola, and Edward Wong, "Musk Said to Have Intervened to Help Free Italian Jailed in Iran," *The New York Times*, January 15, 2025.

101. Ron Kampeas, "Trump Taps Iran Hawks Marco Rubio, Mike Waltz, for Top National Security Roles," *The Jewish Journal*, November 13, 2024.

102. Alexander Ward and Laurence Norman, "Trump Team Weighs Options, including Airstrikes, to Stop Iran's Nuclear Program."

103. See Eric Cortellessa, "Donald Trump: 2024 *Time* Person of the Year," *Time*, December 12, 2024.

Conclusion

1. Former US official, interview with author, April 19, 2021.

2. Transcript of Interview with Robert M. Gates, July 23–24, 2000, College Station, Texas, George H. W. Bush Oral History Project, University of Virginia, https://millercenter.org/the-presidency/presidential-oral-histories/robert-m-gates-deputy-director-central.

3. James A. Baker III, *The Politics of Diplomacy* (Putnam, 1995), 262.

4. Robert S. Litwak, *Rogue States and U.S. Foreign Policy: Containment after the Cold War* (Woodrow Wilson Center Press, 2000).

5. Jeremy W. Peters, "Sheldon Adelson Sees a Lot to Like in Trump's Washington," *The New York Times*, September 22, 2018.

6. Former U.S. official, interview with author, July 28, 2021.

7. Former U.S. official, interview with author, July 28, 2021.

8. Zalmay Khalilzad, *The Envoy* (St. Martin's Press, 2016), 70.

9. These views were relayed in reviews of an early project proposal sent to me in June 2023 via email.

10. Khalilzad, *The Envoy*, 97.

11. Former senior U.S. official, interview with author, April 2021.

12. Ben Rhodes, *The World As It Is* (Random House, 2018), 251–252.

13. Jonathan Swan, Kate Kelly, Maggie Haberman, and Mark Mazzetti, "Kushner Firm Got Hundreds of Millions from 2 Persian Gulf Nations," *The New York Times*, March 30, 2023.

14. Kate Kelly and David D. Kirkpatrick, "Kushner's and Mnuchin's Quick Pivots to Business with the Gulf," *The New York Times*, May 22, 2022.

15. Ben Rhodes, interview with author, November 4, 2024.

16. Ben Rhodes, interview with author, November 4, 2024.

17. Robert Malley, interview with author, November 12, 2024.

18. Robert Malley, interview with author, November 12, 2024.

19. Michael B. Cerny and Rory Truex, "Under Pressure: Attitudes towards China among American Foreign Policy Professionals," Draft Paper, December 9, 2024, https://static1.squarespace.com/static/61362c444f878116b514ec49/t/6757273 41f3f295563cd8a47/1733764917153/Cerny+%26+Truex+%282024%29+-+Working+Pa per+-+Under+Pressure.pdf.

20. Cerny and Truex, "Under Pressure: Attitudes towards China among American Foreign Policy Professionals."

21. The repeated patterns in how analysts and policymakers talk about Iran have prompted satire to illustrate the prevailing stereotypes so dominant in Washington. See, for example, Ladane Nasseri, "How to Write about Iran: A Guide for Journalists, Analysts, and Policymakers," *McSweeny's*, February 16, 2021.

22. See, for example, Thomas L. Friedman, "Sleepless in Tehran," *The New York Times*, October 28, 2008.

23. See Michael Young, "A Revolutionary Identity," blog post, Diwan, April 19, 2022, https://carnegieendowment.org/middle-east/diwan/2022/05/a-revolution ary-identity?lang=en&center=middle-east.

24. For an argument in favor of détente between the United States and Iran, and what it might look like, see Hamid Biglari, "A Reset for Iran and the United States," *Foreign Affairs*, September 6, 2017.

25. Richard Haass presented one such grand bargain approach in early 2025, where he suggested that Iran's growing vulnerability offered an opportunity to elicit greater concessions from Iran on limiting its nuclear program, its missile arsenal, and its support for regional proxies, but would require forgoing regime change goals in addition to offering sanctions relief. See Haass, "The Iran Opportunity: What America Needs to Do to Achieve a Breakthrough," *Foreign Affairs*, January 6, 2025.

INDEX

Abe, Shinzo, 125

abnormal state, Iran as, 164, 167; destined to remain hostile, 12, 168; hostage crisis leads to view of, 15; Persian Gulf shipping and, 35; policymakers frame, 166; public discourse deepens view of, 41; reasons for U.S. view of, 6, 10–11; U.S.-Iran relations affected by, 37. *See also* rogue state, Iran as

Abqaiq, Saudi Arabia, 132

Abraham Accords, 117, 171

Abrams, Elliott, 66, 70, 74, 76, 77, 118, 127, 196n3

Adelson, Miriam, 165

Adelson, Sheldon, 165

Affinity Partners (equity firm), 171

Afghanistan: Al Qaeda in, 68; Biden intends to remove forces from, 141; Bonn Declaration and, 69, 70; Bush cooperates with Iran on, 81, 82, 169; Iran's strategic intentions toward, 83; Javad Zarif works with U.S. on, 102; post-9/11, 88; post-Taliban government in, 63; Soviet invasion of, 18, 29; Taliban in, 62, 65; Trump on, 134; U.S./Iran over-

lapping interests in, 56; U.S. talks with Iranians on, 67, 72; war in, 66, 73, 78, 87, 163, 168

Ahmadinejad, Mahmoud, 82, 86, 90, 96

al-Assad, Bashar, 120, 140, 158, 166

Albright, Madeleine, 16, 50, 54–59, 128

Algiers Accords, 17

Al Otaiba, Yousef, 115

Al Qaeda, 65; attacks U.S., 62, 64, 163; Iran gives U.S. intelligence on, 68; Iran's relationship with, 72, 82, 120; U.S. focus on, 78

Al Said, Qaboos bin Said, 46, 100, 101

Amanpour, Christiane, 55

America First agenda, 112, 113, 164

American Enterprise Institute, 77, 122

American Israel Public Affairs Committee (AIPAC), 53, 94, 97, 98, 103, 107

Amidror, Yaacov, 99

Amini, Mahsa, 131

Amirabdollahian, Hossein, 155

anti-Americanism, 7, 15, 43, 45, 62, 73, 162, 169

anti-Iran stance, 3, 33, 118, 121, 160; policies, 52–55, 113, 165

209

uranium enrichment (*cont.*)
    U.S. zero-enrichment stance, 102.
    See also Joint Comprehensive Plan of
        Action (JCPOA); low enriched ura-
        nium (LEU)
U.S. Embassy, 14, 58, 75, 117, 133; 1979
    takeover, 15, 23, 47, 160; in Israel,
    116; in United Arab Emirates, 171
U.S. foreign policy, xii, 19–20, 169–174;
    Dennis Ross in, 21; human rights
    concerns in, 13; Iran as third rail of,
    162; Iran's distinctness in, 2;
    JCPOA, 109; politicization of, 167;
    toward Iran driven by animosity, 7;
    under Trump, 121
U.S.-Soviet Cold War rivalry, 42
U.S.-Soviet détente, 5
USSR. *See* Soviet Union

Vance, Cyrus, 14
velayat-e faqih, 6
Velayati, Ali Akbar, 44
Venezuela, 11
Vienna negotiations, 149, 150, 152, 158
Vietnam, 4, 16
Voice of America (VOA), 74
vulnerability, Iran's, 120, 140, 142, 155–
    158, 159, 174, 175; Richard Haass on,
    207n25; to Soviet influence, 28

war on terrorism, 18, 78
weapons of mass destruction (WMD),
    54, 62, 81, 96

Weinberger, Caspar, 23, 27, 33, 35, 36
West, the, 170; axis of evil speech, 62;
    in dialogue with Ruhollah Kho-
    meini, 14; Green movement and,
    91; influence in Iran, 29; Iran dis-
    trusts, 96; Iran hostile to, 7;
    Masoud Pezeshkian wants diplo-
    macy with, 140, 159; National Secu-
    rity Decision Directive's
    suggestions to, 28; no deal, no crisis
    status quo, 154
West Bank, 5, 115
Wilcox, Philip, 31
Wolfowitz, Paul, 31, 77
Woman, Life, Freedom protests, 6,
    131, 139, 153, 159, 166
Woodward, Bob, 134
World Jewish Congress, 53
World Trade Organization (WTO),
    79
Wright, Robin, 126

Yaalon, Moshe, 104
Yemen, 5, 117, 120, 121, 155

Zarif, Mohammad Javad, x, 69, 72, 84,
    125–126, 149; appointed foreign
    minister, 102; Bonn Declaration
    role, 70; Edward Djerejian meets
    with, 74; Richard Haass meets
    with, 39
Zayed, Mohammed bin (MBZ), 116,
    117